W9-ACE-539

WITHDRAWN

Gramley Library
Salem Academy and College
Winston-Salem, N.C. 27108

Castings

Castings

Monuments and Monumentality
in Poems by Elizabeth Bishop,
Robert Lowell, James Merrill,
Derek Walcott, and
Seamus Heaney

Guy Rotella

Vanderbilt University Press

NASHVILLE

Gramley Library
Salem Academy and College
Winston-Salem, N.C. 27108

© 2004 Vanderbilt University Press
All rights reserved
First Edition 2004

This book is printed on acid-free paper.
Manufactured in the United States of America

Reprinted by permission of Alfred A. Knopf, a division of Random House, Inc.: From *Collected Poems* by James Merrill, J. D. McClatchy and Stephen Yenser, editors; copyright © 2001 by the Literary Estate of James Merrill at Washington University. From *The Changing Light at Sandover* by James Merrill, copyright © 1980, 1982 by James Merrill.

Reprinted by permission of Farrar, Straus and Giroux, LLC: Excerpts from *The Complete Poems 1927-1979* by Elizabeth Bishop; copyright © 1979, 1983 by Alice Helen Methfessel. Excerpts from *Electric Light* by Seamus Heaney; copyright © 2001 by Seamus Heaney. Excerpts from *Opened Ground: Selected Poems 1966-1996* by Seamus Heaney; copyright © 1998 by Seamus Heaney. Excerpts from *Collected Poems* by Robert Lowell; copyright © 2003 by Elizabeth Lowell and Sheridan Lowell. Excerpts from *Collected Poems 1948-1984* by Derek Walcott; copyright © 1986 by Derek Walcott. Excerpts from *Midsummer* by Derek Walcott; copyright © 1984 by Derek Walcott. Excerpts from *Omeros* by Derek Walcott; copyright © 1990 by Derek Walcott. Excerpts from *Tiepolo's Hound* by Derek Walcott; copyright © 2000 by Derek Walcott.

Library of Congress Cataloging-in-Publication Data

Rotella, Guy L.
    Castings : monuments and monumentality in poems by Elizabeth Bishop, Robert Lowell, James Merrill, Derek Walcott, and Seamus Heaney / Guy Rotella.—1st ed.
    p. cm.
    Includes bibliographical references and index.
    ISBN 0-8265-1452-9 (acid-free paper)
    ISBN 0-8265-1453-7 (pbk. acid-free paper)
    1. American poetry—20th century—History and criticism. 2. Monuments in literature. 3. Literature and history—English-speaking countries—History—20th century. 4. English poetry—20th century—History and criticism. 5. Memorials in literature. 6. History in literature. 7. Memory in literature. I. Title.
PS310.M6R68 2004
811.'509357—dc22
2004001008

To my family,
and for Mary Jane

Contents

Acknowledgments

Acknowledging debts doesn't discharge them, of course, but let these statements mark my intention to remit. Thanks to a lifetime of teachers and a career's worth of students for the lessons of both. Thanks to Northeastern University for a sabbatical leave that helped me complete this book. Thanks to Michael Ames, Betsy Phillips, Dariel Mayer, and the staff at Vanderbilt University Press for seeing it into print. Thanks to Jon Lanham and Edward Doctoroff, of Harvard's Lamont and Widener libraries, for material assistance, including lunch. Thanks to Frank Blessington for friendship and advice, and for models of persistence, precision, and command. Thanks to Mary Loeffelholz for a timely warning about a listing scaffold. Thanks to Elizabeth Burns, Ellen Scharfenburg, and Joseph Westland for thoughtful readings of chapters. Special thanks to Marina Leslie for being a wise and tolerant friend, for insightful responses, and for encouraging conversations at a crucial time. Thanks to the scholars in and beyond the notes for shaping my sense of the writers, the period, and the issues I've taken up. Thanks most of all to the poets for the poems, without which, nothing. As for the rest, in Derek Walcott's words, "let gratitude redeem what lies undone."

Castings

Introduction

Traditionally, monuments remember and remind. They embody exemplary persons or events and the shared ideals they stood for; they prompt an obligation to keep those ideals standing now and forever. Monuments certify a culture's present by securing its past and pledging its future. They assume art's power to maintain what's held in common by joining the particular and the general and by making transient things persistent.

At the same time, monuments have always provoked mixed feelings and been sites of cultural contestation as well as cohesion. Embedded in political, artistic, and social contexts, monuments reflect the faults and fissures of all three; they raise as well as answer questions about who decides what persons or events should be remembered, in what form and to what ends. Because no culture is perfectly united in its beliefs, and because cultures and the beliefs their monuments encode both alter and expire, monumental claims to coherence and permanence are typically controversial. For instance, monumental claims to persistence are belied by monuments that are accidentally or deliberately destroyed, are revised to suit new standards, or remain when the cultures and beliefs they've allegedly fixed forever have disappeared. More generally still, monuments problematically affirm life by resisting time and change, arguably life's very nature. And, of course, monuments are sometimes yoked with power in ways that confuse enforced conformity with cultural cohesion.

Recently, such age-old challenges to monumental assumptions have intensified. Those forms of postmodernism that are particularly distrustful of civilizations—and of art's complicity with them—often judge monuments to be one more arm (or armament) of a culture's disciplinary structures, so that in the second half of the twentieth century, the dismissive command of Nietzsche's *Unfashionable Observations,* "Away with the monuments," was frequently in fashion. At the same time, however, and whether thoughtfully or not, monument making has continued apace. So, too, have the debates associated with it. Meanwhile, many postmodern thinkers and artists have considered monuments and monumentality in ways that fully engage both traditional and more recent critiques of monumental claims, and have done so without either extolling or dismissing the monumental impulse and its manifestations. My particular interest here is in several postmodern poets who are aware of the good reasons urging Nietzsche's order but who don't quite obey it. For them, monuments are neither to be "conservatively" upheld nor "progressively" dismissed, since—to put it crudely—even the best and worst monuments both satisfy and violate public and private needs. Those poets—Elizabeth Bishop, Robert Lowell, James Merrill, Derek Walcott, and Seamus Heaney—are the subject of this book, as are poems in which they address actual or notional monuments precisely in order to consider the unsettled and unsettling political, aesthetic, and more broadly cultural issues that monuments condense.

A brief review of some earlier "monument" poems can serve to outline the terms in which monuments have traditionally been praised and attacked. David Ferry writes that among Horace's equable "commonplaces" are these: "poetry immortalizes; poetry can do nothing against death." In the first phrase, poetry sounds potently monumental; in the second, poetry and monuments alike sound weak. Horace's greatness as a poet is the achievement of poise amid mutually exclusive but coexisting truths. As Ferry suggests, this accounts for his volatility of tone within composed performance.[1] Horace's famous ode beginning "Exegi monumentum aere perennius" (iii.30) inscribes itself within a long tradition of debates among the arts. It privileges poetry as an immortalizing force, placing it above sculptural and architectural monuments ("bronze / And the pyramids of ancient royal kings," in Ferry's translation). One effect of this is to register the poem itself as monumental. That triggers the ode's concern with the claims of monumentality in general, whether sculptural, architectural, or poetic. This is an important reminder that when poetry addresses monuments it also addresses itself and its own claims to monumental persistence, and typically does so in ways that recall poetry's situation within the political and social contexts monuments more obviously inhabit—all major concerns of this study.

Horace begins boldly, confident that his poem will outlast bronze and rulers' pyramids, certain that wind and rain, years and ages won't scatter or erase it. But the calendar of threats performs its own abrasion, and Horace's expectation of future fame is hedged by timeful phrases: "So long as"; "Once." Those phrases support his hope for permanence in terms that also temper or subvert it. Especially apt for my purposes here is Horace's sense that monumental art depends for its persistence upon the political and religious system that surrounds it: "So long as the Pontiff in solemn procession climbs / The Capitol steps, beside him the reverent Vestal, / So long will it be that men will say that I . . . / Was the first." And although it's not directly at issue in this poem, Horace was well aware that the dependence is mutual, that monuments do—and must—earn their keep, a matter recent poets make much of. To return to the poem, the shift from present to past tense in the lines just quoted makes its own comment on lastingness, and Horace contradicts (speaks against) his own confidence in the "endless" exercise of Roman imperial practices—the aegis or conditions under which he and his poem will last—by recalling political and social change ("I, / Born in a land . . . / Once ruled by Danaus, king of a peasant people"). Horace does boast of an achievement that will bring him "praise in time to come" and keep some part of him alive: his carrying a Greek meter over into Latin. But that activity itself bristles with complications: the rich cultural politics of translation, with its mixture of fidelity and betrayal, obedience and rebellion, community and displacement. In the end, Horace "settles" for the present pleasure of being garlanded. Still, the laurel is borrowed from another culture's past, and its placement remains a matter for the future—a future (2,000 years of it now passed, and past) that has continued to bestow the wreath, not least in Ferry's eloquent conveyance of the ode into current English. That gives the matter one more twist, and here's another: Horace's monumental "dulce et decorum est" came to seem a dead and deadly lie to Wilfred Owen in 1918.

Since I'm picking chestnuts, Shakespeare's Sonnet 55 has monumental politics as well. The poem echoes Horace, again elevating poetry above sculptural and architectural monuments in terms of relative eternalizing force: here, the power to give life beyond his lifetime to the worthy young man the sonnet addresses. It also suggests doubts about the stability or meaningfulness of the aesthetic and political activities, structures, and hierarchies the poem depends on, doing so by using the ingenious device (astutely described by Helen Vendler) of "bestowing grandeur" on princely monuments and warfare when they are associated with the young man (and the poem) and "bestowing squalor" on them when they are not, so that in the former case, war is a noble "quick fire" and monuments are "marble" and "gilded," while in the latter, war is a "wasteful" uprooting and monuments are "unswept stone, besmeared by sluttish time." This strategy cracks but doesn't overturn the memorializing foundation it establishes. So, too, does what Vendler calls the poem's "other chief ingenuity," its transformation of a classical, Horatian "commemorative impulse into a [Christian] resurrective one."[2] That takes poetry down a peg; the poem will keep the youth alive, but only "till the Judgement that your [that is, his] self arise." This emphasis points to a difficulty shared by all monumental art, which, after all, makes only the *record* of a person or event immortal and thus praises itself and its maker as much or more than its subject (as in Shakespeare's Sonnet 18). Here, the transference of "full" immortalizing power from sculptor, architect, or poet to God relaxes without resolving that monumental dilemma (of course, for artists dilemmas are opportunities as well).

Horace and Shakespeare praise poetry's monumentalizing memorial power as they indicate its limits in practice. Shelley's more overtly political "Ozymandias" mocks a specific monument in ways that demean the monumental impulse and all its realizations (although, as is usual with mockery, the poem's insult involves a measure of emulation). Ozymandias's monument fails in its architectural, sculptural, and inscriptional aspects and tasks. It's been damaged by time, in the form of natural erosion, and perhaps by political upheaval (the statue is not only worn; it's "shattered"). More important, the monument's intended meaning has been reversed (although in ways that depend upon as they cancel its success as a record). Most of this is in keeping with Shelley's romantic poetics and politics, his preference for ruins and fragments, his commitment to process, and his antiauthoritarian values (although complications in Shelley's position may be signaled by his having chosen to write the poem as a sonnet).

The pedestaled statue and its motto, the verbal underwriting the visual, were meant to decree a tyrant's omnipotence against any and all resistance; instead, they murmur brokenly about the transience of every sort of power. There is some flavor in this of Joyce Appleby's remark that Jefferson's legacy was hostility to legacies, an effect Jefferson intended, as Shelley's king assuredly did not. The import of "Ozymandias" is hopeful, revolutionary. Yet it also implies so expansive—so "barren and bare"—a sense of the impermanence of all artistic, political, and cultural endeavor as to counsel despair, in part because meanings alter unpredictably with circumstances. Similarly, the poem's sculptor—deliberately or not—both reifies and overturns the power the sculptor works for, whether that power is the king of kings, the sculptor's master or patron, or art itself, which the sculptor may be thought either to master or obey, and which apparently has a life of its own in any case. The implications arising from these matters extend to the poet and would be named and valued quite differently by Ozymandias, by the sculptor, by Shelley and his "traveler," and by conservative or revolutionary reader-legislators (acknowledged or not). Shelley's poem wonders whether art and artists can speak back to power or are fated to complicity with it; whether or not they can see into or through an ideology while working within the verbal, visual, or other languages that encode it; whether they resist or yield to natural and cultural change, and to what degree. Such questions about art and artists (even artists supposedly alienated by definition from their cultures and therefore speaking against rather than for them) intensified remarkably in the second half of the twentieth century (not least because alienation—or any position of critique—came to be seen as implicated in the cultural ideology it means to stand apart from).

Intensification implies antecedents in kind if not degree, but before I glance at more recent precursors of postmodern attacks on monuments and go on to catalogue some proximate causes of those attacks, I want to recall that outbursts of fierce iconoclasm in the past (usually driven by religious or military conversion or conquest) typically destroyed monuments in order to replace or reconceive them and thus largely reaffirmed rather than debunked their nature and aims. In its own way, the most recent extreme phase in the history of attitudes toward monuments is also more a matter of renegotiating their meaning, value, form, and function than of discrediting and discarding them altogether. Still, in the past, various "puritan" movements radically distrusted all representations, especially vainglorious monumental ones. Somewhat unexpectedly, given their decidedly "impure" commitments, some postmodern artists and thinkers share that puritanical distrust, particularly when they connect critiques of representation to the suspicion that the monumental impulse is equivalent to imperialist or other modes of repression. At the same time, other postmodern artists and thinkers continue energetically to exercise, examine, and enact the monumental impulse; alert to the ancient and more recently articulated critiques of monuments, they retain some measure of confidence in what monuments might be and do. Maya Lin's innovative (and traditional) Vietnam Veterans Memorial—companioned by praise and condemnation (and "supplemented" by Three Fighting Men, Frederick Hart's more conventionally heroic sculpture)—can serve as an aptly controversial, contested, and memorable example.

Since Shelley's time, attitudes toward monuments have continued to vary. The nineteenth and twentieth centuries were periods of great cultural achievement in the West; cultural achievement encourages monument building—and generates the confidence necessary for tolerating challenges to it. Those same centuries were also periods of profound cultural crisis; cultural crisis discourages monument building—and demands it. The disruption of shared epistemes (the whole set of beliefs and practices defining a culture, including its underlying assumptions about what is "real" or "natural") makes monuments seem debatable, unthinkable, impossible; it makes them seem necessary, too, given their promise to ease or mend disruption (or, less attractively, to ignore, erase, or overwhelm it). In imperial Victorian England, a combination of great cultural unity and extreme social stress produced a dramatic upsurge in the construction of public monuments. Writing in that context, and sharing Ruskin's confidence that monuments comprise cultures, Robert Browning often treated art from the past. He did so in ways calibrated to show how much historical knowledge and imaginative energy are required to comprehend those works in their own terms. This implies that the terms had changed and would go on changing. The sun sets on monuments as on empires, and Browning's poems often measure the gap between the beliefs and practices of other times and places and his own. Such cultural relativism sees monuments as archaeological: they may be maintained or recovered with effort, but their meanings and values are neither transparent nor permanent nor universal.

The historicist, anthropological, Einsteinian, and other relativisms of the late nineteenth and early twentieth centuries—augmented by world wars and economic depression, and by the period's accelerating pace of scientific, technological, artistic, and social and political change—sometimes went further. Along with ingrained faith in progress, relativism and change disparaged monuments, with their apparent devotion to permanence and absolutes, and some modern artists addressed monuments only to impeach them (practitioners of Dada, say). However, to repeat a point made earlier, the same forces that derogate monuments also urge them. For instance, monuments might offer more than momentary stays against confusion, serving as points of coherence and fixity in an increasingly fast-changing and fragmentary world.

Michael North's study of modern monument poems, *The Final Sculpture,* is an important predecessor work to this one (even though our interests diverge and in the one place where we do overlap—we both interpret Lowell's "For the Union Dead"—my conclusions differ markedly from his). North argues that modernist attitudes toward monumental art were intensely ambivalent. Many modern artists harbored deep suspicions of public art, whether because of the simplistic notion that monuments look to the past and the modern looks to the future, because the politics of monuments seem hidebound, because their stability seems inimical to process, or because they're bombastic in actual size or in pretentiousness. But, North says, many of those same artists were also fully absorbed by the dream of a public art that might be both didactic and nonreferential and therefore able to offer to culture the binding agent religion once provided. Concentrating on work by Yeats, Stevens, and Pound, North shows that monumental art both repelled and attracted modern poets.[3]

The adjective *monumental* refers not only to specific monuments but also more generally to that which is memorable, large, or otherwise important. Modernist ambivalence about the monumental in that sense is discernible in modern poets' divided allegiance to imagism, with its formal brevity and focus on the ordinary and small, and to the long poem, with its grand scope and epic ambitions. That dual allegiance is itself subdivided. Some imagist poems make large claims to compress whole worlds, while modernist long poems typically use fragmentation and other disruptions of genre to undercut epic pretensions and insist that their own themes and techniques are provisional and contingent rather than universal. Similarly, many brief or extended modern poems recobble master narratives (those self-explaining, self-justifying cultural etiologies so often expressed by sculptural, architectural, and literary monuments). They do so not only to confirm master narratives but also to show how infirm they are: the exposed seams imply emergency repairs.

Mixed feelings about monuments occur in every cultural moment, but the proportions of trust and distrust in monumental traditions, conventions, and assumptions vary widely over time. I've suggested that some postmodern artists and thinkers surpass modern ones in their intense disparagement of the monumental impulse and its realizations, while others take the reasons for that disparagement seriously without surrendering the monumental impulse. In making that suggestion, I've used the terms *modern* and *postmodern* in their conventional literary historical or chronological sense, where they denote (roughly) the periods from 1900 to 1950 and from 1950 to the present, respectively. This is problematic, since the same terms are also used to define sets of thematic and technical positions and practices that are synchronic as well as diachronic. It can be argued, for instance, that chronologically modern and postmodern poets alike respond to the fragmentation of twentieth-century culture by making self-reflexive worlds in their poetic texts. In that formulation, modern and postmodern poets differ from one another not with regard to chronology but in terms of their attitudes toward their recursive creations. Modern poets are those who see the worlds they make as artificial but still usefully whole or inclusive alternatives to failed systems or fragmented reality, and postmodern poets are those who regard such worlds as falsely imposed structures of containment or totalization, examples of an epistemic tyranny they castigate even as they inevitably reenact it. Such a configuration is useful here; it has obvious application to sorting out attitudes toward the cultural value of monuments. It also confuses chronological with technical and thematic distinctions, since a poet from the modern or postmodern period might reflect modern and postmodern themes and techniques in any variety of degrees and combinations.

Having noted those complications, which I think are more helpful than disabling, I repeat that some artists and thinkers in the second half of the twentieth century have been unusually harsh in their assault on monuments, and that there are good reasons for this. At the same time, I recall that others reach other conclusions and that the postmodern poets and poems I examine here take a more nuanced view of the matter (adding that those views are not characterized by the sometimes static, neatly balanced ambivalence supposedly typical of "modern" poets—it usually isn't).

Among the good reasons underlying the frequent postmodern contempt for monuments is the heightened sense that all cultural systems are arbitrary human constructions rather than reflections of essential or natural absolute truths, whether those systems are religious, political, and social arrangements or the ideas and ideals embodied in monumental works of art. This "constructivist" understanding of things has always been an aspect of human awareness, but it has been increasingly prominent since the nineteenth century and became quite widespread in the second half of the twentieth. Perhaps the uneven acceptance of the constructivist position by individuals and groups in different places and times accounts, among other things, for much of the difficulty of maintaining clear distinctions between modern and postmodern poets. For instance, writing before the terms *constructivist* and *essentialist* became ubiquitous in academic discourse, Richard Poirier observed the somewhat dissonant combination in Robert Frost's work of an intensely "postmodern" alertness to the arbitrariness of language, thought, and literary and cultural structures, and of a more "conventional" tendency to conceive of such culturally determined matters as poverty, war, and human inequality as being inevitable and natural.[4]

As with feelings about monuments, ideas about the respective proportions of the natural and the arbitrary in human knowledge and behavior have fluctuated throughout history, and those ideas also vary within any given age or era. Nevertheless, thought in the second half of the twentieth century leaned remarkably far toward the notion that everything we know, believe, and do is culturally constructed. This idea is itself unfriendly to monuments, since—especially when joined to distrust of existing power relations—it is apt to see public art as enforcing local, temporary, and relative views as if they were universal, permanent, and absolute. The constructivist view is also the source or result (it sometimes seems to be both at once) of a whole set of postmodern events and ideas inimical to monuments and the impulse to make them. Without pretending to be complete or systematic, I want to list some of those events and ideas and suggest their influence on the postmodern tendency to share Nietzsche's drastic aversion to monuments and monumentality, whether that aversion leads to rejection or, as in the case of the poets considered here, to revision.

The horrors of World War II included attacks on civilian populations by rockets, fire bombs, and atomic weapons; the Holocaust; and the not entirely facile conundrum of how well-educated, art-loving people could perpetrate bureaucratic slaughter. Those horrors confirmed and compounded a general twentieth-century sense (visible, for instance, in the post–World War I belief of some people that monuments should repudiate rather than celebrate cultures) that civilization, especially in the form of nation-states and their governments, is less the enemy of disorder and destruction than their source. That judgment was exacerbated after World War II by a subsequent half-century of ideologically driven cold and hot wars, state-sponsored terrorism and gulags, exposés of governmental misconduct and abuse, revolutions betrayed from within or crushed by entrenched powers, and the like. Since monuments are often sponsored by governments or other centers of authority, power, and influence, and since they at least implicitly support the political and social systems they inhabit, monuments themselves may be identified with civilization and its discontents. More narrowly, Fascist, Nazi, Soviet, and other governmental uses of monumental architecture and other arts for propaganda purposes encouraged a sense that monuments (and perhaps artworks in general) are necessarily complicitous with power, including supposedly democratic power.

Postmodern distrust of civilization, governments, cultures, and their structures (including monuments) has been intensified by an increasing sense that the "civilizing" forces of industrialization and technology are creating worldwide ecological disaster: poisoning the earth, air, and water, and pushing plants, animals, and indigenous peoples to extinction. Similarly, the inequities of resource use and wealth distribution, whether they are caused, ignored, or made visible by recent capitalist globalization, convince many that money and power conjoin to impose and sustain arbitrary hegemonies as natural. Such matters lead some to believe that art, especially monumental art, is the partner of self-serving governments, corporations, and other elites in maintaining the status quo—a view that can join some of the others I have mentioned to make any work with large public ambitions seem suspect. Of course, such opinions are debatable; whether as subject or occasion, monuments are often in the fray.

The second half of the twentieth century has also seen remarkably intense critiques of existing social arrangements, which are among the things monuments conventionally help to establish and uphold. Groups demeaned, excluded, or oppressed by those arrangements—whether they're defined by gender, race, class, ethnicity, sexual orientation, or something else—often employ constructivist arguments to show that existing social hierarchies are not natural and inevitable but arbitrary—and therefore both in need of revision and susceptible to it. This can be tricky, since identity politics may imply an essentialism at odds with constructivist views. Nonetheless, these groups have contributed to and made use of the general postmodern tendency to see social reality as constructed rather than natural. Consequent attitudes toward monuments vary. Thoroughgoing constructivists may see all monuments as reifying one or another false hegemony and want to expose or dismiss existing monuments and avoid new ones altogether. On the other hand, some feminists, say, might see a monument memorializing suffrage workers as a proper if not wholly satisfactory corrective to previous errors and wrongs. Similar complications affect postcolonial thought and action; postcolonial peoples and governments—whether practicing identity politics or celebrating hybridity—tend variously to decode the imperialism of particular monuments, to disparage all monuments as necessarily imperialist, or to produce representative monuments of their own. Intensifying shifts toward multicultural societies in the late twentieth century raise the same and similar issues, including the monumental question of whether, how much, and what kind of unity is necessary to sustain a culture, society, or state.

The second half of the twentieth century was a semiotic age. The proliferation of media, advertising, and means for the mechanical and digital reproduction of print, sound, and visual materials—even of the culture of gossip and celebrity—engendered extensive analysis of the sign systems that saturate postmodern life. Among other things, such analysis includes Edward Sapir's idea that "language" (here, any shared system of representation) does not function as a transparent system for problem solving, thought, or communication but instead participates actively in creating what it describes. Thus so-called facts are inseparable from their representations and a culture's language habits (linguistic and otherwise) predispose it to certain interpretive choices while disabling some others. Related ideas include Hayden White's reminders of the subjectivity of history: the now famous textuality of the archive, the notion that facts are no more than events under description, the sense that history is not made up of incontestable data but of ideologically bound interpretations. Those and similar views (Clifford Geertz's in anthropology, say) undermine the value of such concepts as permanence and universality and the value of monuments along with them; they en-

Gramley Library
Salem Academy and College
Winston-Salem, N.C. 27108

courage charges that monuments are complicitous with the systems of power that control the means of interpretation and its dissemination. It's possible, of course, to reach other conclusions. Traditional monuments are still proposed and built, and some exert considerable cultural force. Meanwhile, some artists make monuments (including poems) that acknowledge rather than seek to overcome their limitations, including their provisionality and their inevitable (even if not always immediately visible) involvements with semiotic and other systems.

To return to postmodern reasons for dismissing (or rethinking) the monumental: the implications of the new physics of the early twentieth century later became widely known and accepted. The idea—enhanced by fractal geometry and chaos theory—that everything is an event in a network of events and that even the most objective scientific and mathematical knowledge involves disabling or manageable quanta of indeterminacy may seem at odds with monumental clarity, stability, and extension. So, too, with developments in cybernetics, where nearly everything can be digitized as information, an effect that levels hierarchies, although whether in ways that multiply or shrivel human options remains unresolved. Perhaps, as with monuments, the results, so to speak, depend.

In aesthetic and cultural terms, the postmodern period has experienced a powerful feeling of belatedness: on the one hand, a dispiriting sense that everything has already been done, and on the other, an exhilarating sense that the whole past is available for selective use—whether in filial or parodic ways, or in ways that eclectically borrow styles with or without regard to the epistemes their original practices encoded. Those ideas, too, make monuments seem dubious, particularly when they are combined with a sense that progress is an illusion, that the history of human cultures or the variety of current competing ones is a matter of different but not necessarily right or wrong ways of satisfying the same set of human needs, that we live in an age whose predilection for statistics supplants ideals (the essence of traditional monuments) in favor of seemingly more democratic and achievable but potentially coercive "norms."

The list of factors contributing to the postmodern denigration of monuments might be considerably extended. The poststructuralist exposure of cultures' master narratives as "necessarily" imperialist, classist, racist, sexist, or otherwise exclusive and biased is relevant, for instance, as is the collateral idea that all cultural relations are power relations, with monuments (like schools and museums) supposedly acting as one more lens in the panopticon of a society's conscious and unconscious disciplinary structures. So-called late capitalism, with its emphasis on the consumption of disposable novelties and simulacra, may erode interest in monumental persistence. And the recent blurring (or erasure) of the imaginary line once thought hierarchically to separate "high" from "popular" culture challenges monumental values and value in other ways. But perhaps the point that there are good reasons for postmodern thinkers and artists to disparage monuments has been adequately made. Meanwhile, as it always has, monument making vigorously persists in innovative and more conventional ways. I've already mentioned Maya Lin's Vietnam Veterans Memorial as an example of the former. As I write this, the actor Tom Hanks encourages contributions to fund a World War II memorial on the Washington Mall, and monuments are erected to commemorate the fiftieth anniversary of the Korean War. In Idaho, volunteers dedicate a wildflower meadow and a woodland trail that leads to a waterfall and a group of bronze statues, all paying tribute to smoke eaters who've died fighting forest fires. At the same time, in southern statehouses, there are ongoing quarrels about just what the Confederate battle flag memorializes—valor or racism—and where it ought properly to be placed or barred.

One significant result of the "antimonumental" factors I've been tracing has been the emergence of scholarship that explores critically the place and function of monuments within the cultures that debate, make, and bequeath or inherit them. Kirk Savage's *Standing Soldiers, Kneeling Slaves,* for example, shows how American Civil War monuments—which were required not only to celebrate Northern victory but also to help reunite the nation—typically re-encoded the racist attitudes that made slavery possible in the very act of memorializing and monumentalizing slavery's abolition by emancipation. In *Written in Stone,* Sanford Levinson considers the competing social, legal, and constitutional issues that arise when changing societies respond to the monuments or other commemorations left to them by fallen regimes or by outmoded or discarded cultural, political, and other belief systems. And James E. Young, in *Writing and Rewriting the Holocaust* and *The Texture of Memory,* examines the conflicting tasks Holocaust memorials, including monuments, expect and are expected to perform.[5] Although they don't focus on poetry, those works are of considerable general importance to my own, since they explore related issues with marked rigor and insight. I have learned a great deal from them. They matter to me especially because they assume what the poets and poems I study also assume: that even the best and worst monuments satisfy and violate private and public needs and that even an age deeply distrustful of monuments and the traditions, conventions, and assumptions associated with them will find ways to have monuments of its own. They also practice a generous and critical circumspection I hope (against hope) to practice myself.

Among the strengths of James Young's superb work on Holocaust memorials is his examination of antimonuments, works that seek to record and recall atrocity without submitting to the errors and confusions monuments and the idea of monumentality can lead to. The proposers and builders of actual or conceptual antimonuments ask such questions as these: Can a monument commemorate but not domesticate (that is, can it avoid making what it wants to remember either too easily bearable or somehow ordinary and therefore inevitable)? Can it provoke but not alienate (that is, stir people to critical contemplation and action without forfeiting cultural support)? Can it frame absence or program itself to disappear without seeming to assist in the project it intends to counter, refute, or prevent (that is, avoid the bombast of a too insistent "presence" or of excessive claims to importance, permanence, and universality without appearing to abet, in this case, the Nazi effort to obliterate the Jews, or, more generally, cultural erasures of every kind)? The postmodern peoples and institutions asking those deeply self-conscious, intractable questions don't assume the transparent good will of monuments; neither do they discard monuments as inevitably vicious. Instead, they attempt to revise and revive them for current needs while remaining alert to monuments' inherent and particular limitations. Their various efforts to reconceive monuments and monumentality suggest patterns for the poets I consider here, poets who neither abandon nor dismiss monuments but attend to them while remaining alert to the many good reasons to dismiss them. Rather than praise *or* disparage monuments, Bishop, Lowell, Merrill, Walcott, and Heaney address monuments and the monumental impulse in order to consider the unsettled and unsettling political, aesthetic, and more broadly cultural issues monuments condense: the relations of those who are vested in a culture's ideology to those who are not, art's capacities and limitations (including its being enmeshed in ideology and in some sense complicitous with systems of power), and the competing pleas of change and persistence, meaninglessness and meaning, the self and society, and the relative and the absolute.

Throughout this introduction I've tried to keep two less than perfectly congruent matters in view: one, that monuments have always evoked at least some mixed feelings (a fact recorded in poetry as elsewhere), and two, that the postmodern tendency to constructivist, ideological understandings of human knowledge and arrangements, including verbal and visual language, made monuments particularly suspect in the second half of the twentieth century. This prompts a question: Are there more things under the sun than philosophy compounds, or nothing new? An old play opens when Gloucester, soon to be Richard the Third, speaks—in the wake of wintry battle—of summer and peace and "bruised arms hung up for monuments." Like manipulative rulers before and since, Richard wields the ideology of monuments like a club. Others believe that war's weapons have been converted into safe memorial symbols upholding the order of things; he hints that swords and ploughshares are one and the same, and he arms his plans to usurp and retain power by creating, then crushing illusory threats to public order. The contemporary resonance stings, even if at play's end Richard is defeated and order is "monumentally" restored. That was then. Now, a Sam Gross cartoon in a recent issue of the *New Yorker* depicts a monument to a mouse (or mice), complete with an inscribed pedestal. It's the old story. The cat reading the inscription thinks, "What crap!," its contemporary vulgate marked by centuries-old conviction.

In spite of how dubious and contested monument making has always been and has become (consider the protracted and intractable political struggles generated by almost any proposal to place or displace a public work of art), in spite of how much the human impulse to make monuments has come to seem less "natural" than conditioned to seem so, the monumental impulse persists. To that extent, at least, monuments—and countermonuments and antimonuments—are conventional. And however chastened and beleaguered it may be, the interest of postmodern poets in monuments and monumentality continues long literary and social traditions and is conventional, too. This permits and demands the critical attention to poetry's engagements with history, politics, and culture called for since the New Criticism. It also encourages close textual reading, whether in terms of Alastair Fowler's understanding that the meaning of literary kinds derives from changes over time in their shared conventions, or in terms of David Ferry's observation that conventional themes and situations in poetry permit us to focus on particular performances and to experience any single performance in relation to other ones.[6] As always, of course, poems—like monuments and other works of art (or culture)—earn attention by rewarding it.

Thomas Gardner has written about postmodern poets who find the limits of language a more salutary than distressing reminder of human finitude in an age too much given to hubris, whether in presuming that human beings are unlimited in their capacities or in judging any flaw in a human achievement as damning to the whole of it. Gardner emphasizes an idea shared by Kant, Wittgenstein, Stanley Cavell, and many recent and current poets: the sense that limitations of knowledge (and language and other cultural forms—including, say, monuments) are not failures but the conditions under which we live and work.[7] Perhaps the study of some significant postmodern poets as they encounter the limitations and possibilities of monuments (including poems with a sense of public duty and ambition) can help us to consider how the human impulse to build to last, the impulse to reify our culturally derived and ideologically driven faiths (even when distrust of such drives and derivations—and of reification itself—is among those faiths) might coexist with relativism, multiculturalism, and diversity, those other creeds that define our time and place.

I call this book *Castings*. I have in mind the casting of bronzes as a type for monumental art—with at least a hint of forging. I also imply the shedding (or sailing away) of casting off, and the sometimes flummoxed but hopeful seeking of casting about. Since when and where I could I punctuated writing with fishing, I throw out that line as well.

1

Elizabeth Bishop
"The Monument"

"I hate to see that evenin' sun go down." According to her friend Lloyd Schwartz, that bit of blues (what else?) was Elizabeth Bishop's favorite example of a "perfect" iambic pentameter line.[1] Spoken, it comes close to being one, but sung, as most of her audience was likely to have heard it, it's a syncopated tune. I suspect Bishop meant the variation to clinch rather than to trip up her example, or to clinch it *by* tripping it up, one more version of her famous habit of additive or alternative self-correction (it corrected others, too). Bishop's bluesily bent standard (where regularity and syncopation pair and imperfection's an attribute of perfection) recalls her admiring speculation that Marianne Moore "had been set going to a different rhythm" from birth, "that the old English meters that still seem natural to most of us (or *seemed* to, at any rate) were not natural to her."[2] Bishop's metrics were less "perfectly off-beat" than Moore's, but she mixed iambics with free verse and sped or hobbled accentual-syllabic meters to make a "different rhythm" of her own. Difference, in meter and most everything else, is Bishop's always shifting center, and in something like the poststructuralist sense of the word.

When Bishop says that the old ways "still seem natural to most of us"—"or *seemed* to" seem so, the difference she marks is categorical as well as chronological. Not only does our sense of what is natural alter over time, different people have different ideas about what's natural at the same time, and such alterations and variations dissolve our sense that anything at all is or ever was "natural." Bishop anticipates and shares the poststructuralist understanding of specific human arrangements as constructed rather than natural or essential. She sees personal and cultural systems of meaning, value, judgment, belief, and behavior as the result of provisional choices constantly being made (and adjusted) from among multiple, competing, but not mutually exclusive alternatives—and she believes those choices are exercised without the guidance or guarantee of absolutes or of sustainable hierarchies of any kind. For Bishop, this means that all our private and public structures are (like the blues) "home-made." That condition evicts and frees us from whatever comforting, confining homes we build and try to settle into, whether those "homes" are actual rooms, political realms, religions, or monumental and other works of art. That same condition remodels and restores us to sheltering structures, too.

"I hate to see that evenin' sun go down." Iambic pentameter is the monumental meter of English, the meter of Shakespeare and Milton. By drawing her example of iambic pentameter perfection from the blues, Bishop both nods to and teases metrical proprieties and hierarchies. She challenges national literary and cultural ones as well. The blues is an American form, not beholden to "superior" British performances or precedents. It is also a hybrid form, African-American, a fact attuned to Bishop's view that national identities are no more singular and stable than metrical ones. (American-born but partly raised in Canada and long resident in Brazil, Bishop identified—or didn't—with several and very different places.) Bishop's choice of a blues line as metrically ideal also questions the supposed superiority of high art to popular culture, reconfiguring their relationship as equal rather than hierarchical, or erasing the distinction between them altogether.

"Folk art" is rarely monumental in the usual sense of the term, and Bishop's lifelong tendency to find folk art as meaningful as any other, to see all aspects of a culture as connected and potentially revealing, has much in common with the recent view of cultural studies that everything is a text worthy of attention and likely to reward it. Such matters are an important source of Bishop's characteristic perplexings of all sorts of political, aesthetic, and more broadly cultural "givens." For if everything is a text (birds are "S-shaped" or appear as n's in her work; boats are stacked like "letters"; there's "weak calligraphy" in the weave of songbirds' cages), then, yes, everything has meaning and is worth observing and understanding. At the same time, though, since textual meanings are always arbitrary, multiple, and shifting, no single version or interpretation of anything is final, universal, or sufficient.

Skepticism about givens, about supposedly natural arrangements or authorities whose word is beyond question, is a characteristic feature of Bishop's response to things. It informs her poems, her conversations, her letters, and her childhood memoirs and stories. Recalling in adulthood having been told that her uncle "had read the Bible, Old and New Testaments, straight through three times" as a little boy, she says abruptly, "Even as a child, I never quite believed this." When she was a little girl and that same uncle cited a pious quotation to chastise her for squabbling with a playmate, she rejected the saying's meaning and questioned its provenance, doubting not only its accuracy but its very existence as an "official" text. Part of what attracted Bishop to the Brazilian child's diary she translated from Portuguese is its author's brisk refusal to take authoritative cultural codes on faith; it mirrors refusals of her own: "When a rooster crows at nine o'clock they say that a girl is running away from home to get married. I'm always hearing the rooster crow at nine o'clock, but it's very rarely that a girl runs away from home."[3] Bishop's scrutinizing interest in cultural patterns (from family sayings and "the crudest wooden footwear" to domestic arrangements, literary hierarchies, and systems of government) typifies her feelings, attitudes, ideas, and writing. And even though she began to publish as early as the 1930s, her fascination with cultural codes combines with her ingrained doubt about the absolute legitimacy of any particular code or set of codes to connect her firmly to those artists and thinkers of the second half of the twentieth century who interpret all cultural authority as a fiction and are inimical to or suspicious of monuments and monumentality.

Bishop is fully alert to and sometimes acts on the many (and good) ancient and postmodern reasons to assail the monumental impulse and its realizations, but she also turns to monuments—in her important early poem "The Monument" and elsewhere—to do more than expose or attack them. Like Lowell, Merrill, Walcott, and Heaney after her, Bishop addresses monuments in order to consider the unsettled and unsettling political, aesthetic, and more broadly cultural issues monuments condense. She does so with the "awful but cheerful" sense of things that is her hallmark. Bishop is sure that monuments reflect and exacerbate the human limitations monuments presume to transcend, not least because they presume to transcend them. At the same time, she suggests that when monuments are more humbly conceived, constructed, and comprehended than they usually are, they can help us to express those limitations, and to acknowledge, moderate, and bear them. Bishop considers human shortcomings not so much signs of failure as of a salutary if not always happy human condition (salutary because awareness of limits might keep us from presumption and from the domination of other people and of nature that goes with it). She once said rather cryptically to Marianne Moore, "certain things . . . without one particular fault . . . would be without the means of existence."[4] As her phrasing here implies, Bishop's Christianity was lapsed but vestigial. Her sense of saving faults echoes the fortunate fall; she could sometimes extend that sense to flawed but not quite fallen monuments.

Most monuments are for insiders, however narrowly or broadly defined; Bishop was in many ways an outsider. Redeeming flaws aside, distrust of, even hostility toward the monumental is one of her starting points. In a letter to Anne Stevenson, Bishop wrote, "I don't care much for grand, all out efforts [in art]"; in an interview with Ashley Brown, she said, "I'm not interested in big-scale work as such." Bishop's aversion to the "all out" and "big-scale" is thoroughgoing. It appears, for instance, in her severe dislike for inflated responses of every kind, as in her well-known distress at having claimed to a playmate, at the age of seven, that not only her father but her mother, too, was dead: in fact, her mother was alive but institutionalized. Bishop said that the deliberate lie (her adult term for what might be thought the forgivable exaggeration of a bereft child) had alerted her to the "falsity and great power of sentimentality," adding that whether the lie had been prompted by shame or by a "hideous craving for sympathy, playing up my sad romantic plight," it had made her feel an inescapable "self-distaste." Falsification by enlargement is a besetting sin of monuments, and Bishop's insistence on factual accuracy and precisions of scale (if often shifting ones) led her to attack the monumental in all its guises. Since those attacks are more often oblique than frontal, I'll approach them from an angle.

Bishop shared her generation's admiration for W. H. Auden's verse, but in a letter to Robert Lowell she complained that Auden's "Musée des Beaux Arts" is "plain inaccurate," since the "ploughman & the people on the boat will rush to see the falling boy any minute, they always do, though maybe not to help." Bishop's last phrase moderates her own stricture and exonerates Auden (by reinforcing his view that most people are indifferent to even the most dramatic suffering when it doesn't seem to affect them directly). And she allows that since he's "describing a painting . . . I guess it's all right." None-theless, and not least in the rather grudging allowances she makes, Bishop's distaste for inaccuracy is palpable, especially when some-thing that seems to her to be "plain inaccurate" is used to confirm omniscient authority, to enlarge—or monumentalize—a generalized truth: "they were never wrong, / The Old Masters." She complained similarly to Moore about Auden's redaction of the monumental ec-phrasis of Homer's *Iliad* in his "The Shield of Achilles." She disliked its "air of artificiality," its implicit bowing to authoritative precedent, and she wondered, "why is what's on a shield realer than anything else . . . , as I used to ask myself when I had to translate those endless confusing descriptions when I studied the 'classics.' "⁵ Of course, as with the complaint to Lowell, this is more persnickety than critical (although it's a bit more good humored than I've made it sound); perhaps Bishop's carping at Auden had something to do with profes-sional competitiveness. In any case, the combination of impatience and aggrieved obligation ("had to") indicates Bishop's distaste for the power plays implicit in monumentally grand and aggrandizing aesthetic effects (including effects she may have found masculinist or militaristic). Shields are associated not only with war but also with epics, emblems, and other "classic" monuments; Bishop disparages both shields and the sort of totalizing authority ("realer than any-thing else") monuments typically reach for: Homer's shield claims to contain the whole of the varied world and Auden's to comprise his narrower, grimmer one. Against the impersonal, universalizing grandeur of monumental classics, Bishop preferred the partial, in every sense.

Bishop's partiality for the non- or antimonumental has biograph-ical sources. Her father died of Bright's disease when she was eight months old; when Bishop was five, her mother, judged incurably insane, was committed to an asylum for life. Further disruptions followed. Sent to live with her maternal grandparents in tiny, rural Great Village, Nova Scotia, Bishop settled in, then felt kidnapped when her father's wealthier but less demonstrably affectionate parents returned her to Massachusetts. In their chill and upright Worcester home she felt woefully out of place, lonely, unloved, and guilty, prey to asthma, eczema, and other ailments. With the help of an aunt, she recovered sufficiently to become a successful student at Walnut Hill and at Vassar, but at college she began the bouts of secret drink-ing that persisted at times throughout her life. A small bequest allowed Bishop to travel, but she lived in hotels in New York and felt sharply her lack of a home to go to on holidays, those monumental occasions she always disliked. The homes Bishop did make, in Key West and Brazil, she lost, the former when the island was spoiled, she thought, by the naval expansion brought on by World War II, the latter, when her lover, Lota de Macedo Soares, took her own life. This lamentable list risks the inflated "playing up" of Bishop's plight that she despised, but it can also suggest why monumental claims to permanently settled perfections would have seemed deeply "unlikely" to her. For an asthmatic, to whom something as natural as breathing the air itself could feel contested and unsure, large-scale promises of certitude and stability might seem rigged or askew. At the same time, if everybody's home is a sort of private monument, Bishop's distrust of and desire for homes and houses—a major source of the intense emotion in even her most guarded poems—helps account not only for her disparaging view of more obviously monumental structures but also for her chastened hopes for them.

However that may be, the wider cultural contexts of Bishop's life also discouraged trust in monuments and their implicit but not necessarily capable support for existing arrangements, some of which she may not have wanted to see maintained in any case. Her autobiographical poem, "In the Waiting Room," shows Bishop's childhood awareness of the disorienting threats of World War I. She was a woman in an era when, as Marianne Moore sharply put it, men had power and sometimes one was made to feel it. And Bishop was lesbian at a time when homosexuality was generally thought to be abnormal and, at best, to require dissembling. (Bishop was born in 1911; when she returned from Brazil to the United States in the late 1960s she was disturbed and sometimes delighted by how attitudes toward sexual and other personal and public matters had changed.). Bishop graduated from Vassar in 1934, and she felt the pinch if not the bite of the Great Depression, with its challenges to Americans' widely shared presumptions about the naturalness and superiority of capitalism as an economic system. In her memoir "The U.S.A. School of Writing," she half-mockingly describes the radicalism of her college class as "puritanically pink," while noting without self-pity her own "real need for a little more money" than she had, that is, than she had inherited.

Privileged but not so well-off as most of her classmates and alert to the suffering of others, Bishop elsewhere vaguely aligned herself with critiques of capitalism. She sometimes felt, as when at lunch with the editors of the *Partisan Review,* the pressure of the 1930s proletarian faith that writing must be politically engaged to be serious or important. Yet Bishop disliked political posturing as much as any other kind; she ridiculed the leftist politics of the poet T. C. Wilson for their overheated tone as well as for their content, writing, "This morning Ted sent me some Lenin pamphlets and he has underlined *every* emotional passage and written the most amazingly childish comments in the margin."[6] It might be that since Bishop's doubts about the naturalness and reliability of political and economic as well as other social arrangements were already in place, the lessons of the Great Depression didn't so much shock or revolutionize her assumptions as confirm what she already felt. In politics as elsewhere, she didn't reject one monumental faith in favor of another but kept faith with faithlessness or with more local and provisional beliefs. The militarism Bishop witnessed in civil war Spain and in Europe on the brink of World War II, like the political upheavals she observed in 1960s Brazil, seems also to have cemented her lifelong distrust of authority, especially when paired with power, and her collateral sense that cultural arrangements are conditional, always subject to change and to testing by alternatives. Such views are apt to make monuments and the monumental seem obtuse and obsolete, more arbitrary than absolute, more local than universal, more temporary than permanent, more false than true.

Robert von Hallberg has shown that large numbers of American poets were able to travel to Europe in the 1940s and 1950s on the strength of the U.S. victory in World War II, post-war American affluence, a strong dollar, and the increased governmental support for higher education spurred by the cold war. Many of those poets wrote poems addressing the monuments of European high culture with a proprietary, perhaps imperialist air, as post-war American political dominance extended to include a sense of responsibility for European culture damaged or threatened by war and its accompanying and persistent economic constraints. Bishop's most important European travel occurred before the war. She did not address European subjects in a proprietary way, was more likely to describe a windup toy than works of high culture, and in such travel-inflected poems as "Paris, 7 A.M." and "Over 2,000 Illustrations and a Complete Concordance," took a decidedly anti-imperialist and antimonumental stance. For instance, as Margaret Dickie has shown, the Paris poem anatomizes the continuity among Napoleonic imperialism, the physical shape of Paris (which encodes and reinforces centralized political and military power with its radiating stars and squares), and the histrionics, as Bishop saw it, of monumental and other efforts to memorialize by measuring and resisting the flow of time.[7] In this and other ways, Bishop's choice and treatment of subject matter reflect an antimonumental stance.

Bishop rarely addresses monumental subjects directly; when she does, it's usually to debunk their pretensions. She said she was glad she'd seen the monuments of ancient Rome in ruins rather than imperially whole.[8] In "Over 2,000 Illustrations and a Complete Concordance," she shrinks the grandeur of contemporary Rome's immensely intact St. Peter's by depicting its indifference to inspiring intensities of weather: the basilica's coldness belittles; it makes seminarians antlike, as if the Church's monumental commitment to oddly worldly forms of the supernatural removed it from natural and human contact in appropriate sizes. When something loftily portentous does occur in a Bishop poem, a miracle, say, it's apt to prove wholly an illusion or, at best, to be "working, on the wrong balcony." Similarly, when Bishop turns to artworks in her poems, she doesn't consider masterpieces, works thought great or monumental, but rather conventional landscapes by her great-uncle, paintings that raise questions about art's power to render the world accurately and meaningfully rather than resolve those questions or assume they don't need asking. When an old master does appear in Bishop's writing, the pretentiousness its presence might imply is quickly painted over, as in her story "The Sea & Its Shore": "It is an extremely picturesque scene, in some ways like a Rembrandt, but in many ways not." So, too, with literary works. Bishop alludes to Felicia Hemans's "Casabianca," not to the *Aeneid* or Dante. When she does refer to a famous book, as in "Crusoe in England," she does so to challenge rather than confirm its "civilizing" colonialist assumptions.

Monuments assert their importance by appeals to ideas of centrality and permanence and by sheer physical size. Bishop calls one poem "Large Bad Picture," as if those attributes come paired, and her typical subjects are marginal, small, and fleeting. Her descriptive poems are landscapes and domestic interiors, not history paintings. Of course, the choice of what to depict has its politics, and Bishop, like van Ruisdael or Vermeer, is not abjuring importance but redefining its nature, and the nature of memorial and commemorative

conventions along with it. Nevertheless, Bishop's preference for pe-
ripheries is inimical to the traditionally monumental, whether she is
depicting surreally private dreams, the scruffy harbor of "The Bight,"
the makeshift decorations of "Jerónimo's House," unprepossessing
Varick Street, strong-smelling fishhouses, a squatter's children, an
armadillo, a moose, a run-over chicken, or a filling station. When
Bishop's titles place her poems in genre categories, they lay claim not
to epic or ode but to the humbler modes of the letter, the exercise,
and the invitation, on the pattern, perhaps, of Stevens's notes and
anecdotes. Bishop does sometimes turn to outsize subjects, as in the
prose poems "Giant Toad" and "Giant Snail," but there, largeness
is not the mark of centrality but one more attribute of the outsider,
along with clumsiness, anxiety, alienation, even a kind of terror.
Terror is not an apparent attribute of monuments, which are given
to confidence and poise, but Bishop thought some hint of mortal
terror underlies all works of art. She might have had terror in mind
when she spoke of children as "fearfully observant." Mary McCarthy
captured the fear and pain in Bishop's work. Praising the quidditas
of Bishop's gifted kind of seeing, McCarthy felt admiration but not
its usual companion, envy. About Bishop's famous eye, she said, it
was like having "a big pocket magnifying glass," then added, "*of
course* it would have hurt to have to use it for ordinary looking: that
would have been the forfeit."[9] Bishop's acute vision could make the
magnifications of monuments seem forfeit, too.

Other matters indicate the antimonumental thrust of Bishop's
writing and thinking: her preference for process over products, for
instance (as in her admiration for the desire of baroque prose stylists
"to portray, not a thought, but a mind thinking"), her humility, her
liking for self-interrogating meanings (what she once called "meanings enjambed"), and her wanting to build up effects "by a series of
irregularities." Those leanings are all at odds with traditional monuments, which tend to be stable, proud, declarative, regular, and regu-
larizing. They tend to be adamant, too, as Moore might have been
thinking when she asked rhetorically, reviewing Bishop's first book,
"is not anything that is adamant, self-ironized?" In a notebook, the
young Elizabeth Bishop worked up lists of questions and possible
topics of conversation preparatory to her first meeting with Moore
in 1935; one entry notes the high level of insult conveyed in the expression "It's good for you!" It's the sort of thing most monuments
seem to be saying.[10]

After she met Moore, Bishop reported to her friend Frani Blough that she'd been reading a "Physiologus" trying to find ways to describe the older poet. One candidate was this: "The Centaurs have the upper part as of a man, and from the breast down the form of a horse. So has every man two souls, and is unstable in his ways." That, like her observation that Moore's "combination of understatement and hyperbole is always a little confusing," might apply equally well to Bishop herself.[11] I cite those highly flavored remarks here in part to say how unstable and confused I've been in overstating Bishop's antimonumental views. As with houses, Bishop's distrust of monuments creates as much desire as distaste. A look at Bishop's most overtly "monumental" poem, "The Monument," will show that she not only disparaged monuments but also considered how they might be revised, revalued, and used.

The following passage is from V. S. Naipaul's 1971 novella "In a Free State": "Something like a monument appeared beside the road. It looked like a war memorial or a drinking fountain. It turned out to be a standpipe: a black nozzle sticking out of a large concrete wall with bevelled edges and cut-away corners, PUBLIC WORKS AND WELFARE JOINT ADMINISTRATION 27-5-54 roughly picked out in a stripe of blue-and-white mosaic at the top of the wall. It was the first of eight monumental standpipes. Then once more there was only the road." Naipaul's acid eye for revealing detail (as in the seemingly casual observation "at the top") mirrors Bishop's, and his unprogrammatic postcolonialism recalls such Bishop poems as "Brazil, January 1, 1502" and "Crusoe in England." Naipaul's description, from a brilliantly understated story set in colonial Africa, shares a good deal with Bishop's "The Monument," first published in James Laughlin's *New Directions* anthology for 1939. As in Bishop's poem, the ornamental and official aspects of the quasi-monumental object in question (it has "bevelled edges," "cut-away corners," and a "stripe of . . . mosaic"; it looks like a "war memorial" and was erected by the "PUBLIC WORKS AND WELFARE JOINT ADMINISTRATION") conjoin weirdly with its commonplace and functional ones (it's a "concrete wall," a "drinking fountain," or "standpipe").

But the initial confusion in Naipaul's description ("It looked like a war memorial or a drinking fountain") is quickly resolved ("It turned out to be a standpipe"). Like some bureaucratic Ozymandias, the "monumental standpipes" of Naipaul's story declaim a colonial politics; they allude to a supposedly shared and glorious past ("war memorials") in order to exercise state power. They say something like this: services are benevolently provided; subservience is the unit of exchange. It's an antimonumental analysis with which Bishop might in the main have agreed. But the political, aesthetic, and more broadly cultural issues condensed in the ambiguous monument of Bishop's poem stay in play much longer than they do in the Naipaul passage. Monuments are attacked in the process, but finally, in Bonnie Costello's trenchant phrase, "The Monument" preserves "a place for art after dismantling its idealism."[12] It makes room for monuments and other "impossible" human structures, too.

"The Monument" is an uncanny poem, in part because its explicitness is overdetermined to the point at which detail yields imprecision as efficiently as it does precision. This is a feature both of the poem's descriptions and of what those descriptions signify. It is immediately audible in the tension between the firm specificity of the poem's title and the vexed query of its opening sentence, "Now can you see the monument?" As it turns out, this question has to do not only with the visibility of the object the title names but also with the propriety of placing this particular object within the aesthetic category "monument," where the poem's title and its main speaker both locate it. Whether the poem's dialogue is thought of as occurring between two persons or between competing attitudes within an individual, disagreements about what constitutes a monumental or other work of art generate its debate, as do contending views about the use or value of such works.

The strange combination of errancy and exactitude in "The Monument" has caused some commentators to refer to it as an abstract work lacking any external reference; they classify it with such early Bishop experiments in surreal allegory as "The Imaginary Iceberg." That same combination has encouraged other critics to identify the poem's external object and occasion quite precisely. The candidate most frequently put forward as the source of "The Monument" is the set of Max Ernst wood rubbings (or frottages) called *Histoire Naturelle*. In those works, Ernst took tracinglike impressions of pieces of wood and then assigned or added visual or conceptual significance to the wood-grained patterns. Ernst's surrealism is of the disruptive rather than transcendent kind, and the crossing of exaggerated mimesis with the accidental and willfully arbitrary in his frottage procedures has much in common with aspects of "The Monument," which tries and teases representation and whose shoreline, structure, sea, and sky all seem wooden. In fact, as Costello points out, one of the *Histoire Naturelle* rubbings, "False Positions," actually depicts a pair of vaguely monumental cylinders on a wood-grain base. (Of course, Bishop's construction involves not Ernst's "fretted" yet otherwise bare cylinders but rather ornamented "boxes in descending sizes.")

There's little doubt that Bishop had Ernst somewhat in mind when writing "The Monument." She bought a copy of his frottage collection in Paris a few years before she composed the poem; she thumbtacked six of them around her room (to the maid's consternation), made a number of frottagelike works herself, and admitted that her poem "The Weed," roughly contemporaneous with "The Monument," owed a debt to his work. Like Ernst, Bishop was greatly attracted to wood grain. Perhaps it reminded her of writing paper. Commenting on one of the Bishop watercolors he collected for the book *Exchanging Hats,* William Benton calls wood grain "one of her specialties"; careful attempts to render wood grain appear in many of her writing-page-sized paintings. All of this connects "The Monument" with Ernst's example. But Bishop also vigorously (perhaps defensively) denied that Ernst had affected her work, telling an editor that she "disliked all of his painting intensely" and that the idea of his "ever having been an influence" was "mistaken." She may have feared that too exact an identification of a work's indebtedness would narrow responses to it. More important, Bishop was sure that works of art arise mysteriously and not from single springs. She makes this point in "The Monument" when she writes that the object's generative center or source, whatever is "within" it, "cannot have been intended to be seen." In an interview, she mentioned John Livingston Lowes's ingenious tracking down of Coleridge's sources, then said, "And how do they know? It takes probably hundreds of things coming together at the right moment to make a poem and no one can ever really separate them out and say this did this, that did that."[13]

No doubt many of the "probably hundreds of things" urging "The Monument" are beyond location, let alone separating out. Still, some other possible contexts for the poem seem worthy of mention. "The Monument" was collected in Bishop's first book, *North & South,* published in 1946, and she worried that the fact that none of the volume's poems deals "directly with the war" would leave her "open to reproach." Perhaps the critical word here is *directly,* for however indirectly, *North & South* is very much a war book. During the years leading up to World War II, the years when she was writing "The Monument," Bishop was in touch with what was coming. She had inadvertently booked passage to Europe on a Nazi ship (she described the arms raised in salute when the ship departed as "horrible," "like the dead"); she had experienced the iconoclastic, perhaps propagandistic effects of the civil war in Spain ("the wooden and plastic statues and crucifixes, all periods and quantities, dragged out of a church in Barcelona, lying so that at first one thought they were dead soldiers. There was something suspiciously dramatic about the arrangement"); and she had seen Italy militarizing ("Every 3rd man is in uniform"). Louise Bogan pointed out that one of the poems in *North & South*, "Roosters," "contains all manner of references to war and warriors." Susan Schweik, and Margaret Dickie after her, greatly expanded that insight. Schweik shows how "Roosters" functions as a war poem and indicates the ways in which features of several other poems in the book reflect its wartime context: the natural aggressions and reconciliations of "Florida," "Little Exercise," and "The Fish"; the violence arising from encounters between the civil and the surreal in such poems as "Sleeping Standing Up"; the hint of theaters of war and of art's complicity with belligerence in the stagy literary allusions of "Casabianca" and "Wading at Wellfleet."[14]

Although Schweik and Dickie hint at connections between "The Monument" and war memorials, neither quite considers it a war poem. Schweik implies that she's stretching a point when she includes it in a list of poems in *North & South* that reflect matters characteristic of war literature: the book, she writes, has "naval engagements, border crossings, skirmishes, search missions, even a monument of sorts." Dickie says only that "Paris, 7 A.M." "picks up hints from 'The Monument' of just how vainglorious memorials are" (a view that oversimplifies the latter poem, I think). I want to suggest that "The Monument" is, among other things, a war poem, political in ways Bishop might well have feared would leave her open to reproach, especially from readers sensitive to the antiwar significance it shares with other poems in *North & South*. In 1946, when Americans were sure they'd fought to save civilization from barbarism, Bishop's frequent implication that civilization and barbarity are alike (although not identical) in abusing power would have seemed to most unpatriotic at best. Perhaps the book's famously geographical title, *North & South*, echoes that other civil war as one more indicator of Bishop's risky wartime sense that civility, like literature and monuments, conspires with possessiveness and aggression. At the same time, I want to argue that Bishop's attitude toward monuments, perhaps including war monuments, is less than wholly dismissive.

A poem about monumentality published in wartime, when monuments and memorials matter so much, will have public, political resonance. The most obvious concerns of "The Monument" are aesthetic: it explores the blurred line between representation and abstraction, for instance; it wonders about the fidelity and falseness of artistic versions of the world; and it questions the proper materials, methods, and effects of monumental and other human creations. But Bishop's poem doesn't raise aesthetic issues theoretically. As its dialogue form implies, "The Monument" places considerable emphasis on the nature and public reception of "monumental" art. The poem presents an encounter in which two people—or two competing voices within a single person—look at a purportedly monumental object. One viewer is exact, imaginative, and aesthetically committed; the other is less sophisticated but more pragmatic, interested in art but distrustful of its claims to meaning and importance while at the same time insistent that it have some practical application. The encounter is ambiguously located: perhaps it's set in a museum or some other public space, or perhaps in a private room where a connoisseur displays a recent "monumental" purchase to a less knowledgeable, resistant, but thoughtful companion. One viewer or voice seems to play docent to the other, less fluent party, but each in fact instructs the other. The poem's two voices—each one both actor and audience—are not treated hierarchically. Neither response is represented as superior to the other; each has failings and virtues in something like the way the opposing positions of the speakers in Frost's "Mending Wall"—one arguing for a tradition-based approach to life, the other for experimentation—are, both of them, balanced and thrown over, although not overthrown. The late 1930s was a time of intense reconsideration of art's public roles and responsibilities. The Great Depression, the Spanish Civil War, and the looming war in Europe encouraged many to assert that art must be politically committed in explicit, "realistic" ways in order to matter. Bishop doubted that, but "The Monument" reflects if it doesn't resolve the issue in its concern with "reception," as the political resonance of one of its literary contexts or intertexts also makes clear.

Until fairly recently, Wallace Stevens was usually considered an aesthete whose loftily or anecdotally staged colloquies of imagination and reality played out at an aloof remove from the social and political circumstances of his time and place. James Longenbach, Alan Filreis, and other critics have shown the inadequacy of this view. They demonstrate that *Owl's Clover,* the politically engaged poetic sequence Stevens published in 1936, is less anomalous than characteristic. *Owl's Clover* responds directly to the proletarian requirement that in troubled times art should fulfill its responsibility to the suffering and impoverished masses—its presumed immediate audience—by means of unambiguous political declarations. This general requirement had been applied specifically to Stevens in Stanley Burnshaw's review of his *Ideas of Order* for the Marxist periodical *New Masses.* Although Stevens continued to resist the dogmatism of both the political left and right by maintaining an elusive ambiguity, in *Owl's Clover,* especially in the poems "The Old Woman and the Statue" and "Mr. Burnshaw and the Statue," he respectfully considers the disappointments and irritations the alienated poor and leftist intellectuals might justifiably (if not quite justly) feel in the presence of "uncommitted" art, represented in *Owl's Clover* by sculpture.

Bishop read the Stevens poems when they came out; she commented on them in a notebook that also contains her pen-and-ink sketch of an ornamented stack of boxes. Barbara Page first noticed this connection, and she points out that Bishop's sketch is a visual trial run for "The Monument" (a version of some of its lines appears below the drawing). Page writes that Bishop's creaky monument rejects Stevens's more traditionally stable view of art, and it's true that Bishop substitutes, as it were, her ramshackle structure of crates for Stevens's more conventional equestrian group. But Stevens himself anatomized equestrian statuary in his essay "The Noble Rider and the Sound of Words" (some of it works; some doesn't), and Bishop's comments about *Owl's Clover* in a 1936 letter to Moore suggest that her reaction to Stevens in "The Monument" involves a more nuanced response than rejection. Bishop told Moore that she considered *Owl's Clover* a defense of Stevens's own position and read its statue as representing "ART." The capital letters surely indicate Bishop's distrust of big, authoritative, self-capitalizing works, the sort of pompous thing "The Monument" deflates. But Bishop sees Stevens as practicing similar deflations. She says she interprets "The Old Woman and the Statue" as "confessing the 'failure' of such art" and "Mr. Burnshaw and the Statue" as "a sort of mock-elegy" for it. Those are matters

"The Monument" takes up in ways that preserve as well as dismantle monumental efforts.[15]

T. C. Wilson's poem "Let Us Go No More to Museums" may have provided another, slighter and slightly earlier political and aesthetic intertext for Bishop's poem (intertextuality being, as Barbara Johnson says, one of the "multitude of ways a text has of not being self-contained, of being traversed by otherness," of being, I'd add, less than monumental). I've referred to Bishop's mockery of the emotionalism of Wilson's leftist politics, but the two were friends, introduced by Moore. Wilson lent Bishop books (William Carlos Williams's *In the American Grain,* for instance) and sent her Duke Ellington records. His poems, including the one named above, appeared with hers in the 1935 anthology *Trial Balances,* Bishop's first appearance in book form. The argument of Wilson's poem, like the blunt invitation/command of his title, is straightforward: we should no longer stand in museums "Exalting memorials of some dynasty we have no part in"; we should stand (or take a stand), instead, in the "streets outside," where real physical hunger makes any hunger for art's spiritual sustenance seem truly starved.

In its unknown, unknowable origins, the commemorative object in Bishop's "The Monument" has something in common with the supposedly incomprehensible memorial of an alien culture which Wilson so peremptorily ("some dynasty") dismisses. Perhaps his word "dynasty" was a source for her poem's references to Asia Minor, Mongolia, and an "artist-prince." And perhaps the "realist" voice in Bishop's poem, asking "Why did you bring me here to see it?" and "what can it prove?" recalls Wilson's pragmatic attack on the supposed social uselessness of the art embalmed in museums, as her poem's other voice offers an alternative to that attack. For just as "The Monument" extends and moderates Stevens's mock-elegy for too-exalted "ART," so, too, it queries rather than repeats Wilson's assertion about lost dynasties, wondering just how much or how little part we might have in the art and artifacts that allegedly immortalize or represent cultures now lost to us. Bishop's wonderfully doubtful-certain claim about her monument, "But roughly but adequately it can shelter," is resonant of both the museum *and* the streets.[16]

To return for a moment to the visual arts, the paintings of Giorgio de Chirico might provide another context for "The Monument." Bishop said she liked de Chirico's early work, which often has the hint of mortal terror Bishop thought informs most works of art, and both de Chirico and Bishop frequently use staginess to display and puncture the theatrical or histrionic. Fearful and melancholy, precise to the point of imprecision, the eerie architecture of de Chirico's paintings has a good deal in common with Bishop's poem: in both, the familiar consorts with the deracinated, and the uncanny combination in his paintings of a Cubist-inflected flattening of the picture plane with traditional but inconsistent single-point perspective "estranges" viewers' expectations for painterly spatial descriptions in much the same way the odd angles and overdetermined details of "The Monument" disrupt readers' expectations for writerly ones. De Chirico's "Nostalgia per l'infinito," dated 1911 on the canvas but thought to have been painted two or three years later, seems especially to the point. In it, two viewers are dwarfed by a boxy monumental tower, perhaps of the grim sort from which the Italian nobility fought their neighborhood wars, but lightened (or made more darkly political still) by colorful pennants on poles near the top. Set mostly "against a sky" on a sand-colored piazza, the painting's monument recalls without quite illustrating the tower of Turin's Mole Antonelliana. Like Bishop's more heavily ornamented and less stable monument (the constituent boxes of her structure are tipsily stacked so that corners alternate with sides), de Chirico's tower is both clear and remote, fully present yet implying an "irrevocable past," as Robert Hughes has said.[17] The application to Bishop's poem is almost pat.

Or far from it. In the late summer of 1938, the year she wrote "The Monument," Bishop spent nearly a month and a half in a beach shack near the fishing village and art colony of Provincetown, Massachusetts, at the tip of Cape Cod, on property owned by her friends, the painter Loren MacIver and the critic Lloyd Frankenberg. Bishop described the geography there as "longitudinal," and Brett Millier, in her indispensable biography of Bishop, says that Provincetown's "'longitudinal' landscape became the setting for 'The Monument.'" For that, Key West, where Bishop was living at the time, might have done as well. What Millier doesn't say is that Provincetown has not only a "flat" landscape but a monument, too, a most insistent vertical in that mostly horizontal place. Built on High Pole Hill, the tallest point in town, a tower rises just over 252 feet to put its somewhat boxy top at about 350 feet above sea level. It dominates the land- and seascape, and is, as the current visitors' video introduction puts it, "visible for miles from land and sea." In the words of the flyer handed out by the museum associated with the tower, Provincetown's monument "was erected to commemorate [*commemorate* is perhaps the most charged word in Bishop's poem] the first landfall of the Pilgrims in the New World at Provincetown on November 11, 1620." As the flyer also notes, the U.S. Congress provided nearly half the monument's funding; President Roosevelt came to lay the cornerstone in 1907, accompanied by eight battleships, and President Taft, with his own naval escort, attended the dedication ceremony at the tower's completion in 1910.

Some further details. The pilgrim monument is the "tallest all-granite structure in the United States." Its design "is copied from the Torre del Mangia in Siena, Italy." The weirdly apt political logic by which America's militant protestant separation from Europe is memorialized by an obedient bow to Europe's prior (and Catholic) artistic mastery might well have appealed to Bishop's precisely skewed sense of the way things work. Perhaps the tower's connection to the religiopolitical Pilgrims (the Mayflower Compact was signed in Provincetown Harbor), its association with presidents and warships, and Provincetown's heritage of fishing help account for the odd ornamentation of Bishop's monumental tower, where the political ("flag-poles") and "ecclesiastical" decorations are hard to tell from "fishing poles," a "confusion" that may be intended to recall how church and state and the ordinary citizenry conjoin or conspire in wartime. Provincetown is also well equipped with the sea, sand, and driftwood so prominent in Bishop's poem. Even the museum video has a strange, if surely unintended echo of Bishop's text: asked to explain the artwork in question, Bishop's docent-speaker blandly or desperately intones, "It is the monument"; the calmly proud, only slightly boosterish woman's voice on the videotape says, "It is the Pilgrim Memorial Monument." All of that convinces me to nominate the Provincetown monument as one more of the "probably hundreds of things coming together at the right time to make a poem," in this case, Bishop's "The Monument." On the other hand, Provincetown's monument is made of granite, not of wood. Perhaps that hardness connects both towers to the "adamant" Moore was sure must be "self-ironized." Meanwhile, the mention of Moore recalls that "The Monument" may have yet another source in the boxy representational politics of the older poet's slightly earlier poem "Virginia Brittania."

One strategy of "The Monument" is to deploy precision to create both exactitude and imprecision, and to do so in such a way that the imprecision itself is at once vexing in its undecidability and piercingly exact in its indication of the intricate political, aesthetic, and cultural issues condensed in monumental and other works of art. At every level the poem is distinct and bleary, definitively blurred. "The Monument" involves ecphrasis, for instance, the literary representation of visual art, but it remains unclear whether the poem's ecphrasis is actual or notional (the fundamental differentiating terms of *The Gazer's Spirit*, John Hollander's vivid study of ecphrastic practice in poetry). In some ways "The Monument" appears to describe an actual object (an Ernst frottage, a de Chirico painting, Bishop's own drawing, the monument in Provincetown), but the very surplus of possible objects makes identification suspicious. Meanwhile, the work the poem describes seems almost wholly notional, Bishop's woozily aligned invention.

The poem's language causes similar effects. Declarations abound: "It is of wood"; "It is the monument"; "It is an artifact / of wood"; "It is the beginning of a painting / a piece of sculpture, or poem, or monument." As the last example shows, declarations needn't be definitive. The lines "A sky runs parallel, / and it is palings, coarser than the sea's" multiply strangeness: a paling or fading sky makes sense, but a sky that *is* palings, the boards of a fence, disturbs a range of expectations. Among other things, the disturbance says that the monument (or any work of art) is not a transparent representation of the world. Its material calls attention to itself and affects rather than merely renders or conveys what it purports to represent, in something like the way language not only describes but also creates, and in terms of the necessarily limited cultural assumptions about seeing, knowing, and judging that any language contains and is contained by. Here, since the work is made of wood, we get "splintery sunlight and long-fibred clouds." Furthermore, although the monument is made of wood and is supposedly eroded, dried, and cracked by "The strong sunlight, the wind from the sea" outside it, the sun and sea themselves are also wooden, not realities outside the "stage-set" artifact but properties within it. Sometimes even the viewers of the object seem to be "within the view." All of this both inscribes and erases the conventional boundaries separating works of art from the world and observers from things observed. The questions raised about the relative primacy and power of the actual and notional, subject and object, the knower and the known, have political and social as well as aesthetic force.

I've already discussed ways in which "The Monument" indirectly reflects its Depression and wartime political and cultural contexts. More directly, the poem's title implies an artwork with public and political dimensions, and the monument's "ecclesiastical" and "flag-pole" ornaments refer to church and state. As a result, inquiries that seem to be aesthetic when asked about the monument become political and cultural when addressed to those monumental public institutions. How representative, the poem might be thought to ask, are church and state? Are their structures or constructions absolute, or are they relative to time and place and to limited constituencies and provisional assumptions? Do they invent the reality they claim to describe? Is their authority actual, a matter of fact, or merely no-tional, imagined? Bishop rarely separated art from politics, and she often saw them as complicit. As Millier reports, in Bishop's dreams a writer's tools joined images of war.[18] (She worked out the linkage in "12 O'Clock News.") In "View of the Capitol from the Library of Congress," a band's instrumental brasses want to match sounds with brass ammunition; in "Brazil, January 1, 1502," the delicate art of tapestry enables conquest and colonization. "The Monument" mirrors the pattern; in that poem, political and cultural truths and arrangements fade—but don't quite disappear—along with those of art. The presence there (or presence by absence) of an actual or notional "artist-prince" raises slippery issues of authority. Like his border-crossing title, those issues, too, are as political as they are artistic. The artist-prince may recall Shelley's artist-legislator, for instance, who guarantees art's social value, or he may be one more Ozymandias, a ruler-politician whose adamant, monument-raising will to power is self-ironizing and guarantees collapse. It's even pos-sible that the artist-prince, the poem's very figure of artistic, political, and cultural authority, is nothing more than a language function, merely text. With echoes, perhaps, of sound effects by Coleridge ("In Xanadu did Kubla Khan") or Stevens ("Chieftain Iffucan"), Bishop's artist-prince seems almost produced by alliteration; here's his improbably lettered first appearance: "An ancient promontory, / an ancient principality whose artist-prince . . ."[19]

All of these overlapping political, aesthetic, and cultural issues are explored in the unresolved dialogue of "The Monument," a poem appropriately rich in hyphens, hybridity's punctuation. The first speaker, what I've called the docent-voice, describes the object in question. Her first words, apparently in response to objections that precede the poem, set an inquisitorial, irritated tone. The opening sentence might sound gentle if the word "now" were moved to its end. As it is, "Now can you see the monument?" sounds brusquely impatient. (Does it also echo the U.S. national anthem?) The note of exasperation gives the poem an earthiness removed from monumentally pretentious pronouncements. The description that follows creates the precise imprecisions and skewed perspectives already discussed. It conjoins church and state with art, and collapses the hierarchy between ordinary craftsmanship ("whittled" or "jig-saw work") and more formally artful ornamentation ("fleur-de-lys"). This initial passage is more concerned with perception than cognition or conception, but "The Monument" is always aware that perception is filtered through conceptions, and its opening emphasis on the monument's material raises the issue of whether a structure made of ordinary wood can belong to the category of monuments, usually reserved for loftier (and more "adamant") bronze or stone. Wood ages more rapidly than conventionally monumental materials, as a later complaint from the poem's other voice insists: "It looks old"; it's "unpainted," dry, eroded, "cracked." Given the poem's overdetermined signification, in which the monument stands for so many monumental things (including church and state and works in bronze and stone as well as wood), this also scrutinizes the defining claim of any monument, the claim to permanence. The first speaker's eventual response to this issue (its difficulty made more and more pressing by the other speaker's objections) shifts the poem toward the incomplete but moving resolution it achieves, a partial reconciliation not only between warring theories and ideas about the nature and function of monumental art but between and within people as well.

Admitting that the monument is an "artifact" (both artful and artificial, with perhaps a nod to the "artifice" of Yeats's "Sailing to Byzantium"), admitting that it is "an artifact of wood," the docent-voice makes the monument's "material" fault or flaw a modest virtue: "Wood holds together better / than sea or cloud or sand could by itself, / much better than real sea or sand or cloud." This rejects or revises the polarized terms of debates between monumental and antimonumental positions. The poem has a quiet, unforced insistence; its ramshackle, homely, wooden structure *is* a monument, despite, in fact because of its being subject to erosion and decay. This refuses the conventional (and quite unrealizable) requirement that monuments be immortal immortalizers, inhumanly and unnaturally perfect, permanent, and precious. But it doesn't therefore yield to the contingencies of natural time and change. The poem, like its monument, resists, but only somewhat. The artifact of wood "holds together better" than the stuff of nature itself but not so completely as to deny the realities of time and change and death. It achieves a humble and as it were temporary kind of permanence—no, not permanence, extension.

When shaped by human hands, the natural material wood lasts longer than individual trees or human lives do, but it doesn't assert the timelessness most monuments claim for themselves and for the provisional cultural, political, and aesthetic faiths most monuments encode as if those faiths were absolute and complete. It is precisely this monument's imprecision, its amenability to change, its accommodation (intended or not, occurring in the artist's eye or the beholder's) of altered and altering practices, beliefs, and definitions, that makes it recognizable as human—however imperfectly, relativistically, or subjectively it's understood. "The monument's an object, yet" its indefinite, indefinable decorations "give it away as having life." The undecidable or indeterminate in Bishop's monument, its lack of the wrong kind of confidently "representative" dignity, the uncertainty about exactly what it is or means or represents, gives it a warmth that chillier, conventional monuments lack. This is so precisely because the unspecifiable details of this monument reveal what it shares with every monument (or "painting," "piece of sculpture, or poem"): a perhaps "natural," even "essential" human desire ("wishing," "wanting") to "cherish" and "commemorate." Underlined by Bishop's insistence that paintings, sculptures, poems, and monuments are not so much final products, achieved or completed, as they are works in progress or process, beginnings, "The Monument" cherishes and commemorates (or, more hesitantly still, expresses the shared human desire *to* cherish or commemorate) in ways that correct without wholly abandoning conventional monuments and monumentality, ways that (while gently resisting) live with rather than seek to master change and time as they affect objects and persons, politics, art, and culture. As with claims to permanence, claims to representativeness are thereby denied and redefined, and in terms that swell as they ebb, as if monuments might connect people by relaxing their insistence that they immortalize, represent, or unify some special group of people or their practices.

This monument does "prove" something, perhaps in the way that dough is "proofed"; it is "against interpretation" by being open to its yeasts. The specific forms taken by the desire to cherish and commemorate in the time and place of the artist-prince (if there were an artist-prince) can't now be precisely named, identified, or understood: too much has changed since 1,000 years ago or yesterday, too much is different a world away or down the street. But the desire of "some dynasty," in Wilson's alienated words, to remember this or that, puts us in touch with its otherwise "other," invisible, inaudible (unheard and unheard of) products and people. We take part in their needs and desires if not of their desires' specific, necessarily local manifestations. Bishop's monument promises not mastery but use: "But roughly but adequately it can shelter." Shelters are real but temporary; sufficient perhaps, but rough. The double "but"s in the quoted line keep binary pairs productively askew without maintaining or dissolving their opposition. This useful contact across divides implies contact between the poem's two voices, too. They're not quite reconciled; neither side wins the poem's debate nor are its competing terms resolved. There's no conversion; the second voice is not so much convinced as simply no longer heard, and while the docent-voice softens from imperious impatience to more patient explanation, it isn't moved to tenderness. Still, as Anne Colwell has pointed out, the final words of the poem's first (and last) voice ("Watch it closely") reinforce rather than discredit the demand for accuracy and application of the more resistant second voice, just as the second voice upholds as well as saps the other's claims when she calls the "shoddy" monument a "temple of crates." [20] A tacit, rickety communion is celebrated there; in wartime, it might seem a kind of peace.

Several critics interpret "The Monument" as a postmodern rebuff to modernist poems that treat art as a kind of monumental last resort against cultural fragmentation and collapse. Such readings overestimate modernism's hopes for art and underestimate its skepticism about it. (I'm recalling that the mastering container of Stevens's "Anecdote of the Jar" is also "gray and bare," that the golden nightingale of Yeats's "Sailing to Byzantium" is both a totalizing object and a trivial toy.) Those readings misconstrue Bishop as well, overstating her skepticism and understating her hopes. Bonnie Costello provides a helpful corrective when she places Bishop's poem in the line of other poems on monument making, but she errs, I think, in describing "The Monument" as conventionally hierarchical because it shares the awed contemplation of art objects characteristic of ecphrastic texts. As John Hollander points out, ecphrastic poems also often, if latently, resist such awe.[21] Bishop's attitude to her monument, as to other human structures in her work, especially those private monuments, houses, is neither skeptical dismissal nor hieratic awe but a kind of tempered affection, sometimes exasperated, always shakily firm. In many ways the structure described in "The Monument" elaborates that of another early Bishop poem, "Jerónimo's House." Papery, provisional, "left-over," "glued with spit," this makeshift home gives temporary "shelter from / the hurricane" that, certain as change, decay, and death, is surely coming. In Bishop's great, late poem "The End of March," the monument once more becomes the notional "proto-dream-house," "crypto-dream-house" it may always actually have been. (Perhaps to echo "The Monument" Bishop calls this poem's house a "crooked box.") The house, she says, is "dubious," also "perfect! But—impossible." It's a limit no monument can master. Still, as in the blues, conventionally improvised memorable shapes console, if they're not too monumental.

2

Robert Lowell
"For the Union Dead"

All poets revise; Robert Lowell revised notoriously. In "North Haven," her elegy for him, Elizabeth Bishop made the tart but friendly observation that Lowell had deranged as well as rearranged his poems. Frank Bidart worked with Lowell on the revisions of *Notebook*. He records that Lowell couldn't stop making changes and altered even final copies of poems they'd prepared for the printers. Lowell named remorse his second alcohol and, in Seamus Heaney's phrase, "thirsted for accusation." Lowell accused himself of addiction to revision (among other things), saying he treated even already published work "as if it were manuscript." Asked by an interviewer whether he revised a great deal, he answered, "Endlessly." Lowell called "revision . . . inspiration." Some readers find his "endless" rewriting outrageous; it led Helen Vendler to judge Lowell's manuscripts the most interesting since Yeats's.[1]

Lowell typically revised by negation or reversal, a practice that gave one critic the "sinking" feeling that everything is "arbitrary." Lowell might have felt that, too, given his remarkable capacity for both willfulness and abjection; what Vendler says of his last works might be said of his poems more generally, that their endings don't fulfill but annihilate their beginnings. Jonathan Raban reports that Lowell's "favorite method of revision was simply to introduce a negative into a line," reversing its meaning. He says Lowell would have put "a 'never' or a 'not' at the essential point" in almost any sentence he ever wrote "if he thought it made a better line." Raban cites an example, then concludes, "It made perfectly good sense either way round, but the one did happen to mean the opposite of the other."[2]

Arbitrary reversal may be a sometime feature of Lowell's revisions (he spoke with relish of a poem that started out lovingly called "To Jean" and ended titled "To a Whore at the Brooklyn Navy Yard"[3]), but Raban's example contradicts what he says about it. In the revised and expanded edition of *Notebook,* the poem "Les Mots" ends with these lines: "the supreme artist, Flaubert, was a boy before / the mania for phrases dried his heart." The diagnosis is Flaubert's mother's, and Lowell extends to himself her fatal charge that the writing life parches actual living. In *History,* Lowell revised "Les Mots," retitling it "First Love." Now the poem ends this way: "the supreme artist, Flaubert, was a boy before / the mania for phrases enlarged his heart." As Raban suggests, a reversal occurs in the change from "dried" to "enlarged," but the one does not "happen to mean the opposite of the other." The revision doesn't cancel the earlier version; it refutes and reinstates it. If the writing life enlarges rather than dries the artist's heart, then it ripens and swells rather than shrinks its capacity, making it more mature, more responsive, healthier. But an enlarged heart is also diseased, dangerously swollen, in physical and psychic peril. Lowell's first version abuses art and artists; his revision exonerates and assails them.

Lowell once said that if a person is "intense and honest enough, the half-truth of any extreme position will in time absorb much of its opposite," but the characteristically tense inclusion of contradictory meanings and evaluations in Lowell's revision has little to do with resolution or closure.[4] The rival forces at work are not dissolved, unified, or held in balance; they are primed to explode. To moderate the terms only slightly, contending forces here and throughout Lowell's poems tear at without finally destroying one another—like figures in Dante's Hell. The frequent result is to challenge the capacities of language, literature, and other human systems to achieve accurate knowledge or judgment—and, of course, to challenge those capacities while striving to apply and enlarge them.

In a 1964 interview, Lowell told Stanley Kunitz that a poem "needs to include a man's contradictions." This has the ring of then still fashionable New Criticism and its exaggerated preference for poems that hold opposed ideas and feelings in static equilibrium (perhaps a reflection of then contemporary liberal policies of geopolitical containment). Lowell shared liberal views, and he had been taught by leading (and conservative) New Critics, Allen Tate and John Crowe Ransom. With those, as with all authorities, Lowell's real obedience included "sincere rebellion" and his honest mutinies, considerable compliance. In the Kunitz interview, Lowell describes the tipsy mix of liberal and conservative political and philosophical views in his own outlook, and his sense that either view can be "a form of death." He concludes, "In the writing of a poem all our compulsions and biases should get in, so that finally we don't know what we mean."[5] Compulsion, bias, ignorance—those crumple any notion that Lowell's strategy of inclusion achieves some reasoned and reasonable, stable clarification. However encompassing, Lowell's reversals are imperfect, damaged, incomplete. They aim at accuracy and disclaim it.

The analogies, parallels, and other structures that make up Lowell's poems are similarly damaged, and, however oddly, such damage helps preserve his poems from impasse, that defect of New Critical virtues. Something like disequilibrium is an aspect not only of Lowell's revisions but also of his overall (and all over) view of poetic, political, and human possibility. No matter how strenuously Lowell's poems compose their remarkable variety of competing thoughts, feelings, discourses, images, and terms, the poems remain both compulsively and deliberately off kilter, uncombed, as Lowell once said his soul was. A sense of something always out of whack underlies Lowell's often-remarked mixed metaphors, a "stuffed duck" that "craned," for instance, and his characteristically jarring adjective-strings: for example, his description of his grandfather's summer house—and his grandfather—as "manly, comfortable, / overbearing, disproportioned," where the terms are variously compatible and discrepant, and in varying combinations. To paraphrase Vereen Bell, such devices subvert unity or identity by the very force that sustains them.[6] Strain compels and discredits significance throughout Lowell's work; it does the same for signification.

To return for a moment to the matter of Lowell's revisions, now in a slightly different sense, one of Lowell's favored compositional strategies was to negate or otherwise alter proverbial truths. In the poem "Fall 1961," for instance, "Nature holds up a mirror," and "One swallow makes a summer." The first revises Aristotle, Shakespeare, and imitative theories of art of every stripe; the second cheerily reverses an Italian proverb at the expense of social pieties about frugality, restraint, or standards of evidence. The stakes in such revisions can be high. "Anne Dick 2. 1936" has "swords forged from ploughshares" and makes a weapon of forgiveness. That inverts whole gospels, as do these lines on spirit and flesh from "Jean Stafford, A

Letter": "the spirit is very willing to give up, / but the body is weak and will not die." Bell says those lines convey Lowell's belief that "the common wisdom of the race never prepares us for what turns out to be the common truth of human life," a version of what Vendler calls Lowell's awareness "of the disproportion between human aims and life's events."[7] Just so, and yet, as with Lowell's other off-kilter devices, his reversals of adages and epigrams are incomplete, partial in both that word's ill-sorted senses. Lowell's denials depend upon and thus recall and reinscribe the common truths they alter or refute, as well as the common wisdom that produced them. Again, the result is not cancellation, confirmation, or standoff but struggle, lively, threatening, abrasive, and alert.

This description is accurate as far as it goes, I think. Lowell tends to a dynamic and uncombed rather than stable and well-kempt inclusion of the many and conflicting attitudes, beliefs, and reference frames at work within himself, his language, and his culture, and does so in ways that challenge poetic and political strategies of containment. But Lowell also knew that awareness of complexity can itself disable action and choice; it was a dilemma—or escape—for many intellectuals and artists of his generation. I've already mentioned that Lowell's disequilibrium, his "damaged" analogies, parallels, and inclusions resist such impasse. In addition, even Lowell's more resolutely irresolute poems harbor a contrary desire for clear-cut knowledge, action, and expression, as in his self-accusing attack on how easily the "simple word" gets "buried in a random, haggard sentence, / cutting ten ways to nothing clearly carried." For a poet to whom translation mattered so much (both translation of one tongue into another and of experience into language and back again), such miscarriage severely chastens. It should chasten critical generalization as well. Writing on "Poets in the Theater," Lowell engineered a characteristically witty reversal: "The English stage's most terrible affliction is not Milton, its enemy, but Shakespeare, its friend." Then, as a bridge to self-correction, he wrote, "Here I falter a moment: the trouble with criticism is that it makes points." With the corrections or adjustments made, though, Lowell went on to apply his initial observation. In a letter to one of his critics, Lowell wrote, "You are not altogether right to trust what I say. Emphasis confuses." The word "altogether" adjusts in its turn. Lowell turned (or twisted, no, wrenched) a phrase to describe continuities and disjunctions between and among the poems of John Crowe Ransom; it applies to consistencies and anomalies of thought and feeling within Lowell's poems as well: at every level, they "stick apart."[8]

Lowell's offbeat revisions sap and buttress establishments of every kind, and his responses to the political, artistic, and cultural formations he encountered, including monuments, typically involve colliding urges both to enlist and to mutiny. Lowell's capacity for worship was matched by his capacity for heresy and sacrilege, a combination further complicated by the fact that his affiliations and rebellions were as principled as they were driven: as Ransom said, he "would have revered all his elders if they were not unworthy."[9] Lowell adored and desecrated a wide range of precedents and pieties. His strict and volatile mixture of attitudes toward received political, aesthetic, and more broadly cultural truths has multiple sources and outcomes, many of them connected to familial and other issues of authority and power.

Lowell was, of course, a Lowell on his father's side, scion of a Massachusetts "first family," and on his mother's side, a "Mayflower" Winslow. In the background were old Boston money and influence (both somewhat waning in Lowell's time), and an imposing array of religious and civic leaders, founders and presidents, war heroes and poets. Bishop had those connections in mind when she confessed envy of Lowell's seriousness and confidence as a poet, qualities she attributed to his only having to put down the family names for his work to seem "significant, illustrative, American." An inveterate outsider herself, Bishop sees Lowell as the consummate insider. She's right. When Lowell titles an essay "Epics," the choice seems as inevitable for him as it would have been inconceivable for her, just as Lowell seems destined to practice the large, public genres and to treat monumental subjects directly while Bishop seems destined to avoid them or to treat them obliquely. But Bishop realized that Lowell's privilege was also a burden: "In some ways you are the luckiest poet I know!—in some ways not so lucky, either, of course."[10] Lucky or not, Lowell was never at ease with his inheritance, whether familial, social, national, literary, or cultural; like Bishop, he handled monuments in ways that raze and rehabilitate and raze (and raise) them.

One important source of Lowell's mixed attitudes toward received authority is parental, as, for instance, his mother's nearly cultlike idealization of masculine power, which she located in Napoleon, in her own father, and in herself, as she found that her husband—Lowell's narrowly competent, genial, unambitious father—lacked it. I recommend Lowell's memoirs and his biographers for fuller discussion of these intricate matters and rely on shorthand to suggest how family experience helped produce in Lowell a temperament urging him to both adulate and demolish the powers that be. Lowell said of his experience in the lower grades at his Beacon Hill school, where the upper levels were open only to females, "To be a boy at Brimmer was to be small, denied, and weak . . . I wished I were an older girl." Later, at all-male St. Mark's, Lowell developed a reputation for bullying, often—and paradoxically—in the service of what Ian Hamilton calls his "almost monastic reverence" for self-restraint. At home, Lowell defended himself and his father against his mother's scarifying strength, and he joined his mother in regretting and mocking his father's weakness. He knocked his father down in a quarrel about a girl and felt justified and unshakably guilty about it all his life. He adored his mother and was crushed and relieved—and crushed to be relieved—by her death in Italy. It eventually sent him into a manic phase of the manic-depressive illness he suffered all his life. (Its highs and lows were brought under relative control only in the late 1960s when he began treatments with the lithium carbonate he called "salt for the brain.") Before his breakdown, or on route to it, Lowell dithered as his mother lay dying and arrived in Rapallo only after her death. There he wept desperately with the nurse who'd witnessed his mother's final days. He obediently observed the Winslow formalities, escorting her body home by ship and arranging her interment in the venerable family graveyard at Dunbarton in New Hampshire. Then he punctured propriety by observing that her Italian undertakers had wrapped her body in tinfoil like a panettone.

Many aspects of Lowell's life and work reflect his dual capacity for worship and desecration. For instance, his youthful and temporary but thorough conversion to Catholicism was an act of disloyalty to his family's Protestant religion and to its ethnic and class presumptions and decorums: idolatrous Catholicism was the faith of the bumptious Irish and Italian immigrants who were usurping Brahmin hegemony in Boston. But conversion to Catholicism also permitted Lowell impassioned enlistment in a faith more ancient, ritualistic, and rigorous than the one he'd rejected, a faith—at least as he saw it—demanding total loyalty to absolute beliefs and obligatory practice.

Lowell's choice of poetry as his vocation also both insulted and

honored inherited values. His parents sharply discouraged his interest in literature and judged poetry impractical, wasteful, and trivial.
Lowell's mother equated verse with mania and illness, blaming one
of her son's hospitalizations for mental disorder on Tate, whom she
thought had encouraged him in what she called "the emotional excitement" of poetry. Lowell rejected his parents' pragmatic view of
poetry; he thought they were philistines. That satisfied his need for
rebellion. At the same time, especially in the context of the mid-
century elevation of poetry to a substitute religion, his acolyte's embrace of verse as a time-honored, disciplined calling satisfied his need
for affiliation—in fact, given the number of poet Lowells, his choice
provided allegiance to the family it repudiated. Similarly, Lowell's
departure from Harvard and his alliance with the southern New
Critics and their exalted view of verse at once abused the Lowells'
New England pieties and preserved the conservative cultural hierarchies the Lowell view of Harvard and New England relied on. There
were further twists. The New Critics briefly made their sort of poetry
a church; Lowell took the sacrament. But his later reinventions of
self and style profaned the creed and its associated icons and rites.
Like other poets of the second half of the twentieth century, Lowell
came to see language and poetry as complicitous with the establishments they sought to examine, ignore, or replace—so that poetry for
Lowell (like the Catholic Church) became both a revered alternative
to institutions he had to reject and a reviled establishment itself.

Mutiny and deference characterize Lowell's most overt political actions, too: his declaration of conscientious objection and refusal of conscription during World War II, his participation in the
protest march on the Pentagon, and his public refusal of President
Johnson's invitation to the White House during the Vietnam War.
As Richard Tillinghast says, Lowell's dramatic "anti-social" gestures
of denial, made in the name of higher values, were characteristically
handled in formally courteous letters "consistent with upper-class
social protocol." Such anomalous combinations typify even Lowell's
manic episodes, with their anarchic outrages against decorum and
their identifications with the most rigidly authoritarian despots.
Tillinghast suggests Lowell's ideal hero would have been a legitimate
king who was also an outlaw.[11]

The list I've been making risks seeming to reduce Lowell's most
profound cultural critiques and affirmations to effects of conditioning or illness. They're the result as well of Lowell's piercingly intel-

ligent feeling and thinking about vital historical and contemporary matters of politics, art, and culture. I hope my discussion of "For the Union Dead" will show that and show, too, the extent of Lowell's achievement in finding poetic resources for the conveyance of that feeling and thinking in all its abrasive and bracing complication—particularly as the poem responds to monuments and to monumental assumptions and ideas. Meanwhile, I want briefly to extend the list marking Lowell's capacity for worship and desecration.

Lowell often quarreled with or otherwise bitterly tested his warmest acquaintances, and he was married three times. Yet as Peter Taylor said at Lowell's funeral, he could claim to have "never lost a friend," and he never "wanted to give up a marriage entirely," being less often divorced than reconciled.[12] As with those more intimate social arrangements, so with more public ones. In the poem he addressed to "Margaret Fuller Drowned," Lowell writes: "you knew the Church burdens and infects as all dead forms / however gallant and lovely in their life." On this occasion, Lowell seems almost content in his explosive view of tradition as both admirable (elegant, beautiful, noble) and hateful (oppressive, sickening, sick). Perhaps the implication here that conventions have life spans—that they serve admirably a while and only then betray—eases his conflicting judgments by permitting them to be sequential. Evaluations of a particular present moment as fallen from a prior golden age are characteristic, especially of Lowell's earlier work. In his later work, time seems less a matter of decline than repetition, and cultural conventions are more apt to ennoble and infect at once, so that respect and disdain for them coincide—or "stick apart"—and strain intensifies. In some Lowell poems, including "For the Union Dead," competing views of time as regressive, progressive, and repetitious all appear at once, further ratcheting stresses. In any case, however they're inflected by theories of change and time, patterns of worship and desecration persist throughout Lowell's widely varied career. Whether his terms are Catholic, familial and psychoanalytic, enraged, resigned, or nearly nihilist, he praises and attacks the things he loves—including monuments and master narratives of every kind—because they erect and fail to meet their own high standards.

Alan Williamson captures an important aspect of these matters when he writes that Lowell is a poet "of the intelligent mind enmeshed in institutional commitments that no longer justify themselves as right and human, or even as harmless."[13] The trouble with this illuminating formulation is emphasis, which, as Lowell said, confuses. Williamson bases his conclusions on Lowell's affinities with the argument of the radical Freudians Norman O. Brown and Herbert Marcuse that the forms of civilization are at war with human needs and instincts and therefore deform and destroy them. The affinities are real, but they are at odds with another Lowell belief: that without the forms of civilization, human needs and instincts deform and destroy the self, other people, and community (itself a human need). Those positions make an untenable pair or grouping. Lowell held them, and for all his myopia, he held them with a capacity for anomaly as sanely clear-eyed as Bishop's. The positions appear together, for instance, in his attitude toward the "institutional commitment" of poetic form, that exemplum of inherited ritual, convention, and tradition. Lowell butchered and feasted on it. They're visible, too, in his choice of subject matter for the only commissioned poem he wrote besides "For the Union Dead." Asked for verses to mark the U.S. bicentennial, Lowell didn't elect the obvious George—George Washington—but George III. Fealty and revolt rupture and cohere in both the gesture and the poem.

In graveyards, on commons, and in other public spaces, monuments mark, enforce, and authorize perpetual remembrance, at least for a while. Bishop avoided monuments; on the lone occasion when she addressed one, she replaced pretentious stone or bronze with more modest and perishable wood. When she depicted gravestones in a painting, she drew "for sale" signs where the names and dates would go. Lowell was a much more frequent and pious monumental and graveyard poet than Bishop. In subject and theme, he was committed to bronze and stone and to considering their largest aesthetic, political, and cultural claims. But he always had both a reverent and a wrecker's eye on past and present forms and their persistence. He could imagine the statue of a farmer-soldier near the rude bridge in Concord as still standing firmly "on guard" or "melting down like sculptured lard." Lowell distrusted monumental grandeur and hungered for it.

Robert von Hallberg says Lowell believed what his translation of Gongora asserts: that "Words / give marble meaning and a voice to bronze," adding that Lowell reached for memorable lines as though the stonecutters were waiting. He did, but von Hallberg's example of a Lowell "wisdom line" shows how strenuously Lowell could interrogate or subvert what he sought to attain. Here's the phrase von Hallberg cites: "fame, a bouquet of forgetfulness." That is a wisdom line, and memorable, but it's more at odds with itself than monumentally stable. Immortal fame is the ancient goal of warriors, poets, and nations; what monuments boast they possess and provide. But Lowell's line, however cut out for the carvers, wears itself, no, all but wears itself away: "forgetfulness" insists that fame won't last; "bouquet" recalls and reinstantiates it; bouquets—whether they're made of flowers, stone, or words—are infamously fragile.

In the mid-to-late 1950s, not long after his parents' deaths, Lowell had to see to the removal and relocation of the family graveyard, which was about to be inundated by an Army Corps of Engineers flood-control project. This bitter-comic confusion of ends and means might have suited Lowell's wry sense of things. The break in continuity it effected hurt him. He wrote to his cousin Harriet that he had long looked forward to taking his children to play among ancestral tombs as he'd once done and now was "more upset than anyone alive." In the reestablished graveyard, Lowell's parents' monuments still carry the words he wrote for them; his authorship appears in his own name carved below the block inscriptions. The effect is monumental but a little skewed by the graveyard's relocation and perhaps by these odd facts. Lowell attended kindergarten at Boston's Brimmer School. Then, while his Navy officer father was stationed in Washington and Philadelphia and his mother fumed that she'd been banished to the provinces, Lowell attended school and graduated from printing to writing script. When the family returned to Boston and Lowell's parents sent him back to Brimmer, his teachers constrained him once more only to print. It affected his handwriting all his life. Mutinously obedient, he had his name on his parents' gravestones cut in cursive.[14]

Lowell had an abiding, perhaps obsessive interest in authority, power, and permanence; need and knowledge drove him to ratify and demean them. And since monuments condense issues of authority, power, and permanence in all their political, aesthetic, and more broadly cultural implications, Lowell wrote often and directly about them. He did so in ways that extol and eulogize and smash the monumental all at once. Lowell's use of the word *bronze* as both blessing and curse can graph his mixed feelings. I limit myself to a single example; its immediate concerns are aesthetic, but it bears on Lowell's attitudes toward political and cultural actions and forms as

well. "Fishnet" is one of Lowell's several valedictions to the writing
life. Echoing the stitching and unstitching of Yeats's "Adam's Curse"
and Bishop's "At the Fishhouses," it compares the work of making
poems to the practical labor of working a net. "I know I've gladdened
a lifetime / knotting, undoing a fishnet of tarred rope." This joyful
activity is not an end in itself; it makes it possible to fish; it nourishes. When the fishing ends, "the net will hang on the wall when the
fish are eaten, / nailed like illegible bronze on the futureless future."
This partly ratifies the poet's labor, his authority and power, his access
to permanence: when his weaving and fishing are done, he bequeaths
a bronze and noble trophy, fixed in place forever. It demeans them,
too. Rope rots; tarred rope rots more slowly; bronze persists but is
dead, mere decoration, husk, or skeleton: out of touch with action
and time, the monumental bronze is fixed in a timeless nowhere,
unreadable, unnourishing, unread. Lowell's terms (poem, net, fishing, bronze, "nailed," "illegible," "futureless future") both suggest and
skew clear contrasts between process and product, indelibility and
erasure; it's one more way their resonance is uncontained.

Exalted and defiled, bronze is much at issue in "For the Union
Dead," Lowell's most monumental poem. The term *brazen,* implying
hubris, associates with *bronze,* as in the bronze or brazen age, and
when Lowell commented on the distinctive amalgam of private and
public history in his oddly cobbled but seamless text, he said he'd
included the personal in order to avoid "the fixed, brazen tone of the
set piece and official ode." A celebrated bronze memorial—an official
set piece—is among the poem's threatened and treasured objects,
and the word *bronze* appears in it twice, in familiarly off-kilter alloys
of respect and disdain: they disturb without destroying whatever is
fixed and set, or settled, the very stuff of monuments. But before I
turn to such matters in "For the Union Dead," some discussion of
the poem's history of composition, publication, and reception is in
order, as is this caveat: Lowell's reminder that "meaning . . . is only
a strand and an element in the brute flow of composition."[15]

"For the Union Dead" both is and isn't a commissioned poem,
and its public nature stems from more than its occasion. Most of the
poem's parts existed in separate drafts before the commission to write
it was given; nevertheless, the commission galvanized the joining and
shaping of the parts into the final version. "The Old Aquarium" and
"One Gallant Rush: The Death of Colonel Robert Shaw" had already

been sketched out in 1959 when Lowell accepted an invitation to read a new poem at the 1960 Boston Arts Festival, to be held in the Public Garden in June; they were combined and revised to become "For the Union Dead." The poem was read and reread to a large and enthusiastic audience on that occasion, when Lowell introduced it dryly by describing present-day Boston as "a rapidly emerging center of highways and parking places." Later that year "For the Union Dead" was published in the quintessential Boston magazine, *The Atlantic.* Then, in 1961, retitled "Colonel Shaw and the Massachusetts 54th" ("Colonel Shaw and His Men" had been another working title), it was tipped into the paperback reprint of *Life Studies* as its final poem. In 1964, with its earlier name restored, it became the title and concluding poem of Lowell's next book, called, of course, *For the Union Dead.* In a letter to Tate, Lowell described "For the Union Dead" as "the most composed poem" he had ever written. He may have meant that as a compliment to Tate, whose "Ode to the Confederate Dead" had been an inspiration, although an inspiration that encouraged defiant revision as well as respectful imitation: Lowell's erasure of the "brazen" genre of the ode, for instance. Lowell may also have meant the phrase as an insult to himself, since he increasingly thought of composure in life and art (the well bred, the well made) as forms of fraud. Strong feelings about the poem persisted. In the early 1970s Lowell was asked to select his best poem; he said if he knew what it was he'd keep it a secret, then chose "For the Union Dead."[16]

I said above that the public nature of "For the Union Dead" stems from more than its occasion. Many of the poem's places, objects, and subjects have public dimensions: the Boston Common; small-town New England greens; graveyards; the Statehouse; the old South Boston Aquarium; Augustus Saint-Gaudens's bronze memorial relief for Colonel Robert Gould Shaw and the men of the Massachusetts 54th (it stands on public ground at the northeast corner of the Common, opposite the Statehouse); the public speeches accompanying the memorial's 1897 unveiling; a television broadcast; a moment in the 1950s struggle for school desegregation; the disruptive construction of a public parking garage beneath the Common; and an advertisement, that most relentlessly public form. The poem also evokes large-scale public events: the American Revolution, the Civil War, World War II, and the civil rights movement. And it addresses broad public issues: the decay or preservation of public spaces and social institutions; government morality in the conduct of warfare and in regard to such matters as commerce and race; the relation of art and the artist to public life.

Public as it is, however, "For the Union Dead" is marked by private history as well. Lowell lived much of his life on Beacon Hill and in the Back Bay, and the poem's places, buildings, and sculpture were his neighborhood. He was distantly related to Colonel Shaw, visited the aquarium as a boy, was deeply interested in local and national history and connected to them by family tradition, went to jail for conscientious objection during World War II, watched public events on television, saw the Common gouged to build the underground garage, and, of course, as an artist observed himself observing. Furthermore, while Lowell was writing the poem, his wife, Elizabeth Hardwick, was preparing a magazine article on the decline of Boston and editing a selection of letters by William James, who had delivered a speech at the Shaw memorial's dedication. Oliver Wendell Holmes Jr. also spoke at an event related to the dedication, and Lowell, who had recently become a member of Boston's Tavern Club, found a copy of Holmes's remarks in the club library. In life as in the poem, the private and public met, collided, and intersected. One of the poem's implicit arguments is that the two can't be disentangled.

From the beginning, "For the Union Dead" has been seen as an important poem, both within the Lowell canon and in more general terms. It has been written about extensively and been much anthologized, partly because its political concerns speak to a generation of critics formed by the experiences of the civil rights movement and Vietnam. But while responses to Lowell's poem agree about many of its particulars, those responses tend to divide dramatically in judging the effect of its troubling mix of private and public anger, shame, and assessment: some commentators find the poem harshly satirical but finally ameliorative and affirming; others find it wholly nihilistic, whether enraged or despairing. As much of what I've said so far implies, I think it's all of that. But before I try to say so, I turn to two of Lowell's finest critics to represent the terms of the debate.

Steven Axelrod says "For the Union Dead" accuses America of obliterating its past, so that the nation lacks identity and inherited moral values and repeats ancestral crimes in ever more monstrous patterns. Nevertheless, he thinks the poem is hopeful. Commenting on Lowell as both the maker of the poem and a character in it, Axelrod concludes that as Lowell's morale declines, his moral consciousness increases. Eventually he matures into a "visionary hero . . . as necessary and ambiguous as Shaw himself." Meanwhile, "Lowell's national elegy ultimately becomes a 'song of praise' . . . for the enduring forms and values of human civilization." Vereen Bell considers Lowell a genuine nihilist and views ameliorative readings of "For the Union Dead" as a kind of critical wishful thinking making the poem more palatable and palliative than Lowell intended. Bell describes the Lowell who appears in the poem as a brilliant but withered and finally isolated and escapist observer unable to alter himself or the fallen society he inhabits. Of the poem's ostensible hero, Colonel Shaw, Bell says that because genuine nihilism precludes the heroic, he is finally "a forlornly symbolic figure, only absurdly grand."[17]

Understandably, criticism does not associate Lowell with the action painters or with the poets more obviously linked to them, Charles Olson and John Ashbery, for instance. Yet in a conversation with A. Alvarez, Lowell said he had "a lot of argument" with those painters when he was writing the poems immediately preceding "For the Union Dead." He added that although his own desire for "a sort of Tolstoyan fullness of representation" was at odds with the action painters' antirepresentational strategies, he supposed there was "some connection" between their work and his. However unexpectedly, and in spite of its representational specificity and historical depth, "For the Union Dead"—and much of Lowell's later work—shares action painting's interest in all-over or field composition and in techniques for "energy transfer." Perhaps Axelrod had something like that in mind when—in a gracious, exaggerated phrase—he called "For the Union Dead" an "emanation of total consciousness."[18] In any event, however full their readings, Axelrod, Bell, and other interpreters of Lowell's poem emphasize one or another aspect of it in their conclusions. It seems to me, though, that "For the Union Dead" neither ultimately affirms nor negates culture and its representations. Lowell's poem is not a statement or argument but a kind of representational action painting, a gesturally rendered field of competing, confirming, qualifying strands that actively drip and spill and stream, over- and underlap, collide and intertwine, choir, quarrel, and converse in order to "transfer" to the reader Lowell's irresolvably multiple and competing feelings and thoughts about the political, aesthetic, and cultural heights and horrors monuments condense.

I follow that woozy sentence with something more capably pedestrian and begin with the poem's title. I've already mentioned that in calling his poem "For the Union Dead" Lowell nods to and negates the "brazen" generic grandeur of Allen Tate's "Ode to the Confederate Dead." Lowell's double gesture has multiple implications. For instance, it reduces his own poem's generic stature while putting the whole idea of generic stature or hierarchy in question, including the lofty status traditionally accorded to monuments. At the same time, though, however humbled or paradoxically exalted it is, Lowell's title also shares with Tate's a graven, monumental quality, and both poems memorialize and ennoble heroic, idealistic soldiers in monumental terms. Nevertheless, Lowell's title is openly adversarial, and not only against generic monumentality, the unreconstructed South, and Tate, but against itself as well. In choosing loyalty to the North of his birth rather than the South of his New Critical education, for instance, Lowell—as he had in *Life Studies*—breaks with Tate's view of the poem as a poised (if tense) and stable object in favor of a more event-based and pervious model. He breaks, too, with his one-time mentor's agrarian belief in permanent and hierarchical social arrangements in favor of a liberal commitment to social change, especially in the area of race, as the poem will show.

At the same time, as the poem will also show, Lowell's commitments to aesthetic and social change are partial. "For the Union Dead" is formally roughened but still in quatrains, and while the poem judges monumental permanence and its attendant hierarchies to be deadening and deadly in their unnatural resistance to change, it also decries the meaningless destruction of mere material "progress" and assaults the civic vandalism and military and commercial barbarity that come with it in terms perfectly congruent with agrarian assumptions. These matters are audible in the title, which not only aligns with and secedes from Tate but also is at civil war with itself. As every reader notices, the phrase "the Union Dead" both pays tribute to those who died to preserve the Union and mocks their sacrifice as meaningless, since, its values abandoned, the Union is dead. The flickering mobility of Lowell's terms is tellingly at odds with the stability of Tate's comparable ones: there's a pun in the phrase "Confederate Dead," but it confirms rather than subverts the ideal of soldierly brotherhood. Lowell's parallel words, "the Union Dead," perform contradictory double duty, or duty and dereliction. So, too, does the intertextual dimension of Lowell's title—and of the poem as well, for as Axelrod has shown, Lowell's text is in edgy conversation with many poems, speeches, and other representations. The title's gesture to another text both acknowledges descent and dissents from monumental traditions. Perhaps even the shift in prepositions from "to" to "for" implies a competing mode of address.

An unstable mixture of respect, resistance, and revision in response to received textual, monumental, and other traditions is displayed throughout "For the Union Dead." It appears in the poem's epigraph as well as in its title. The inscription on Saint-Gaudens's memorial to Colonel Shaw and the African-American soldiers of the Massachusetts 54th, the first free black regiment to fight in the Civil War, is borrowed from the motto of the Society of the Cincinnati, an elite military club celebrating the virtues of the Roman citizen-soldier as reflected in officers of the American Revolution: Colonel Shaw belonged by right of family descent. Lowell in turn borrowed the monument's inscription as the epigraph for his poem. As the sequence of borrowings attests, this is a matter of handing down traditions, and Lowell is in line to inherit. He contests the will while accepting the bequest. The motto inscribed on the memorial relief is "Omnia Relinquit Servare Rempublicam" (he sacrificed all to serve the republic). Lowell's epigraph—"Relinquunt Omnia Servare Rem Publicam" (they sacrificed all to serve the state or public good)—revises what it repeats. The shift here from singular to plural, like the other titles Lowell considered for his poem ("Colonel Shaw and His Men"; "Colonel Shaw and the Massachusetts 54th"), exposes and corrects the racial and class bias implicit in the memorial and in those who raised it: the monument's inscription seems to refer only to Shaw; the white officers killed in battle are listed by name on the statue; the slain black foot soldiers aren't (or, rather, weren't until their names were added in 1982).

The artistic and political achievements and shortcomings of the Saint-Gaudens memorial are complex and much debated; I'll return to them later. For now, I want to stress Lowell's faithful and mutinous handling of his local, national, and Western (classical) inheritance, while recalling that mutiny when the nation fails to maintain its ideals—the belief that all are created equal, for instance—is itself a way to keep faith. Lowell was deeply alert to the modeling of America's institutions on Roman examples; he knew how easily the Roman republic became imperial and imperialist, how inextricable Roman grandeur could be from Roman brutality. Lowell's modulation of the monument's Latin inscription is one way he names and acts on his fears for his own increasingly imperial nation (in this, he follows one of his poem's many intertexts, William Vaughn Moody's "Ode in a Time of Hesitation"). Finally, Lowell's epigraph also sets up one of the poem's major verbal and evaluative patterns, an uneasy cluster of terms whose meanings are variously congruent, opposed, or more queasily related: *servare,* serve and service, servility, servant, slave.

In private and public terms, "For the Union Dead" addresses relatively recent and contemporary events (World War II bombings, the Holocaust, school desegregation, the building of the underground garage, rampant commercialization), matters of history (the American Revolution, the Civil War, the 1863 deployment and the 1897 commemoration of the Massachusetts 54th and Colonel Shaw), and details that are both prehistoric and atavistic, in that they involve the persistence of the past in the present ("dinosaur steamshovels"). As that last description implies, these chronological categories are themselves unstable, and many aspects of Lowell's poem are both at once clear and blurred. Throughout the poem, objective events are inseparable from their subjective representations, for instance, and Lowell in the poem is remarkably alert, yet morosely passive, even enervated. Similarly, the analogical method of "For the Union Dead," in which comparison and contrast are the means of analysis and evaluation, is both exercised and disabled. That is, the analogical relations among the poem's varied materials ramify so powerfully and in ways at once so exact and so nearly unconstrained as to simultaneously confirm and demolish their meanings. To put it in other terms, "For the Union Dead" encourages, blocks, and skews analogy, so that logic, knowledge, judgment, language, and the fundamentally comparative activity of poetry itself all seem both sound and hollow in it.

Lowell's monumental poem opens by describing a public institution—itself a kind of monument—in ruins. The old South Boston Aquarium is deserted and vandalized, broken, arid, and cold. Nevertheless, it still "stands" in the "now" of the poem's beginning. "Once" the aquarium had been intact, and the child Lowell had been a visitor there. By the end of the poem, even its ruins are "gone." The slightly dizzying sense that the poem's present is unusually porous to the future and the past prepares for Lowell's manipulations of tense and sequence and of private and public history throughout. It prepares, too, for the poem's examination of how personal and social commitments to the past and the future can both nourish and poison the present, for Lowell's view of time is neither purely regressive nor purely progressive: either resisting, encouraging, or yielding to change can warp and sustain—and human consciousness precludes pure living in the present. But to return to the aquarium, its presence in the poem as intact, in ruins, then gone implies an inevitable decline. Even so, that declension is complicated by signs of resistance, for as the poem opens, the aquarium windows are not only broken but also defensively boarded up. Construction, preservation, and decay; ruin, repair, and obliteration; reverence, rebellion, and revision are all at work in "For the Union Dead," as Lowell addresses monuments and monumentality (and their companions, institutions and institutional memory) in order to consider a range of unsettled and unsettling political, aesthetic, and more broadly cultural matters.

Lowell's description of the decayed aquarium introduces the poem's concern with private and public acts of judgment and justice and with their monumental and other representations. The aquarium's "bronze weathervane cod has lost half its scales." An apt decoration for an institution exhibiting fish, the bronze cod is also the traditional symbol of Massachusetts and her colonial riches; another cod hangs in the statehouse, as if to preside over its legislative deliberations. Perhaps in Lowell's view it both blesses the Commonwealth and exposes her sometime tendency to govern in the service of private wealth instead of the public good. The cod's wrecked role as weathervane implies a damaged if not wholly destroyed sense of physical, governmental, and moral direction, and the pun on the cod's lost "scales" suggests that justice has lost its balance. In any case, the description of the ruined aquarium prompts Lowell's memory of a childhood visit there. He says that his nose then "crawled like a snail" on the glass of the tanks. This is an image of rapt attention and of identification with other forms of life. (A little oddly, the fish, too, are said to have noses; the slight element of strain in this both underlines and undermines connections, as if to affirm and question the legitimacy of this and any comparative procedure.) The image of the nose crawling on glass is also faintly unpleasant, snail-trail snotty, yet it recalls the snail's role as cleaner in aquarium culture.

Similar complications mark other aspects of the child's visit. His hand "tingled" with the excitement of an intense desire to know and make contact with the alien beings from whom he's cut off by the glass wall of the tank. It tingled, too, with an impulse to possess, control, and destroy the other, as if the "cowed, compliant fish" called to something aspiring, sympathetic, and tyrannical in Lowell all at once. It is as if his urge to "burst . . . bubbles" forecast not only his lifelong straining toward uplifting structures but also his lifelong courage in deflating such structures when they proved false and, as well, his sometimes manic pleasure in destroying structures no matter what beauty, validity, or value they actually possessed. Lowell suggests all of this with his usual self-assessing and self-accusing candor. The imagery of breakage and bubbles builds associations as the poem develops. I'll return to it later.

Meanwhile, the depiction of the "cowed, compliant fish" raises competing issues of institutional containment, repression, and imprisonment, matters lent further nuance by the next stanza's introduction of "the dark downward and vegetating kingdom / of the fish and reptile." On the way there, so to speak, Lowell engages in sleight of hand to return the poem to the present. The hand that "tingled" in childhood now "draws back." This involves self-discipline, an act of will, as Lowell connects his desire to linger in the past to the persistent present temptation (he says he sighs for it often) to luxuriate in the dark, downward, and vegetating realm of the pre- or nonhuman. Lowell resists both those desires, but his deliberate drawing back signals a troubling loss of intensity and contact as well as a maturely human reining in of destructive and escapist urges. This knot can be loosened a little if not untied by returning to the terms *cowed* and *compliant*. Both words describe obedience, but where *cowed* implies being made sheepish by fear (to jumble flocks and herds, schools, perhaps even schooling), *compliance* suggests responsiveness and choice. Then again, *compliance* also invokes the conformity-inducing threats of policing. Perhaps all the elements of this unstable pair of opposed and parallel terms (they echo *servare,* with its yield of both servility and service) are involved in any act or institution of self- or social control. The aquarium contains and constrains the fish in something like the way other human institutions seek to control, direct, or moderate our so-called animal instincts. But institutions also imprison and repress; repression may warp instinct or cause us to forget that our animal urges are part of who and what we are, a snail trail we ignore at our peril. At the same time, part of the aquarium's institutional value is precisely its reminder of those animal urges and their attractions as well as their dangers.

Lowell draws back from regressive indulgence in memories of his personal past (the childhood recollection) and in the more distant biological memory of our shared nonhuman origins (the downward kingdom), but he does so in a manner that affirms the necessity of such returns to a full recognition of the self as rooted in rather than released from its psychological and evolutionary inheritances. In this way Lowell conveys the sense that human life involves irresolvably conflicting needs to acknowledge, constrain, and express or set free the "base" self. That densely textured sense of things informs Lowell's view of monuments and their attendant assumptions. I said that the phrase "draws back" describes an act of will; it does, but it implies a reflex reaction as well, just as it indicates a shift from action to contemplation in ways that blur the line between them.

The notion of blurred lines can introduce the intensifying concern of "For the Union Dead" with barriers, and with social, political, and aesthetic boundaries and enclosures more generally. In the poem's present, the adult speaker now recalls a moment in the relatively recent past. Long ago, the child had nosed and "tingled" at the aquarium's tanks; one morning just "last March" the adult Lowell had "pressed" against a new barbed-wire fence installed on the Boston Common. As throughout "For the Union Dead," a great deal is condensed in this description. The fence surrounds the construction site for the underground garage. Does its presence serve public safety or abrogate the "commonness" of the Common: its public ownership and access? Whom does the fence protect, and from what: Does it secure the public outside the fence from injury, or does it shield the "insiders" from public scrutiny (accusations of graft—the abuse of public office for private gain—swarmed around the construction project)? More abstractly, who determines what constitutes the inside and outside of such structures? And how is construction distinguished from destruction? The idea that the answers to such questions depend upon subjective points of view is among the poem's conditions—as is the fact that the parallels between the child's and the fishes' noses, between aquarium glass and fence, and between the words *tingled* and *pressed* generate meaning and judgment while also suggesting that meaning and judgment are always both partial and overdetermined. Meanwhile, the poem maintains its efforts to understand and judge within those conditions—and to be tempered by them.

The barbed-wire fence is also called a "cage." This evokes images of Nazi concentration camps (images given wide circulation in the postwar decade and a half before the poem's composition), and it suggests that the corruption that rots a society's institutions and the cowed and other forms of compliance that sustain them lead to the same horrific conclusion. These views bear importantly on the poem's later concern with the conduct of World War II and on its attitude toward the very notion of civilization, whether expressed in institutions, governments, wars, or monuments. Meanwhile, the depiction of the fence as a cage also recalls the fish caged in the watery zoo of the aquarium. "Behind" this fence-cage, "dinosaur steamshovels" crop and grunt as they dig at the Common. (Lowell places them "behind" rather than "within" the cage, thus further blurring distinctions between inside and outside and perhaps implying that human structures of containment necessarily fail, or even that they're actually tricks to conceal the instinctive or deliberate unleashing of selfish forces.) The "dinosaur steamshovels" evoke brontosaurs in a primeval marsh, or perhaps in one of those museum dioramas where surmises about the past appear as material facts. Museums, like aquariums, zoos, and fenced-in sites, are framed displays that conform to and distort what they contain. So, too, perhaps, are poems and other works of art. Alert to such complications, "For the Union Dead" employs the enclosing structure of quatrains and persistently breaches their frames: its four-line stanzas are unrhymed, in very irregular lines, and harshly enjambed across stanza breaks. In this, as in its references to aquariums, cages, and fences, Lowell's poem registers and attempts to adjust itself to one more congruent, discordant matter: what we see and know in art and politics and life are not things and events themselves but their culturally determined and determining representations.

The word *pressed* has the energy of scrutiny in it. It also implies energy blocked before it's converted into action. The poem's many barriers and blockages at once drain and spur Lowell, both the Lowell who writes the poem and the Lowell who speaks it. For instance, although Lowell as a character can only press against the fence, both he and the poet Lowell see through it well enough to describe the forces behind it and to reveal his complicity with them. (I wrote *his;* perhaps I mean *their:* for now I'll surrender the dubious, attractive effort to keep character and poet separate.) The poem has already presented Lowell as tempted by escapist dwelling on or in the past and as sighing for the vegetative realm where fish and reptile reign. This associates him with atavistic portions of the self in general and with the dinosaur steamshovels gouging the Common in particular. At the same time, it is precisely Lowell's acknowledgment of his machine and animal aspects that allows him to see and reveal his complicity with those who threaten the common good and to judge those menaces without presuming superiority to them. However sapped the poet's forces are (Lowell called *For the Union Dead* a book of witheredness), his unflinching accuracy here and throughout the poem is a form of moral and artistic action. Its more practical political weight remains to be taken (it can't quite be measured).

The personal versions of public matters discussed so far are conveyed in the poem's first four stanzas. Beginning with the fifth stanza, the speaker's "I" recedes from the poem, not to reappear until near its end, and the poem's voice becomes more "removed," more distant, public, authoritative, and judgmental. Nevertheless, those qualities are tempered by the preceding emphasis on the personal, subjective, and complicitous. In this sense, Lowell's poem is structured to insist that no authoritative voice can escape or transcend its partialities, but to do so without wholly disabling judgment. Overlap between the poem's private and public voices is audible in the description of the statehouse as "tingling." The term resonates with the word applied to the eager child's hand (*tingled*); like the association of the childish word *sandpiles* with the supposedly adult garage construction project, this keeps subjective involvements and complications on show while a somewhat more objective, judgmental treatment of more broadly public matters goes forward.

Excavations for the underground garage (Lowell calls it the "underworld garage," suggesting the involvement of organized crime in its construction and perhaps a hubristic profanation of sacred ground) not only threaten the Common but the seat of government as well. (Although in saying so, it's good to remember that in Lowell's vision these things, like monuments, may and may not merit preservation.) Efforts are made to protect the statehouse from damage: the building is girdled and braced by a framework of girders, recalling the boarding up of the aquarium's windows. Nonetheless, vibrations from the project affect it. If the statehouse building is kept intact, its governmental functions are disturbed. (Perhaps even its survival is in doubt, since the neglected aquarium, although once protectively boarded up as the statehouse is currently braced, eventually disappeared completely.) Lowell describes the statehouse as "shaking over the excavations." The precisely chosen preposition indicates both the statehouse's physical position on higher ground above the Common and its "superior" responsibility for oversight, including the protection of public works from corruption. Here, the statehouse seems more likely to overlook than to oversee. Its view obscured by girders (a weird and telling externalization of its internal structures), the statehouse shakes with an unstable mixture of anger, fear, impotence, and a kind of vibratory complicity, as if the institutions built to contain and control our baser urges were built upon and reflect them—as the child at the glass-walled tanks is father to the balked man at the fence, as vegetable, animal, and human, past and present, dinosaurs and steamshovels overlap.

Construction of the underground garage also threatens the Saint-Gaudens Civil War relief, which stands on the corner of the Common and "faces" the statehouse in partnership and confrontation. As ambiguous as the aquarium or statehouse, it is described as both "shaking" and "propped." Lowell's consideration of this monument and all it stands for in historical, political, aesthetic, and cultural terms is at the center of "For the Union Dead" and comprises more than half its length. In a study addressing poems addressing monuments, I'll seem to have been a long time coming to it. That's part of the point. For Lowell, monuments are metonymically continuous with other cultural expressions, from institutions like aquariums, governments, and churches to social movements, wars, automobiles, television programs, poems, ads, flags, commercial photographs, and seemingly private gestures. Any one of them can stand for the others. In this, Lowell combines the traditional view of history as the business of great men and great events with the more contemporary sense of history as the material reality of everyday life. Similarly, as the poem's emphasis on representation suggests, Lowell is alert to the textuality of the archive and sees history and its markers, including monuments, as a set of competing subjective narrative interpretations deliberately or otherwise designed to encode, make "natural," and enforce personal and public beliefs and existing power arrangements. In all of this, Lowell recognizes the need to maintain and to level hierarchies. To put it another way, the Saint-Gaudens monument is central to "For the Union Dead" in ways that call into question monumentality and centrality, and along with them social, artistic, and political regimes.

Saint-Gaudens's sculpture commemorates the deaths in service to the Union and the cause of racial equality of many of the black soldiers of the Massachusetts 54th and of Colonel Shaw and several other of the regiment's white officers in a battle at Fort (or Battery)

Wagner near Charleston in 1863. It recalls in every way that monuments are sites of contestation as well as unification. The regiment itself was raised and deployed for a range of variously conflicting and congruent purposes. For instance, its existence asserted or promised eventual equality between the races, yet its black troops were led by white officers. Because he and his family were committed to abolitionist ideals, Shaw overcame initial doubts and volunteered for a position unlikely to advance his military career (opposition to black recruitment was still strong in the North, inside and outside the military), and he did so in spite of the South's decree that white officers of black troops would forfeit military courtesy and be subject to execution. Yet for all his idealism (and despite the fact that captured black volunteers faced execution or reenslavement), Shaw privately expressed doubts about whether black men could maintain military discipline and fight. There are other anomalies as well. Whatever ideals inspired its formation, the decision to field the 54th and other units like it pragmatically exploited a source of manpower the South couldn't. (It also reflected the practical hope that the presence of black troops in battle would engender slave revolts and siphon Confederate forces from the front.) At the same time, the unit was rapidly trained and thrown into battle, in part for propaganda purposes (or so it came to seem in retrospect). Meanwhile, its men behaved with valor under fire and provided a source of racial and abolitionist pride, not least because so many died bravely as martyrs in defeat.

This kind of anomalous coherence marks the history of the Saint-Gaudens monument and its reception. Kirk Savage tells the story best in *Standing Soldiers, Kneeling Slaves,* his brilliant study of race, war, and monuments in nineteenth-century America. Savage shows that the first, aborted effort to commemorate Shaw in a monument was made by freed slaves in South Carolina. For various reasons the monies raised for that project were diverted to found a free black school, named for Shaw, like others of its kind. The effort that eventually resulted in the Saint-Gaudens memorial was also begun by a former slave, Joshua Smith, who lived in Boston, committed his own money to the project, and raised funds in the African-American community. Smith had in mind a traditional, free-standing equestrian statue, but, as Savage points out, public discussion of the project and the views of Shaw's father made clear that Shaw's importance was intertwined with recognition of his black troops and that a statue of him alone would be inappropriate. (He was, after all, a relatively junior officer, and his actual military achievement was small, however large in symbolic and other terms.) Progress on the monument's design stalled; after a time the memorial project was taken up by a group of elite white Bostonians (or Brahmins), and its origins in the black community all but disappeared from the monument's official history and archive, to be recovered by Savage from other sources. Nonetheless, and paradoxically, it was the Brahmin committee that transformed the original impulse for a traditional statue celebrating Shaw as an heroic white emancipator into a memorial commemorating free black soldiers acting on their own behalf as well. Elite artists were commissioned, and eventually—almost thirty-five years after the event and the first efforts to commemorate it—the work by Saint-Gaudens was dedicated.

The tale of the monument's emergence is fascinating. As Savage demonstrates, Saint-Gaudens, who had replaced earlier artists, over time developed a design that celebrated both Shaw and his men and reimagined the entire genre of Civil War statuary. Most Civil War memorials served the postwar need to reunify North and South by narrating a tale of white emancipators freeing slaves, rehearsing that tale in the sculptural terms of Savage's title: standing soldiers and (grateful, still inferior) kneeling slaves, a configuration that reinscribed the myth of white superiority emancipation was supposed to have erased. This dismal development is understandable. The representation of black soldiers as agents of their own freedom would have bruised Southern sensibilities, challenged the continuing racism of the North, and retarded reunification. Saint-Gaudens's bronze relief responds both to that cluster of issues and to the inextricability of Shaw's importance from that of his men, while retaining, rejecting, and revising the traditional nobility of the equestrian statue and its celebration of a single and singular hero. Shaw appears in the foreground, grandly mounted on horseback, yet he as much accompanies his troops as leads them, checking his charger's pace to match his men's. The black soldiers, on foot, as military reality required, are represented in terms of the harmony essential to a military unit as well as in terms of distinctive individuality of appearance and carriage. In this, they are treated as ideal American soldiers: marching, they are united by their uniforms and by military discipline, yet they maintain the individuality of a free people and express it, as Savage says, in the angle of a hat brim, the tilt of a rifle, the way a blanket is rolled or set on a pack. Meanwhile, the dramatic tension between the black soldiers' controlled eagerness and Shaw's abstracted restraint conveys their related but differing positions and stakes in the matter at hand.

The Saint-Gaudens relief is a masterpiece, however unfashionable the term. Nevertheless, and however much Saint-Gaudens's wholly respectful portraits of black soldiers counter his own conventional racism, the Shaw Memorial has racist elements (as that choice of name for it conveys). I've already mentioned that the monument carries a roster of the regiment's dead white officers but not (until the 1982 amendment) of its slain black soldiers, and that its borrowed motto emphasizes Shaw's sacrifice at the expense of those of his men. Lowell's revision of the monument's motto in his epigraph comments on these matters, as does his insistence—both in working titles for the poem and in the poem itself—that the monument commemorates Shaw *and* his men. Some readers of the Saint-Gaudens memorial go further. Albert Boime argues that the representation of the black soldiers on the monument is itself racist, but I agree with Savage that the evidence of the sculpture contradicts Boime's claim.[19] In any case, there is a great deal more to be said about the monument, including the history of how well and badly Boston has cared for it at different times, and including, too, the tricky issue of what to call it. (Most names for the memorial emphasize either the commanding officer, his men, or the genius-artist who made it, with all the aesthetics and politics such choices imply.) For present purposes, though, what's been said so far can suffice.

"For the Union Dead" is interested in the character and action of Shaw and his men. It is interested in the monument that represents them. It is interested, too, in the monument's reception (or rerepresentation). This is one way Lowell insists that however much this or any monument makes a moment in history permanent, it nonetheless remains enmeshed in history itself. Like other human artifacts—commons, aquariums, governments, poems—the monument remains subject to damage, neglect, revision, and other changes in meaning: it is an interpretation subject in turn to interpretation. This keeps the monument central and decenters it, as does Lowell's complex awareness of the many competing representations of Shaw and his men that preceded and followed Saint-Gaudens's relief: poems, ranging from widely circulated doggerel to verses by Phoebe Cary, the remarkably named Anna Cabot Lowell Quincy Waterston,

James Russell Lowell, Emerson, Benjamin Brawley, Percy MacKaye, Paul Lawrence Dunbar, William Vaughn Moody, and John Berryman, among others; a musical interpretation, "The 'St. Gaudens' in Boston Common" section of Charles Ives's *Three Places in New England;* and essays and addresses by Thomas Wentworth Higginson, Frederick Douglass, and others. (Lowell took the phrase "one gallant rush," which he used to title one of the sketches that became "For the Union Dead," from Douglass). Axelrod provides a richly nuanced treatment of this intertextual aspect of Lowell's poem. I refer to it here as one more indication of Lowell's insistence on the multiplicity of representation and interpretation. It serves as a reminder and rebuke to his own poem and to the monument it honors, dismisses, interrogates, and revises.

The memorial to Colonel Shaw and the Massachusetts 54th was erected in its privileged place across from the statehouse on the Common and dedicated in 1897. (Savage reports that the procedure in which a group of—usually elite—private citizens commissioned a public statue, saw to its funding, design, and execution, placed it on public ground, and then turned it over to the government for safekeeping was standard nineteenth-century practice.) The dedication was an impressive affair, and it provided another set of rerepresentations of Shaw and his men and of Saint-Gaudens's monument for Lowell to ponder: a poem by Thomas Bailey Aldrich, "Shaw Memorial Ode," and speeches by government officials and by two national luminaries, William James and Booker T. Washington. Axelrod describes Lowell's poem as standing in ironic contrast to the optimism of the speeches by James and others. (Oliver Wendell Holmes's tart words were referred to in an early draft of "For the Union Dead"; references to James's talk remain in the final version.) I'll return to that. Savage cites Washington's remark that the "real monument" to Shaw and his men was being built in the South by blacks themselves.[20] As we'll see, this, too, became part of Lowell's complex celebration, critique, and revision of the Saint-Gaudens monument in "For the Union Dead."

As I've said, the Saint-Gaudens memorial, like the Common and the statehouse, is also threatened by work on the underground garage: the relief is "shaking" and "propped by a plank splint." As with the aquarium and the statehouse, several competing attitudes are displayed in its depiction. The monument itself, the event it memorializes, and the meaning and remembrance of that event are all represented as worthy of preservation against corrupt or merely careless forces of change and destruction. Meanwhile, we see that some attempt at protection has been made, although given the parallels among the propped statue, the boarded but ruined and soon to disappear aquarium, and the girdled statehouse (which ignores or abets what it ought to check), that effort may be merely palliative and futile; it may even be a charade to conceal indifference or active malice. At the same time, the threatened and propped monument is also depicted as not quite worthy of protection. As the word *splint* implies, the relief is already broken; perhaps it always has been. That description extends the judgment—registered in Lowell's revisionist epigraph—that the monument is flawed in racial and other elitist terms. Throughout the poem, respect for the Saint-Gaudens monument, for monuments in general, and for monumental assumptions about knowledge, hierarchy, and permanence is shadowed by doubt and disparagement. Similarly, Lowell both celebrates the actions of Shaw and his men and questions Shaw's motives; related mixtures of admiration and censure appear in Lowell's treatment of intersections between monumental and other artistic and cultural representations and the political realities of warfare, commerce, and race.

Perhaps Lowell's most strenuous praise for the Saint-Gaudens memorial comes in this sentence: "Their monument sticks like a fishbone / in the city's throat." Picking up images of the half-scaled cod and the aquarium (and perhaps the statehouse and its own "sacred cod"), this treats the statue as a persistent spur to idealism and action which Boston's people and government can't dislodge, even if they can't or won't swallow it. Thus Lowell acknowledges art as a public force and compliments monumental permanence, but he does so in a way that insults them. For no matter how persistently the monument keeps a model of idealistic action in public view, it's also a merely skeletal remain: it makes nothing happen, as Auden said about poetry. The pronoun *their* (as opposed to, say, *our*) underlines the monument's inability to transfer the commitments of Shaw and his men to contemporary Boston and the nation. On the other hand, "their" includes both Saint-Gaudens and William James, who spoke at the 1897 dedication. This implies that the actions of Shaw and his men did outlast their moment and continue to inspire others, including monument makers. That, too, is qualified in Lowell's typically layered, congruent but skewed presentation.

Lowell has already chastised Saint-Gaudens by revising his

monument's inscription. When he writes that James at the dedication "could almost hear the bronze Negroes breathe" (echoing James's
remark that the soldiers are "so true to nature that one can almost
hear them breathing"), Lowell is praising James's lively sympathy,
so different from the reflex response of the contemporary citizens
who choke on the monument's fishbone. And Lowell shares James's
celebration of the monument's revivifying, immortalizing power,
the sort of claim so many monumental poems and other works of
art make for their subjects, themselves, and their artists. But James's
naïve realist and redemptive or reformist aesthetic (his speech's hope
that a statue so "true to nature" will give life to the dead and "save
us from degeneration") is also mocked by the content and style of
"For the Union Dead": its insistent description of death and cultural decline, its quick cuts, weird conjunctions, and overdetermined
image patterns, its antimimetic stress on multiple and competing
representations

The impossibility of separating persons, events, and objects from
their representations is a feature of Lowell's description of Colonel
Shaw, whom he depicts as he is depicted on the monument. At
the same time, though, Lowell neither valorizes the monument's
representation nor permits it to be monolithic. He not only interprets its representation himself, he also recalls that the monument's
version of things is rerepresented by others, as in James's speech at
the dedication. Lowell produces similar effects by including in his
poem the monument's context, its historical surround. For instance,
Lowell makes connections between Saint-Gaudens's and other war
memorials, considers the attitudes of Shaw's family, and presents in
starkly factual terms the event the monument idealizes, noting that
two months after leaving Boston, "half the regiment was dead."
(This not quite accurate estimate serves both to heighten Shaw's
and his men's idealism and to chasten the statue's idealization of
it.) Lowell's treatment of Colonel Shaw as a flawed hero partakes of
similar complications.

Lowell's Shaw, as filtered through Saint-Gaudens and the historical archive, is idealistic and brittle, gentle, vigilant, and prudish.
He is in some ways a conventionally idealized Brahmin figure. As
"lean as a compass-needle," he is associated with the monument as
virtue's remnant fishbone in the city's throat and seems to possess
the sense of direction the cod weathervane has lost. But in Lowell's
version, if Shaw is puritanically moral, he is also priggishly moral-

istic, painfully isolated as well as socially committed: "he seems to wince at pleasure, / and suffocate for privacy." The very rigor that permits Shaw's self-sacrifice in the service of a (flawed) vision of racial equality keeps him rigid and removed from contact with his men; for whatever mixture of reasons of temperament, race, and military and class decorums, "when he leads his black soldiers to death, / he cannot bend his back." (Is this praise or denunciation? One branch of Lowell's family has a Latin motto saying it's better to bend than to break: when applied in the poem, it accuses Shaw of inflexible righteousness, but it also accuses the state, its institutions, its citizens, and Lowell himself of failing in the firmness rectitude requires. This exposes limitations in the motto itself and in a comparative method that requires choosing between apparently opposed positions or values; it also exposes the risk that refusing to choose means bending to the point of breaking.)

Lowell's picture of Shaw includes comparisons to animals: he "has an angry wrenlike vigilance" and "a greyhound's gentle tautness." These images are attractive, especially when compared to the "giant finned cars" of the poem's conclusion. They also associate Shaw with violence, and they may recall the psychological and biological inheritances implied in the poem's opening stanzas. Whether they do so in terms that admire Shaw or diagnose him is deliberately less clear. Does Shaw's vigilance arise from righteous anger, or is his apparent moral vigilance a socially acceptable expression of some less than altruistic psychic rage? In comparing Shaw to a wren, Lowell may have had in mind Edward Howe Forbush's anthropomorphic depiction of the bird as a compulsive fighter. (Lowell had been reading Forbush—in a letter to friends he called him the most eccentric writer of our time;[21] it's a title Lowell might have garnered for himself, although for other reasons.)

As some of these matters begin to suggest, Shaw is in part a Lowell self-portrait, in terms of contrast as well as similarity, especially in that while Shaw took decisive action, Lowell, since he is a poet not a soldier, is more likely only to observe. One of Lowell's ancestors, Charles Russell Lowell, himself a Civil War hero, was married to Shaw's sister: he appears, birdlike and otherwise conflated with Shaw, in the early Lowell poem "Falling Asleep over the Aeneid." Lowell was fascinated by military heroes and shared some of his mother's adoration of them. He had tried to enlist for service in World War II. But during the course of the war Lowell became appalled by what he considered the indiscriminate, illegal, and immoral bombing of civilian populations by American forces, refused to take the induction physical when drafted (the same physical he had failed when he'd attempted to volunteer and would likely have failed again), and was jailed as a conscientious objector. At the time of "For the Union Dead," he was increasingly disturbed by the militarization of postwar U.S. culture and by "the bomb," that is, by the arms race in nuclear weapons and the doomsday follies and fears attendant upon it. Those mixed attitudes toward military matters inflect Lowell's depiction of Shaw as both portrait and self-portrait. But one aspect of Lowell's treatment of Shaw is all but unalloyed, perhaps as close to purity in such matters as Lowell could come.

Lowell says of Shaw: "He rejoices in man's lovely, / peculiar power to choose life and die." Lowell championed such idealistic self-sacrifice in his contribution to a 1962 *Partisan Review* symposium on "The Cold War and the West." He wrote, "No nation should possess, use or retaliate with its bombs. I believe we should rather die than drop our own bombs."[22] Lowell had remained distressed and outraged by the U.S. bombing of German cities during World War II, and by the atomic bombing of Hiroshima and Nagasaki; those feelings were exacerbated by the more immediate contexts of the Berlin crisis and the Cuban missile crisis and by the intense fears and debates about nuclear weapons and the arms race those events had engendered. (In the poem "Fall 1961," Lowell spoke of the "chafe and jar / of nuclear war," eerily adding "we have talked our extinction to death.") Lowell's symposium statement is starkly clear; it requires an unselfish heroism parallel to Shaw's. And yet in a 1961 letter to William Meredith, having said he probably ought to join the group supporting unilateral disarmament, Lowell added, "but I hate that arid, logic-chopping debater's world of the righteous cause." Similar complications haunt "For the Union Dead."

A moment ago, I described Lowell's praise for Shaw in the quoted lines as all but unalloyed, and Shaw's action seems far removed from logic-chopping debate, his rejoicing anything but arid. Still, Lowell doubts the likelihood of a purely motivated altruism in others as in himself. Even companioned by *lovely, peculiar* seems a dubious word. Does marking the power to choose life and die as peculiarly human indicate a risky forgetting of humanity's animal inheritance and recall those "superior" aspects of Shaw that are wincing, suffocating, and unbending: aspects that are, in a word (or words), monumental, brazen, or bronze? Can a willingness to die be wholly distinguished from a death wish? Lowell stresses such complications by refusing to allow his most monumentalizing praise to stand alone as an independent sentence—it's joined by a dash to the phrase about Shaw's inability to bend and its implication that even in life Shaw was on his way to becoming a brazen thing. Perhaps the prefix in *rejoices* implies a mindless and violent repetition of ingrained habits and cultural assumptions and presumptions. Of course, that same prefix recalls Shaw's noble reception, reenactment, and handing onward of his familial and cultural traditions.

As "For the Union Dead" proceeds, Lowell's meditation on Shaw and the Saint-Gaudens on Boston Common leads him to a brief but broader consideration of the Civil War statues on "a thousand small town New England greens." As with other features of the poem, it unsettles what it settles, expanding Lowell's celebration and critique of monuments and the monumental, and of the aesthetic, political, and cultural issues they condense. Generic mass-produced commemorative statues of Union soldiers became a minor industry in the later nineteenth century, as one response to the need for national reunification in the wake of civil war. The relaxed pose of many such works (in Lowell's version the men depicted "doze over muskets / and muse through their sideburns") stresses watchful tranquility over battle. But in his speech at the Saint-Gaudens relief's dedication, William James distinguished sharply between the highly specific memorial to the Massachusetts 54th and to Shaw, on the one hand, and "the abstract soldier's monuments . . . reared on every village green," on the other (as in the almost breathing bronze passage earlier in the poem, Lowell echoes the language of James's speech directly, although this time—as a courtesy, perhaps—without referring to James).

Savage convincingly argues that James's intention in making his distinction was, first, to separate the Shaw memorial from other Civil War statues because it commemorates something nobler than military prowess—the end of slavery—and second, in discussing Saint-Gaudens's statue itself, to separate military valor from civic valor, rather than, as was more commonly done, to use the sculpture to equate them. James asserted that military valor is instinctive, as generic and common as the "abstract" monuments raised to confirm it, but that civic valor is principled and rare, faithful to independent moral ideals rather than to the group or to collective institutions, and therefore appropriately recorded and urged in the specificity of Saint-Gaudens's relief. The increasingly pacifist Lowell suspected that civic virtue always rests on military force and is subverted by its platform. He might have sympathized with James's maneuver: it offered a way to praise Shaw while muting his militarism. But Lowell recognizes the price James pays for his achievement and refuses to share the expense. As Savage says, by making Shaw stand for a private and noble civic valor ignored in standardized military monuments to ordinary men, James almost erases the black troops from his consideration: it's as if James inadvertently revised Saint-Gaudens's monument back in the direction of those statues of standing soldiers and kneeling slaves Saint-Gaudens had so brilliantly reimagined.[23] Lowell avoids and corrects this unintended consequence in the remainder of his poem, just as he has already questioned James's tendency to valorize realist art as redemptive and, by challenging presumptive hierarchies, complicated James's tendency to assume the centrality of exceptional individuals to political progress and of monumental masterpieces to the history of art.

Perhaps Lowell's doubts about the consequences of James's argument are implied by the way this section of the poem trails off in ellipsis, as if it were going to sleep with the dozing soldiers. (The word *muse* recalls what's at risk for the poet who too compliantly relaxes vigilance.) But before turning to Lowell's adjustment of James's tactic, I want to glance at another aspect of Lowell's treatment of the "abstract" statues' soldiers. He describes them as growing "slimmer and younger each year—/ wasp-waisted." This implies the statues' erosion and mocks presumptions of monumental permanence. It recalls that statues committed to assisting in the cultural task of post–civil war reunification or of national and cultural unity in general have to forget as much as they remember. It marks Lowell's own aging. It may also indicate the nation's increasing historical distance from its past and its intensifying failure to remember the past and its lessons. In a typically precise Lowell tangle, this suggests both that monuments fail to provide what they claim to—a continuously accurate and useful tradition, say—and that the culture fails to learn from flawed and accurate monuments what lessons it could learn, including the contradictory need to maintain, reject, and revise monuments and the memorable and forgetful traditions they record. Several commentators on "For the Union Dead" have suggested that the slim soldiers evoke by contrast the fat and insulated affluence of the American 1950s, another postwar era. Similarly, the "sparse, sincere rebellion" of an earlier America contrasts with the poem's swollen and meretricious present. In another twist, Shaw's leanness connects him to the slim soldiers, as if to invalidate James's distinction between the Saint-Gaudens relief and the "abstract" statues on every green. More strangely, in the sort of uncanny, wildly comic combination at which Lowell excels, the poem's images of leanness contrast with the braced and girdled statehouse, as if to say that 1950s slimming is a matter of illusion, of fraudulent appliances for holding up and holding in the body and the body politic.

Perhaps the punning term *wasp-waisted* recalls the elision of the black troops in James's "Brahmin" speech and in the standard Civil War statues of standing white soldiers and kneeling slaves or of ordinary white soldiers at their ease. It's an elision Lowell won't practice, although he'll have to adjust his own "individualistic" emphasis on Shaw in order to avoid it. Lowell brings his dreamily drifting ellipsis up short as if to announce such intentions. In deliberately harsh language, the poem returns abruptly to the monument as a site of contestation and to its racial context. "Shaw's father wanted no monument / except the ditch," he says, "where his son's body was thrown / and lost with his 'niggers.' " The emphasis on actual bodies here abuses the idealizations of military monuments generally and of Saint-Gaudens's almost breathing bronze relief. Shaw's father's position recalls the monument embroiled in debate rather than as a stable, realized presence. And the word *lost* hints at racism within abolitionist idealism and perhaps at its persistence in the present, as the word *niggers* does with greater force. Axelrod locates a source for Lowell's use of the term in a bit of doggerel about the 54th; a popular poem claimed to quote the orders of a Confederate officer intending to insult Shaw by burying him with his black troops; Lowell's ancestor, Charles Russell Lowell quoted it in a letter to his wife, Shaw's sister.[24] Shaw's father made an honor of the intended insult. Lowell uses the doggerel's racist slur to put race back in play in a manner that shows the limits of the emancipatory narrative that James, Civil War statuary, and America too contentedly relate. It's a simple matter no monument can overcome: emancipation is incomplete; American racism persists.

Lowell will say more about how contemporary matters of race

in America comment on the virtues and limitations of monumental narratives of several sorts. First, though, he adds matters of warfare and commercialization to his layered presentation: angled more like an ice-jam than any shapelier lamination, Lowell's structure has, to repeat a phrase, an anomalous coherence. "The ditch," Lowell says, "is nearer." This reverses the historical distancing of earlier maneuvers in the poem and suggests that the failure to learn history's lessons destines dreadful repetitions. The meanings of the word *ditch* ramify fearfully. It is, for instance, the ditch where Shaw and his men were buried, the excavated and desecrated Common, the mass graves of the Holocaust, the crater of the Hiroshima blast, Lowell's approaching death, the divide of race, the gap between American promise and achievement. As "For the Union Dead" returns to the present, Lowell notes that even the flawed public efforts of nineteenth-century monuments have been abandoned. The last war (for this poem, World War II) has no statues here. Perhaps it's too monstrously near to be comfortably remembered (since as Lowell's meditation on monuments shows, remembering requires selective forgetting): the splinted Saint-Gaudens took nearly thirty-five years.

For Lowell, the abandonment of the monumental process has its own horrors, for however flawed and falsely self-congratulatory that process and its products are, they reflect some moral and civic effort. More horrifically still, it turns out that World War II actually does have monuments in what might be called the popular culture: the general cold war sense of impending apocalypse, for instance, and an advertisement on Boylston Street across the Common. It shows "Hiroshima boiling" (the echo in "Boylston" stirs the pot) above a safe that survived the blast, nicknamed or trade-named "Rock of Ages." Lowell's phrase is "boiling / over"; like the ditch, the preposition ramifies. It means physically above and places the mushroom cloud as perversely hovering Paraclete; it implies an uncontained boiling over, suggesting failures of containment and control of every sort (an effect increased by the phrase's enjambment across the ditch dividing stanzas); and it hints at apocalyptic ends in which everything is "over." The delusion of safety in nuclear contexts (with the Mosler safe some weird sort of bomb—or tax—shelter), the mad privileging of money and objects over people, and the ugly appropriation of the Hiroshima bombing and religious imagery for commercial purposes all suggest, to recall James's terms, the death of both military and civic valor.

The hideousness of these transformations almost crushes Lowell as a character in the poem; it leaves him crouching to his television set, one more balked citizen at a glass-walled barrier or fence between reality and the self. This crouching posture gives credence to the view of many commentators that Lowell is enervated or defeated in "For the Union Dead." The sequence from "tingled" to "pressed" to "crouch" and the worsening public situation seem to say so. And yet, there are alternatives. The cultural critique of "For the Union Dead" is withering, and *For the Union Dead* is a book of witheredness, as Lowell said. But as one of Lowell's finest critics, Stephen Yenser, has pointed out, Lowell's books are typically structured as inverted triangles in which a descent toward negation is countered by a return toward chastened affirmation. *For the Union Dead* is no exception, and "For the Union Dead" is its final poem. Moreover, judgments of the poem as despairing depend upon a belief in history as decline which Lowell finds as dubious as a belief in history as progressive. Throughout "For the Union Dead," Lowell both employs the evaluative power of chronological comparison and contrast and implies the alternative view that every moment shares the same set of struggles in different terms. Perhaps Lowell's "crouch to" his television set hovers a little off balance between defeat and a more affirming, almost religiously intent, if secular attention—although, of course, attention isn't action.

Lowell sees "the drained faces of Negro school-children rise like balloons." This image of African-American children attempting to integrate schools under federal law and against armed states-rights segregationist resistance provides the civic version of military valor James sought in the Saint-Gaudens, but it does so in a way that avoids James's near erasure of Shaw's black troops by putting the "Negro school-children" (and not, for instance, Lowell as leading citizen or artist) at the center. In this sense, Lowell does imply a kind of progress. Fearful and brave (their faces are "drained" but not colorless), the children confront the forces arrayed against them. Lifted by their own ideals, they rise. As usual with Lowell, a good deal goes on here, some of it contradictory. For instance, the children recognize the unfinished work of emancipation and continue the communal (rather than individualist) effort to complete that work, accepting and extending the tradition handed down by their "plural" black forebears in the 54th. In this, they recall Booker T.

Washington's statement at the Shaw memorial's dedication that the real monument to the 54th was being built in the South by blacks themselves. Perhaps the shape of balloons (with all their irony about child's play) connects the children to the "bell-cheeked" infantrymen of the 54th.

But in an image the poem will soon restore, the balloons also recall the bubbles drifting up from the "cowed, compliant fish," those bubbles the child Lowell had ached to burst. These children may be cowed, but they are not compliant. If Lowell admits some realistic or manic temptation to burst their idealist bubble, to disillusion them with his adult knowledge of history and the world (a despairing counter to hopes for ameliorative progress), he also "lowers" himself (in the nonpejorative sense but perhaps with hints, as well, of condescension: Lowell never 'scapes whipping while he holds the whip) to watch in vigilant admiration (with the further self-accusing twist that he remains a mere observer of the drama and not an actor in it). The outbreak of parentheses marks my own balked effort to trace—without straightening out or otherwise obscuring—Lowell's zigzag track.

Colonel Shaw makes a brief reappearance in the poem's next-to-last stanza: "riding on his bubble, / he waits / for the blesséd break." As he does throughout the poem, Lowell uses the present tense in describing Shaw. This honors the persistence of his example and keeps him alive as a monument might; in a poem so marked by distrust of monuments and by such intricate chronological shifts, it also suggests once more that Shaw's idealism, like other forms of monumental pretentiousness, put him out of touch with time and change and other people in unbendingly unattractive and unnatural ways. Meanwhile, the image of the bubble unhorses Shaw and frees him from monumental weight while it also marks his ideals as an illusion. Similarly, the collocation of bells, balloons, and bubbles connects Shaw by likeness and contrast with the children, his regiment's men, and with Lowell. Perhaps the most important detail here is that Shaw "waits" for the "blesséd break." The break may signify release from monumental delusions and a breaking back into life beyond wincing at pleasure and suffocating for privacy. Or it may indicate a desperate yielding to temptation: the idealist desire to experience the cleansing breakage of apocalyptic destruction which unveils the meaning of human action or reveals it all as illusion, the bubble finally burst. Or perhaps the break hints at a hope that the children will break through to realize their own more modestly idealist dreams and desires. Maybe what matters most is Shaw's antiapocalyptic willingness to wait, especially in the nuclear context of Lowell's present moment.

The poem's close is bleaker: in part because the contemporary situation is bleak; in part, I think, because Lowell is leery of the sort of reifying self-congratulation he's abused in monuments and wants to avoid in his poem, which, by its own logic, will require revising in its turn. "For the Union Dead" has revered, reviled, and revised Saint-Gaudens's monument to Shaw and the Massachusetts 54th, along with the remarkable range of aesthetic, political, and cultural issues the monument implies. Lowell's poem subjects itself and its maker to similar critiques. For example, Lowell's reimagining extends—both follows and corrects—those of Saint-Gaudens and James by putting the "Negro school-children" at the center of America's then-current version of the Civil War, the struggle for civil rights. But it does not assume that in doing so it's monumentally sufficient, final, or transcendent. Those commentators who see Lowell as attacking the monument and replacing it with his poem are (partly) wrong. It's one more matter of emphasis, and as Lowell said, emphasis confuses. Perhaps "For the Union Dead" is like those monumental flags the poem memorializes: "frayed," they "quilt the graveyards of the Grand Army of the Republic"; like them, Lowell's poem comforts and decays.

The final quatrain of "For the Union Dead" is monumentally despairing. It declares the aquarium's disappearance and then, as if all the institutional and monumental containments it stands for have failed, reports the outcome: "Everywhere / giant finned cars nose forward." "Everywhere" is apocalyptic. Humanity's brute, acquisitive nature has been crossed with machines and freed from constraint, force has been wedded monstrously to compliance, so that the body politic and artistic is fish food or sleeps with the fishes. Lowell's disgust is an audible hiss, a palpable smear: "a savage servility / slides by on grease." But perhaps this is one more confusing emphasis. The poem's thorough insistence on the historically situated partialness of things makes "everywhere" seem dubiously extreme—an apocalyptic desperation at odds with the courage of the infantrymen of the 54th and the children, and with James's cautious "almost" and Shaw's patient waiting. Lowell's own strenuously worded anger bespeaks the watchful citizen on guard against destruction and contrasts with compliant sliding by.

Perhaps Lowell's earlier self-vigilant confession of his tingling desire to burst bubbles should make us vigilant against his nihilist deflations here. Similarly, the poem's several reminders that monumental and institutional containments repress as they constrain and therefore only partly merit preservation might temper Lowell's fishy fears: after all, those fears reflect, with Lowell's usual thirst for honest self-accusation, his Brahmin aversion to "greaser" immigrants and their gaudy or exuberant tastes. In fact, here, as often in Lowell, something jokey infects and inoculates his most profoundly serious moments. The nosing fish echo the poem's earlier noses, portentously, to be sure, but also in a way that recalls that poems, like monuments, are nosily overdetermined. The inundation of Boston's streets by big-finned 1950s cars mimes barbarian hordes; does it also restore the poem to more ordinary civic considerations? One of the nearest things to a rhyme in "For the Union Dead" comes in the words *cage* and *garage* in its fourth stanza. Might the parking garage, for all its graft, its desecration of the Common, and its threats to monuments and institutions, be built to cage those crass, commercial, automotive (and atavistic) fish? But maybe this is just my ploy to make Lowell's clairvoyant, dreadful vision somehow assuaging. I think of Lowell as he described himself singing: a catbird breaking his sweetest song with some harsh squawk—think of him, too, as he used to stand: his chin supported by a palm or fist, his elbow braced on nothing but thin air.

A final word. Throughout this book I use the term *condense* to indicate the ways in which monuments stand for the many aesthetic, political, and cultural attitudes and issues described in my introduction. Because he sees monuments as one more link in a metonymic chain that spreads from postures, TV shows, and ads to systems of government and religion, Lowell unpacks those attitudes and issues. But if "For the Union Dead" finds ways to reimagine monuments and monumental poems without the hierarchies, certitudes, reifications, and sense of completeness, permanence, and closure that usually attend them, it's in no way Lowell's last word on the matter. "For the Union Dead" is a hinge or pivot poem in Lowell's career, in terms of its placement at the end of two different volumes and its association with the moment of his leaving Boston for New York and other places, and in terms of the closing of one stylistic period and the opening of another. Lowell's later work extends his dark illumination of what politics, art, and culture might mean in private and public spheres where ideals we tingle (lovingly, greedily, violently) to reach may destroy what they're meant to uphold.

3

James Merrill
"Losing the Marbles" and "Bronze"

James Merrill was as canny about the guises and disguises of the self as he was about the conventions and inventions of literary kinds. He called his autobiography *A Different Person.* Merrill's experimental memoir follows biology's synecdoche, in which single cells carry an entire organism's DNA. It frames the events of a few youthful years in Europe to represent the elaborating constants of his larger life. In the autobiography, Merrill recalls an instance in which he was accused of "un-American gentility." He answers the charge this way, "It's not fair. We're as American as lemon chiffon pie." With its measure of admission and portion of tart rebuttal, the retort is characteristic. By approximate citation, Merrill preserves the apple pie adage; he respects it enough *almost* to serve it again, then comically changes the menu. The altered dessert acknowledges varied tastes and is laced with citric self-assertion. It might be put like this: in his remark, Merrill (who was, among other things, a wealthy, well-educated, homosexual artist) allows that, to some, lemon chiffon pie might seem elitist or arty or gay compared with proverbially democratic, workmanlike, and conventionally domestic apple, but he also insists that both are kinds of (American) pie. This implies an oppositional *and* inclusive sexual and cultural politics (and an oppositional and inclusive gender and literary politics as well, since the context of Merrill's riposte involves Ernest Hemingway's supposedly manly person and style).

Merrill's remark also implies social and literary practices in which presumed boundaries between the trivial and the serious blur or disappear, so that—as in anthropology, for instance—cooking can codify culture. It suggests as well that every human construct—whether an adage, a canon of taste, or an established (or antiestablishment) hierarchy—is subject to recoding. It's a modestly radical method. Merrill applied it to everything from preferences in pie to revisions of epic. It reflects a quality he admired in Dante: Merrill says the Italian poet's "conceptual innovations . . . refigure rather than refute the thought that preceded them." Merrill's innovations also refigure rather than refute preceding views and versions. One form this takes in his work is the polite allusion politely amended. For instance, Merrill recalls and refigures Dante when he titles one of his books *Divine Comedies;* elsewhere he approvingly quotes Wallace Stevens's adage, "There is no wing like meaning," then adds, "Two are needed to get off the ground." Such practices typify Merrill's handling of matters ranging from sexuality and identity to language, literary tradition, and belief. They typify, too, his treatment of monuments and the political, aesthetic, and more broadly cultural issues they condense.[1]

"All stone once dressed asks to be worn," Merrill writes, in the poem "Losing the Marbles." Epigrammatic syntax ballasts the sentence; generalizing, definitive, memorable, it invites belief and repetition, the response of faith. But the epigram's central terms are rocky (or wrinkled). In the context of stone, *dressed* and *worn* evoke clothing. The effect is both compatible and incongruent. (We speak of seams of rock; in *The (Diblos) Notebook,* Merrill observes that cloth-of-gold's rough seams abrade the wearer.) Under their slippery guise in Merrill's adage, the words *dressed* and *worn* invite not rock-fast repetition but interpretation and revision, the response of doubt. It's part of Merrill's point that the competing invitations to skepticism and faith are not quite mutually exclusive, since doubt is vital to belief, interpretation is a rite of nearly religious attention, and revision is a version of repetition. To put it another way, Merrill refigures epigrams (and other structures and systems) even as they're uttered; neither rote nor rejection, his strategy stitches faith and doubt together but leaves the seams displayed.

To dress stone is to cut, chisel, or otherwise shape it for human use, for building, say, or for making statues. And in Merrill's epigram, dressed stone, meant to wear on, wears out. The formula is familiar from poems on the futility of efforts to immortalize ourselves and our private or public ideals in monuments or verse. "Losing the Marbles" echoes such poems, and (echoes are never exact) it revises them as well. Merrill's epigram (and poem) suggests that whatever humans shape in their search for permanence wears out; it also suggests—as the awkward, suitable pairing of *dressed* and *worn* shifts ground from harder stone toward softer cloth—that we wear what we shape for a time as fitting dress. We wear it, that is, until styles change or a garment (or ideal, belief, or monument) comes to feel ill-fitting, too loose or too tight, or just wears out. Here's the phrase again: "All stone once dressed asks to be worn." It implies that in stone as in cloth what wears away is also donned and worn, and persists at least for a while, wearing well as well as wearing out.

In a further complication, Merrill's phrase also implies that in both supposedly timeless monuments and supposedly transient fashions we not only wear what we make but also are made by what we wear. Man (*sic*) makes the clothes (or culture—or cooking), and clothes make the man. As Merrill said of the rural Greek who told Aesop's fables as if he had made them up, "that they had made *him* up was closer to the truth."[2] A postideological poet in some sense, Merrill hedges and hampers his commitments; endlessly reconsidered, they're neither final nor wholehearted. Yet Merrill is also sure that ideologies or epistemes (our culture's fables, going in and out of fashion) more or less create us. The extent to which they do—and direct for good or ill our personal and political behavior—is one of Merrill's central subjects. He pursues it while keeping his own and others' centers plural and awry. He interrogates and seeks to limit epistemic power without presuming to escape it.

"Losing the Marbles" doesn't repeat or refute the attack of, say, "Ozymandias" on political and creative power. It refigures it in ways both stonily firm and fabric-supple. Merrill's poem is in part a catalogue of time's erosions of permanence in private and public realms: the loss of memory that accompanies age, the deaths of friends, forgotten versions of heaven, a temple so abraded that it has become featureless, whole cultures displaced and dissolved. The list seems patently antimonumental, but the structure I've used to describe it sets transience too starkly at odds with endurance and is somewhat misleading. In "Losing the Marbles," erosion (with its companions, death and forgetfulness, dissolution and displacement) not only cuts off endurance but partakes of it as well, for better and for worse. For example, the title's lost marbles are the colloquial ones associated with senility, but they are also the so-called Elgin Marbles. Scoured by the ages, threatened by the decline of ancient Greek civilization (and by negligence and Ottoman occupation), but preserved (or looted, or both) by Lord Elgin, those fragments of the Parthenon's ruined frieze imply destruction yet are safely housed (or imprisoned) in London's British Museum. Meanwhile, nationalistic contemporary Greeks loudly lament the monumental marbles' loss (or theft) and demand their return to the homeland. Tied to myths of origin, those citizens are sure that repatriating worn and broken stones will certify the continuity and wholeness of their culture's epistemes (or, as Merrill might see it, shore up wholeness's remains, or dress up the illusions with which we make do in its absence).

Not only memory and monuments (those metonyms) wear out and wear on in Merrill's poem, so, too, does writing, their coconspirator in the arts of preservation. When Merrill describes a set of poetry worksheets damaged by rain, one more human scheme for indelible inscription seems all but washed away. "All but" because—to repeat—at the same time that "Losing the Marbles" describes decline, collapse, and erasure, it also describes what resists them—and partly resists them itself. Memory can be recovered, if only partially (and never impartially). Some monuments are preserved, if only in pieces, out of context, and under assumptions apt to be honorable and dubious at once (those of British imperialism, say, or Greek nationalism, or the sort of respect for history, tradition, and art that gets mixed up with manipulation of and by them). Even a rain-drenched text can be restored—although recovery and invention blur in the restoration process. Merrill blends a sense of his poetry's worth with awareness of his own and any art's fragility. He plays on the tradition that what we have as Sappho's works were recovered—their gaps filled in by scholarly guesswork—from papyrus fragments used for stuffing crocodile mummies. In one section of "Losing the Marbles" Merrill gives us a page of his own rain-wrecked drafts—a worksheet reduced to fragments, lacunae, and a few likely guesses—and in another section provides a restored text in finished sapphics. The effect is that neither of the poem's categories (which overlap in any case) quite overcomes the other—not its examples of time's destruction nor its exempla of human resistance to time's erosion. Like Lowell and Bishop, Merrill is less concerned with dismissing or upholding whatever lasts—the dressed stone of monuments, say, or the personal and cultural beliefs they codify and enforce—than he is with exploring their fulfilling, failed, and fraught relations to public and private occasions and needs.

In "Losing the Marbles" Merrill's "conclusions" are provisional and comic. For instance, it's unlikely that the recovered "sapphic" poem provided there accurately retrieves the original, now corrupted text from which it works (if there ever was such a text). Nevertheless, the combination of threatened loss and attempted restoration does inspire verse, in an activity that accepts loss as generative as well as painful, and honors product and process, permanence and change. One implication of the word *asks* in the dressed-stone epigram is that stone has a life of its own and participates in a natural cycle of building up and breaking down, as persons and cultures do. The pleas of dressed stone for its own gradual demise in wear-resisting (but) temporary use (to recall the wavering sense of *worn* discussed above) both criticizes monuments—the Parthenon, a poem—for their denial of change, the very stuff of life, and refigures them as willingly immersed in the timeful change they resist for a little while.

Poets' (or anybody's) views of such matters have to do with attitudes toward aging and death, and "Losing the Marbles" can be read as one of Merrill's several revisions of Yeats's great poem on aging, "Sailing to Byzantium." An earlier Merrill work recasts the mode of transportation and the destination of Yeats's poem; it's called "Flying from Byzantium."[3] "Losing the Marbles" does similar work less directly. Yeats, in his poem, sees physical decrepitude and the attendant loss of sexual and artistic power as a wholesale and alienating disaster. In response, he elects to abandon the body and enter the eternity of art. Yeats cunningly counts the cost of that exchange: the enameled nightingale he chooses as an alternative to human form is monumentally potent and precious (it functions nobly and all at once as historian, chronicler, and prophet—and as muse), but the bird is also almost absurdly tiny and toylike, at best artificial, and perhaps merely fake. Even so, Yeats's preference for "Monuments of unaging intellect" over tattered, paltry flesh is intensely real in "Sailing to Byzantium." His embrace there of supposedly immortal art as a desperate alternative to age, decrepitude, and death is tragic and dramatic.

In "Losing the Marbles," on the other hand, Merrill (in similar circumstances) is comically good-humored; he might think of aging as *growing* old—and of Yeats as melodramatic. However that may be, Merrill sees the "blinkings-out" age wreaks on memory as also wreaked on marble, so that works of art (whether poems or golden nightingales or monuments) are alternatives to flesh at most in degree and surely not in kind. (I'll come back to that.) Meanwhile, Merrill also responds to the erosions that signal decline and death with equanimity rather than with anguish or despair—or with rhetorical heroics. Invoking yet another prior text (Keats is a presence here as well, of course, and by multiplying precedents Merrill mutes—without silencing—the authority of any one of them), Merrill suggests that Dylan Thomas's famous exhortation to "Rage against the dying of the light" may be excessive in the way of "the Athens press, / Breathing fire to get the [Elgin] marbles back"—as though too strenuously resisting death in life and art is equivalent to overheated political posturings that conflate identity and possessiveness. Both Thomas and the Athens press have a point, Merrill implies, but they exaggerate their claims.

At the same time, though, Merrill also agrees with Thomas and Yeats (and perhaps the Athens press): the "blinkings-out" of age and death and other losses are "Capital punishment, / Yes." Meanwhile—as the ionic, iconic, "monumental," political, "I"-effacing joke in *capital* suggests—he also feels that they're a kind of "grace," an "utmost clemency at work" upon the self and state. It's characteristic in every way that when Merrill tries to extend that insight into a conclusive argument, closure (artfully, of course) collapses. Suddenly at a loss, a befuddled, aging speaker drifts toward blank inconsequence: all this "to prove—hold on, don't tell me . . . What?" Forgetting's clemency lends solace by calming several sorts of excess—including, perhaps, the sometimes frantic faith that it's the individual's permanence that matters—or the individual culture's.

"Losing the Marbles" doesn't so much refute Yeats's anxiety about aging, then, as it refigures it comically. To Merrill, aging and its attendant losses are part of the nature of things, and the loss of personal persistence is compensated for by contributions to the larger human and natural communities or systems of which the self is part. Thus, as dressed stone asks to be worn, Merrill counsels that we accept age and its discontents as necessary experience rather than too rigidly deny them. At the same time, no selfless rush to death is recommended or encouraged. Addressing another long-lived poet, Merrill says, "It almost seems / Death has forgotten us." "Shh!" his friend replies, "A cautionary finger to his lip." Once more, the tone isn't anxious but light, conspiratorial, second-childhood-like, marked by wonder, tenderness, and a real but muted and therefore bearable distress.

To return to a point made briefly above, Merrill also refigures rather than refutes Yeats's view of art as an alternative to bodily aging, decline, and death. If "Losing the Marbles" sees monuments erode with equanimity, it also admires art's power. But where Yeats sometimes conceives of art's potency as defeating or outlasting time, immortalizing either art's patron or maker, its cultural source, or the artwork itself (all traditional tasks of monuments and writing), Merrill (refiguring Yeats) sees art as one more participant in a broader process of growth, decay, and recycled growth that encompasses clothing, persons, stones, and everything else, albeit at differing rates. Merrill hopes that art—precisely because its heavens are fickle and "counterfeit" (a still tougher, less solacing term than Yeats's *artifice,* which has the glamour of "art" in it)—can insulate us from the rigid, disillusioned, sometimes destructive fate of those who adhere at any cost to objects or ideas they assume or insist are immune to change. It's typical of "Losing the Marbles," written, as Merrill says, from the "high wire / Between the elegiac and the haywire" and involving a poet who wishes he'd been an acrobat, that in it the word *adherents* flippantly unglues cultural, political, and artistic attempts to stick around. Typical as well is the poem's postmodernist challenge to those monumental, unifying, and immortalizing aspects of modernism that have come of late to seem too much committed to "authoritarian" politics and poetics.

Meanwhile, at the same time that Merrill thinks recognizing art's status as counterfeit provides protection against ideological rigidity and its sometimes dangerous consequences, he also fears that his more playful view of art—implying a high-wire act performed above the fray of quotidian choices and commitments—might in its own way distract us from the reality of life and process, the difficult acts of committed choosing that produce not only politics but works of art as well. He worries that a private, disengaged view of art (where *counterfeit* might mean valueless, unable to function as legal tender, impotent to transact with others and with the broader culture) is escapist and risks alienation from the cyclical economy everything inhabits, including works of art. In that economy, "the will- / To-structural elaboration [may] still / Flute up, from shifting dregs of would-be rock, / Glints of a future colonnade and frieze." It's a process in which the flutes of musical and columnar elaboration slip and overlap, in which decaying and decayed creations beget renewed if never "original" making—or remaking. (Merrill's shift to long-term geological views in these lines—a strategy frequent in his work—puts individual desires for immortality in ironic perspective and offers a solacing grandeur of temporal—but not eternal—expansion in which otherwise divided individuals and communities practice constructive collaboration across the ages.)

Merrill's provisional solution to all of these matters is, I think, to keep them *in* solution. "Losing the Marbles" offers, "in conclusion," not so much an idea or an argument as a set of interrelated images: a vanished seaside temple, a pile of "wave-washed pebbles," and a pouch of toy (or playing) marbles. Like "a palindrome," the ruined temple (that of Artemis at Ephesus) has "laid its plans for stealing back." The pebbles (like the temple) once belonged to the seven wonders of the world; now they're recycled when chosen by topless women at the shore "To use as men upon their checkerboards." The marbles, "targets and strikers," were given to the aging poet in reply to jokes about losing *his* marbles; he set them randomly between the slats around his swimming pool, creating one more counterfeit, consoling, constellated heaven—placed firmly underfoot, not overhead. Those images have many implications. In general, as bits and pieces remaining from earlier monuments now lost or destroyed, they become building blocks in the renewing play of further structural elaboration. More specifically, each involves a kind of amusement, pastime, or diversion. Palindromes (a favored toy in word games) read the same from right to left as they do from left to right. They recover themselves as they unravel or return as they depart—and the reverse; they also recall some of Merrill's fondest images for composition as a process of creation, decay, and (pun intended) recreation: the jigsaw puzzle worked to completion and then dismantled; the craft whose (wakeful) stern mends what its sharp prow scissors; the magician who saws his (one presumes, well-put-together) assistant in half without harming her.

As to the topless women playing checkers, they seem as much like goddesses, fates, or furies as exemplars of contemporary Mediterranean seaside fashion. Their checkerboards (like targets and strikers, those warrior victims and attackers in marble[s]) threateningly recall and playfully refigure the doom of men in war. They do so in something like the way the Ouija-board poetics of *The Changing Light at Sandover* antiapocalyptically warn of Armageddon and, in an effort to help to prevent it, pacify epic commitments. In *Sandover*, Merrill refigures the epic's monumental urge to immortalize individuals, cultures, or nations by converting warfare to a board game, battlefields to banquets, and culture wars to conversations. If we recall that Yeats makes his nightingale both monitory sage and aristocratic tchotchke, we see again how Merrill (whose marbles are elegant and playfully pedestrian) refigures without quite refuting Yeats and other prior masters. But I'm getting ahead of the story. "Losing the Marbles" appeared in Merrill's next-to-last collection, *The Inner Room,* published in 1988. Merrill's late accommodation to (and of) monuments and monumentality in "Losing the Marbles" and elsewhere is one eventual outcome of a lifetime's fluently disciplined, often antimonumental work.

Taxonomy skews the ecologies it classifies. It would serve my argument—or at least its arrangement—to divide Merrill's career into discrete categories: an early phase of fixed or monumental views, a fluid or antimonumental middle stage, a late period whose fluent refigurings recover monuments for human use. But that configuration is at best (although also at worst) a half-truth, balked and blocked repeatedly (although also encouraged) by Merrill's immense capacity for complication at every stage of his career. The skeins of affinity and variance in Merrill's work are tricky to represent and always changing. One solution might be to put my taxonomy forward while also admitting anomalies encountered along the way—both letting them in and confessing to them. The result would certainly be rocky— little avalanches set off when hilled-up statements and qualifications exceed their angle of repose and tumble roughly toward momentary (never stable) rest. It might sound something like this.

The image of conjuring flutes and fluted columns in "Losing the Marbles" conjoins music with stone, just as the poem's dressed-stone epigram combines rock with clothing. The effect is neither antithesis nor synthesis but modulation and alteration, a fluid set of reciprocal relations. In some of Merrill's earlier work, however (although not in his earliest), the flow of tunes or tunics (or torsos) is more apt to oppose than it is to transpose, refit, or refigure the rigor (mortis) of marble and other monuments. In Merrill's early play *The Bait,* for instance, all the characters save one are rendered grotesque by the hardenings of self toward change brought on by inflexible commitments. The lone not-so-hardened character says, "our cold virtues, once thought durable," in fact are "frail as snowflakes" becoming "lazy water in the sun." "Fluidity is proof against major disasters," he adds, "The marbles melt and wink" at us. These theme-clinching lines dissolve stone and corrode the monumental; they firmly associate the drive to durability with the cold, the outsized, and the catastrophic.

At the same time, though, as is often the case with Merrill, this acid judgment is sweetened some (and my initial version of it chastened). Stephen Yenser notes that Merrill himself winks at the moment when the marbles do: within his character's speech about marbles melting, the passage's prose—in implicit contrast to its content—"has crystallized to verse." That complication is an apt reminder that even in early work Merrill avoids schematic oppositions and finds subtle ways to remain of many minds at once. Most generalizations about Merrill's performances require a corrective *but* (or several); his conjunctions, as Yenser puts it, "force us to that conjunction." In *The Changing Light at Sandover,* for instance, the poem's matter (which is hierarchical and deterministic) and its manner (which is disruptive and fluid) abrade and adjust one another. But *Sandover*'s meanings arise less from the conflict of matter and manner than from our "submersion in and resistance to" both—and from the many layers of interplay between them. Merrill admired Rossini's "Musique Anodyne," with its relief from singleness of mind and related headaches, including ideological and aesthetic ones. As Merrill observed, Rossini's multiple settings of the same brief text for several solo voices show "how many different tones"—"tragic, romantic, mocking"—"can channel a given statement." It's a compositional strategy Merrill often deploys himself, framing alternatives so that they seem not opposites but rather "aspects of one another."[4] Nevertheless, while a preference for inclusiveness and complication, for variety, nuance, and variation, saturated Merrill's career, he sometimes took sides against the monumental with a Nietzschean dismissiveness his later work redresses.

As I said, this way of representing things is rocky. Assertions elide objections and abrade what they're meant to describe. Qualifications detour and delay—and impede the flow of statement. So be it. Deferral connotes not only hesitation but also good manners. Perhaps a deferred, disrupted, hindered approach to Merrill's (almost) antimonumental observations is properly respectful, courteous to the poet; after all, he works by ever-shifting emphases, not verities or declarations. Merrill shares an aim he attributes to skilled interpreters of Dante: the desire to be "ever more complex and less obscure." Merrill's means for reaching toward that always put-off, optative goal include interruption, postponements, and repeated new beginnings.

Applying every sort of flexed and fractioned verbal operation, he subtracts and adds, takes square roots, and multiplies across parentheses. His methods convey a covert content of their own; arithmetically, geometrically, they expand, contract, and ramify to supplement, curtail, and complicate his poetry's more overt matter.

Even in moments of epigrammatic concision ("All stone once dressed asks to be worn," for instance), Merrill's designs, as Helen Vendler says, have more to do with unending elaboration, however terse, than with the fixed finality of aphorism. When Merrill speaks of the "glaze of custom to be neither shattered nor shattered by," *glaze* connotes something both dully dazed and brightly beautified, and *custom* something worthy of preservation and respect while also subject to resistance and alteration. No wonder Merrill lauded Ponge for creating texts "perfected . . . without 'finish' "—and commended his method: exposing poetry's (and culture's) mechanisms.[5] In the current context, all that might come to this: Merrill's antimonumental stance avoids rigidity precisely by being rigorously thorough; after all, an antimonumental view that's not exposed to alternatives and interrogation becomes (what else?) a monument itself, inviting ruin.

Merrill's distrust of monuments (once again, it's a hedged distrust, where alternatives are aspects, not mutually canceling extremes) has multiple sources. Some are personal. To simplify (and commit a Merrill sin against the Holy Ghost), one of his formative experiences was the divorce of his parents, the financier Charles E. Merrill and his second wife, Hellen Ingram, in 1939, when Merrill was thirteen. The child's desire to ignore or resist this momentous change, to retain or recover a family unity he'd assumed was permanent and keep his parental monuments intact, appears in many of Merrill's poems, most notably in "Scenes of Childhood," "The Broken Home," "Days of 1935," and "Lost in Translation." In all of these, of course, the child's dread of alteration isn't merely recorded; it's filtered through adult reconsiderations of the nature, meaning, and value of time, change, and human behavior—and instructed or adjusted by those considerations. A few of Merrill's earliest poems (all preceding the ones just named) reflect attitudes that might seem likely in a child wounded by divorce: a preference for immutable arrangements and a view of the poem itself as a perfectly arranged object that fixes experience (corrects it, makes it permanent).

But many poems of his middle period (including the ones just

named) are attempts to convert the child's dread of time and alteration to hope or trust in them, an effort to reconceive as natural and
bearable even seemingly catastrophic change: divorce, illness, death;
the Proustian truth that "the loved one always leaves"; the fluidity
or relativity of all arrangements once deemed universal, permanent,
and natural—whether families, cultures, systems of government,
or works of art. Such attempts are fundamentally opposed to the
monumental, as is Merrill's aim to recognize breakage (in private and
public affairs, and in poetic form and content) as something to be
accepted and instructed by—however much, and perhaps because,
its lessons never settle. For instance, this phrase from *The (Diblos)
Notebook*, "I understood it better later," grants time an educational
function while implying that final understanding won't and needn't
be attained. In "Yánnina" (which stages a scene of instruction where
the surrender of wholeness yields wholeness enlarged, not fractured),
these words do the same: "That the last hour be learned again by /
Riper selves." Something similar is implied throughout *The Changing
Light at Sandover.* There, increasingly authoritative revelations from
more and more highly placed instructors are routinely corrected and
supplanted so that, as Merrill said in an interview, what seems "the
last word" when delivered always turns out to be "penultimate."[6]

To return to my present focus, Merrill's frequent view that time
and change are heuristic—and more nearly sacramental than sacri-
legious—is sharply antimonumental. This term, if not quite fairly,
fairly well defines a good deal of Merrill's work from all but his earliest (somewhat "monumental") poems until the period of the *Sandover* trilogy and his final three volumes, where—as Merrill ages—
monuments are again and still more nimbly than before refigured.
Altered and warily restored for human wearing, their abrasive seams
are exposed as their fit and fittingness are modeled. Meanwhile, the
frequent distrust of monuments marking much of Merrill's career
isn't merely a matter of recovering from the trauma of his parents'
divorce or from his own initially "static" reaction to it. It reflects his
later, larger experience of "love and loss" and can also be understood
as a critique of several inherited aesthetic, political, and cultural traditions. I'll consider that critique more fully before turning to the
great accommodation of (and to) the monumental in Merrill's late
poem "Bronze."

Leslie Brisman writes that for Merrill life is "less impossible to
mend than to replace." This captures a key component of Merrill's

vision, although *vision* isn't the word: like Bishop, Merrill demoted "visions" to more earthly, provisional "looks"; he called his own work not visionary but revisionary. His main complaint against monuments and monument makers is that they replace life rather than mend it. Too fearful to accept life's alarming, incurable, but—Merrill thinks—also ultimately healthful and surely bearable identity with time and change, they substitute something dead and deadly in its place: monumentally singular objects, visions, and systems, including artistic, political, and cultural absolutes. Those "monuments" reject all alteration; they wear like iron, seeking forcefully to dominate or destroy alternative arrangements. Putatively permanent, their resistance to process makes them inflexibly hard and unforgiving. They break themselves and damage others.

Merrill's view of the human situation is milder and more comic, a matter of toleration, inclusion, and adjustment, of multiple arrangements, rearrangement, and repair. Such attitudes—and the politics they imply—are tricky to account for. There's temperament, of course, and Merrill's unusual combination of moral subtlety and mannerly consideration. In still more general terms, there's Merrill's commitment to both change and reconciliation in poetry and life. It's as if he combined the first rule of tinkering—keep all the parts—with the inventor's trust in innovation and the botanist's or florist's faith that color breaks may yield more varied and more fulfilling arrangements. Sure that everything breaks but can be mended although not restored, Merrill doesn't coerce the shards of a shattered bowl or damaged text or broken home to reproduce some supposedly perfect "original" configuration; instead, he adjusts and refigures the original pieces and incorporates new material, producing revised and provisional patterns for altered circumstances he expects will alter again and require further amending. His is the renovator's motto: "nothing lasts and nothing ends." (The phrase is from Merrill's poem "Flèche d'Or," which introduces a golden arrow into a door of flesh.)

In tonal terms, at least, Merrill's sexual orientation offers a case in point. Merrill was homosexual in a culture that at worst demonized his affections and at best labeled them deviant. Later in his life, things changed (as Merrill memorably put it, he didn't come out of the closet; instead, like Sarah Bernhardt descending a spiral staircase by standing still and letting it revolve around her, he stayed "in one place while the closet simply disintegrated"). That improvement aside, however, Merrill's trust in political and cultural authority had already been (constructively) damaged. Since the "normalizing" powers that enforce heterosexual codes as the only natural and acceptable ones denied the conditions of his own existence, perhaps the other conventions authorities impose (marriage, monuments, meter) are fraudulent as well—or are better understood as cultural constructions than as absolutes. But such doubts no more wholly soured Merrill on conventions (including literary ones) than conventional disapproval kept him from living an unconventional sexual life—all while realizing that homosexual culture has conventions of its own to be abided by and challenged (as do both experimental and "traditional" writing).

In regard to sexual (as to other) conventions, Merrill managed neither to be shattered by nor to shatter the "glaze of custom." Like a good slice of lemon chiffon pie, his rich and generous response to circumstances—as with his parents' divorce or his long, loyal, sometimes difficult relationship with his lover, David Jackson—was tart but never bitter. A similar flavor marks Merrill's disparagement of monuments and the monumental, and of the aesthetic, political, and cultural views they represent. Meanwhile, since my recipe mixes metaphors so freely, here's another appetizer—one more reminder that Merrill keeps on hand the elements (or ingredients, or aspects—including monuments) he momentarily puts aside. As J. D. McClatchy writes, "Merrill would have agreed with George Balanchine, who once said that the true figure for the artist should be the gardener or the chef: you love everything because you need everything."[7]

Merrill's antimonumental political and cultural stance (although, to say it again, his positions aren't firmly two-footed) is frequently conveyed through comments on aesthetics. For instance, in an essay on Corot, Merrill indicates a preference in art for unpretentious landscapes over grand religious spectacles and history painting. (Similarly, in *The (Diblos) Notebook,* a character explains that certain paintings are moving because they are so slight.) Merrill is pleased to think of a particular Corot canvas as "lighthearted, a spoof on certain big moments out of Titian or Poussin." He especially praises Corot's versions of Rome, describing his "rapidly brushed" depictions of that imperial, monumental, "eternal" city as providing us instead with "the city of our dreams: physical, somnolent, unimperially casual and even-tempered." He highlights the painter's "wonderful trees";

"dwarfing the monuments they frame," they cut Rome's gigantism down to size, just as the speed of Corot's brushwork twits Roman cults of permanence and perfection.

The sense that monuments violate the properly human scale of things is a frequent Merrill theme. Describing a visit to Istanbul in *A Different Person,* for instance, Merrill prefers the mosque known as the "little Hagia Sophia" to its immense and more famous neighbor. He approves of its intimate space, "perfectly scaled to the play of human attention." He admires still more the common things to be seen there: an "artisan's cotton smock hung, limp with wear, one pocket torn, from a row of five wooden pegs painted orange." Merrill also observes that the building's apse has been "reoriented" toward Mecca "by an oblique dais." Perhaps *dais* puts the orientalist Said on stage in anagram. In any case, Merrill's directionally angled puns make geopolitical points. The little mosque is a converted Catholic church; in it, Merrill refigures what has been remodeled already. Neither Catholic nor Muslim, he takes a secular communion, "drinking in those humble objects the tide of daily life has filled brimful." Back in Rome, Merrill venerates the "tiny church of San Carlo alle Quattro Fontane . . . with its pearl-gray cloister no bigger than a brooch"; he praises Borromini, some of whose paintings are housed there, celebrating his antimonumental "taste for perishable materials" and "preciousness of scale."[8]

In such ways, Merrill asserts an anti-imperial, antitotalizing politics without being politically explicit. Merrill thought political directness invited the "tread of a stone guest" within his house. He told an interviewer, "The trouble with overtly political or social writing is that when the tide of feeling goes out, the language begins to stink." Richard Saez was right, then, when he said that Merrill avoids the topical, and he was also right when he listed the important contemporary topics Merrill nonetheless addresses. The catalogue might go like this: ecological destruction, terrorism, political assassination, nuclear arms, overpopulation, religious zealotry, and the whole ensnarement of selves and states in the conceptual structures or constructs they inhabit. But when Merrill takes up such matters (all related to enforcing some ideology or other as absolute and permanent—that is, as monumental), he typically does so obliquely. Again, his comments on art and artists offer reorientation. Here, for instance, what seems a tourist's casual description of architecture and setting reveals the fate of militant beliefs that people kill or die for:

"The cold pink of cherry blossoms lightened Albi's fortress church, and the Tarn moved on tiptoe eddies. The eponymous heresy, with its 'dualist doctrines' for which thousands perished, seemed harmless enough by now, like brick structures massive against clouds but, once reflected, going to pieces in the slow green river." This dissolves the "massive" edifice of religious and political faith, perhaps reducing its (monumental) force for harm. The solvent is reflection, that shimmering term. Meanwhile, although Merrill often discounts the content of belief and chides fanatical commitments, the feel and feeling of belief as it comes and goes is something else. Merrill prefers the sacraments of dailiness to those of churches, but he knows that *secular* and *sacred* share an etymological root and that making and unmaking faiths is an everyday occurrence. While he never wants song to "curdle into scripture," his phrasing acknowledges that each is an aspect of the other. Merrill puts it this way in remarks on Bishop: the value of "a world relieved of theological apparatus" is that it permits poetry to go on being what Montale said the ancients called it, "a staircase to God."[9]

Elizabeth Bishop's work (no "oracular amplification"; no "stilts") is often Merrill's model for poetry that avoids the monumentally out of scale without sacrificing access to the numinous (and to political and cultural critique). He admires her "way with systems," which "tend to fade beside her faith in natural powers." Those are qualities Merrill found lacking in the major (male) modernists—he calls them "giants"—who "transcend human dimensions" in order to create their totalizing, monumental structures: say, *A Vision, The Waste Land, Paterson,* and *Cantos.* For similar reasons, Merrill also distrusted the supposed alternatives to modern monumentalism put forward by *his* generation, finding in them a difference without a distinction: he said of the confessional poets, for instance, "I didn't care for . . . the way they blew up, I mean, inflated, magnified their sufferings." Once more, Merrill's antidote is Bishop, who "Refused to tip the scale of being human / By adding unearned weight." But those sharp contrasts don't quite capture Merrill's nuanced views. The off-kilter weave of companionable and conflicting aspects he observes in Bishop's portrayal of titanic, treasonous Ezra Pound in prison comes nearer: she "define[s] *and* disarm[s]" him, "while sympathizing with his predicament, if not with his politics."[10] Merrill, too, defines and disarms, evaluates and sympathizes, whether discussing poets, monuments, or churches.

As I've said and sometimes demonstrated, Merrill's aesthetic comments gather and convey political and cultural resonance. His aesthetic practice does so as well. A brief diversion into (potted) U.S. literary history can help show how this is so and further describe Merrill's "refiguring" poetics. Political and cultural fragmentation characterized the modern age. Modern poets typically responded either by seeking to reverse or retard fragmentation and the changes that caused it, or by seeking to hasten them, depending on whether they saw the past as a locus of stability and coherence or as the site of oppressive traditions in need of being smashed (often, of course, single poets felt both ways). By the 1930s (a period of economic and social ferment in its own right), modernist poetry had run its course, and a critical approach to it had begun to emerge. Its theorists and practitioners were called New Critics, and they—like *some* modern poets—sought conservatively to protect perceived cultural centers against supposedly alien disruptions. They elevated "high" or tradition-centered modernism above other poetic styles, and (by stressing continuities between high modernism and seventeenth-century verse, for instance) they healed—or papered over and ignored—the modernist rupture with tradition. Their intention was to restore political and cultural unities as they did so. Those activities may be judged preservationist or reactionary. In pursuing them, the New Critics developed remarkable skills for interpreting "difficult" texts, and for a time their analytical, "scientific" method provided literary study with cultural capital in universities increasingly committed to technology and business.

Meanwhile, the New Critics not only ignored alternative poetic styles but also tamed the style they celebrated. They domesticated the technical radicalism of modernism by favoring poems that conceived of themselves as objects rather than events and that were regular in meter, rhyme, and stanza form. They also domesticated modernism's often radical themes by favoring poems that hold pairs of conflicting ideas or attitudes in monumentally stabilized suspension within sets of linguistic and figurative tensions, irony most prominent above them. At least in retrospect, those preferences seem related to U.S. cold war politics and policies concerned with maintaining (or enforcing) stability at home and a balance of powers in the world.

New Critical preferences were systematically applied as a dominant critical, classroom, and editorial practice in the 1930s, 1940s, 1950s, and beyond. For a time, they were confused with poetry itself and produced a period style in verse: the impersonal, ironic, self-contained, and formally regular set of conventions called "academic." Replete with allusions to high culture (on the principle that recourse to traditional models could retain or recover cultural centers), the academic style dominated the literary education of Merrill's generation of poets. But while Merrill's contemporaries were baptized in the New Critical creed, most refused to be confirmed and fell away (or soared) into various heretical rebellions. They rebelled against cold war politics and culture as well. Christened in the New Critical faith at school, Merrill also defected. As usual with him, he refigured rather than renounced the catechism.

As New Criticism was conditioned by political and social forces, so, too, were the uprisings of Merrill's contemporaries against academic poetic practice. To them, the cultural coherence the New Critics meant to defend from alien forces came to seem alien itself—and oppressive. A reductive version of the situation might go like this. In the early 1950s (when New Criticism was in its ascendancy and Merrill in his mid-twenties), persisting effects of the unified effort required to fight World War II joined fears of a return to prewar economic depression and of Soviet Russia and enforced a conformity of appearance, ideas, and behavior that briefly concealed serious divisions of race, class, and social and political opinion. Soon, this "unity" was challenged from several sides. In the half-century since the mid-1950s, such factors as the civil rights movement, various forms of youth rebellion, the political and social crisis of the war in Vietnam, movements for women's, lesbian, and gay liberation, the shocks of a series of political assassinations, an intensifying distrust of established institutions and professions, the multiplication of media, and various demands for a society more responsive to multicultural differences all eroded actual cultural consensus or exposed consensus as an illusion at odds with the nation's self-definitions and actual conditions. The result, including several strains of neoconservative response, was a culture "abob with centers" (an A. R. Ammons phrase that Merrill once admired).

Poetry was also abob with centers in the decades following the early 1950s. The "academic" consensus was fractured by multiple alternatives, most embedded in movements too narrow to capture Merrill's more protean practice. For example, beat, projectivist, confessional, and neosurrealist poets challenged the academic claim to present universal truths by containing conflicting views within impersonal, ironic, and formalist structures. Depending upon affiliation, they insisted instead on the authority of personal experience and thus on autobiographical presentation, or they emphasized the relativism and artificiality of artistic acts. They also insisted that perfected "closed" forms are mechanistic constraints out of step with nature (and with science's recognition that everything is a relational event), and they judged traditional forms inferior to experimental, "open," provisional, or contingent organic ones. Meanwhile, other poets—working from ethnic, racial, class, gender, sexual, and even regional roots—also challenged consensus views. Committed to identity politics, they questioned the priority, propriety, and privilege of high cultural models, and (replaying a modernist debate) they considered the literary or cultural past less a resource for repairing rupture than an oppressive obstacle to desirable transformation. More recently, poets influenced by ideas related to literary theory have doubted the existence, coherence, and authenticity of the self, asserted the constructed rather than essential or necessary nature of all human systems, suspected that we are more nearly produced by language than producers of it, and insisted that art conspires with power even when seeking to chastise it. Such views contest not only the New Critical or academic model but also many of the earlier alternatives to it, especially those based on the assumed authenticity of autobiography or of identity politics. Meanwhile, neoformalists have recently reasserted the values of the tradition, usually without attempting to restore the hierarchical divide between high and popular culture which the New Critics took for granted and their detractors dissolved or revalued.[11]

I introduced this detour through literary history as a necessary diversion; it may have seemed more like distraction (in the sense G. K. Chesterton had in mind when he recalled the word's connection to the Latin term for being torn apart by horses). In any case, Merrill partook of the poetic and political developments conditioning his generation but wasn't circumscribed by any of them (just as being wealthy didn't wholly align him with the establishment, nor being gay fully estrange him from it—as the clichés of his time demanded they should have done). Merrill's "ever more complex" positions within the political and cultural debates of his time are suggested by his border-crossing (and crisscrossing) aesthetic performances. As Mutlu Blasing has brilliantly shown, Merrill avoids the false "progressive" logic that insists traditional poetic forms are the obsolete associates of political reaction, while "experimental" ones are politically and culturally "advanced." Instead, Merrill's conventions are as apt to fracture custom (or power) as to reinforce it, and his breaks with custom are as likely to refresh convention as to subvert it. Perhaps this is part of what David Bromwich meant in saying that Merrill can be as "exquisite in sobriety" as "in extravagance."[12] What matters most for present purposes, however, is that Merrill's aesthetic practices indicate political and cultural views that interrogate the monumental assumptions apparent not only in the New Critical or academic rules for verse but also in many of the supposedly antimonumental revolutions against them. They do so while allowing that even monuments might have refigured uses.

Merrill mastered the prosodic and other formal skills the New Critics granted pride of place, and he practiced them with the aplomb of Pope or Auden. But like any beat or other rebel against tradition (with the difference that he saw rebellion as part of tradition, one more convention), when needed Merrill broke and abandoned formal patterns without apology. He mixed iambics, quatrains, or terza rima with free verse, blocks of prose, undigested Ouija-board transcriptions, and such editorial impediments as asterisks, crossings-out, a bracketed question mark, even footnotes. In one poem he has a schoolmaster-speaker rhyme *pentameter* with *er,* a patently plodding and padding interjection that subverts (and celebrates) the prosody it practices. In another, he disruptively includes both a mathematical formula, complete with its radical sign, and a compass with the cardinal points revised (north, south, east, and west deflected—or trued—to *nought, sought, eased,* and *waste*). Merrill's transgressions have multiple directions. He revered Eliot and Yeats as the New Critics taught him to, for instance, but he also critically revised their more mandarin posturings. Once, while dutifully citing a much admired phrase, he irreverently rhymed the dismissive words "So what?" with the quoted author's name: "T. S. Eliot."[13]

Unlike the beats, confessionals, and other rebels against New Critical high modernism and the academic, however, Merrill avoided mirroring inversions. He preferred those not quite revolutionary (rather, refiguring) moments when the "inessential"—as proscribed by any hierarchical code, whether radical, conservative, or temperate—is suddenly (and temporarily) felt "as essence." His interests were in revelation *and* in its presumed enemy, reconsideration, rather than in either one alone, so that if he interrupts the well-made poem, he is equally likely—within some looser structure—to crisp to quatrains or sonnets. Similarly, Merrill brilliantly deployed the densely condensed lyric, the "object" poem New Critics and academics considered poetry's highest art, but he indulged its foes—digression and interruption, the poem as an event (and sequence)—to equally glittering effect, and he often mixed both modes together. So, too, Merrill experimented with fiction and drama, violating the New Critical hierarchy of genre, and in his poems he freely used autobiographical and other narrative and dramatic devices the New Critics had disparaged or ignored. But he typically did so without assuming the stability, authenticity, and authority of the self on which beat and confessional rebellions—as well as those associated with identity politics—were founded. As to those more recent poets concerned with exposing the constructedness of systems, Merrill concurs, but without nihilist despair or utopian conviction, more like Ashbery, say, than the language poets. He assumes the complicity of art with culture's exercise of power, but he also thinks that, properly conceived (as collaborative or intertextual, for example), art's power is "comparatively clean." (For Merrill, relational terms are diagnostic.) In much the same way, Merrill is at ease with the collapse of academic distinctions between high and popular culture, but rather than replace the prior hierarchy with a new one, he mingles grand opera with a Tyvek jacket, an obscene graffito with epic: on Merrill's Walkman one might find music by the Neapolitan street singer Roberto Murolo, the Grateful Dead, Richard Strauss, or Arvo Pärt.[14]

The list of Merrill's refiguring responses to competing aesthetic, political, and cultural positions might be considerably extended. Perhaps a few further points will do. Like other thinkers and writers of his generation, Merrill made the linguistic turn and saw language as a "glaze of custom," more opaque than transparent and perhaps more likely to control its users than to be controlled by them. But Merrill's reaction to this as to other situations was never pat, as his comments on puns (those meaning-sapping, generative fiddlings in the crotch of language) can demonstrate: "A pity about that lowest form of humor. It is suffered . . . with groans of aversion, as though one had done an unseemly thing in adult society, like slipping a hand up the hostess's dress. Indeed, the punster has touched . . . upon a secret, fecund place in language herself . . . The pun (or rhyme, for that matter) 'merely' betrays the hidden wish of words." The name of that wish might well be propagation. Lee Zimmerman nicely describes the overall quality of Merrill's strategies, applying terms from N. Katherine Hayles's comments on literary versions of the "field" models of biology and physics (where propagation also matters greatly): "the 'distinguishing characteristics' are 'its fluid, dynamic nature, the inclusion of the observer, the absence of detachable parts, and the mutuality of component interaction.' " Such qualities are palpable in these few words from Merrill's "Yánnina": "See through me. See me through." There, the self is illusion and instrument, and in need of help; the politics of unquestioning loyalty and critical analysis fluidly interact in shifting terms and syntax more translucent than transparent or opaque. In an essay called "The Beaten Path," Merrill recalls boardwalks in watery Bangkok. He exclaims: "No wonder the Siamese are graceful! What it must be like to be always stepping on planks of varying flexibility." One thing it's like is Merrill's way with language (he called it "thread and maze").[15]

In the poem "The Will," about willfully resisting and by acts of will accepting inheritances more or less inevitable in any case, Merrill says of his mother and her bridge-playing friends, "They love their sweetly-sung bloodthirsty games." He might be speaking of any inherited cultural apparatus, low or high—say, epics—and the resisting, receiving work in which their makers and readers engage. No comma divides *sweetly-sung* from *bloodthirsty,* and the words *spears* and *spares* in the poem are less concerned with keeping distinct the contrasting arts of war and peace than they are with performing as mutually implicating anagrams. Willy-nilly, our inheritances come from family and home, and from the systems of politics, art, and culture we inhabit, whether card games or Homeric poems. Fateful as it is, it might seem tragic.

Merrill shares a good deal with the Rilke that Stephen Yenser cites, the Rilke who says the messy world we inherit "fills us. We arrange it, It breaks down. / We rearrange it, then break down ourselves." But Merrill refigures the residue of self-regarding sentimentality in Rilke's knowingly tragic final phrase. For Merrill, rearrangement persists beyond our momentary selves, or literary modes, or individual states or cultures. He distrusted the selfish "thirst for pattern, whether . . . of words on the page or stresses in the universe." He called that thirst the "hubris that invents tragedy for the glory of undergoing it." Since hubris and glory are tragedy's essence, to include them within its dismissal half restores what's been sent packing. Part of Merrill's point is that since tragedy *is* invented, its inheritance might be revised and thereby partially resisted. It's altogether characteristic that the sort of alternative he seeks is not something "original" but an inheritance available already. In a notebook entry, Merrill describes a newly discovered fragment "by Stesichoros: the 'proto-Oedipus.' It antedates Sophocles, and by a somewhat cooler telling of the story (Oedipus lives on, blind but fed & cared for, while Jocasta goes on reigning upstairs) shows the more famous poet as over-reliant upon the loud pedal." Without soft-pedaling how much we get what's coming to us, but committed, too, to forgiveness, care, and carrying on, to adaptation and modulation rather than revolution or exile in families and kingdoms, Merrill's work accepts and refigures what he inherits (Oedipally and not) from powerful parents and potent artistic predecessors, whether persons, genres, stories, or forms—and including monuments and the aesthetics, politics, and cultural signs and systems they imply. As he says with not quite symmetrical reversibility in "After the Fire," "Everything changes; nothing does."[16]

More than thirty years after its first appearance, Merrill refigured his early poem "The Broken Bowl," recasting the monuments referred to in it as alternatives to tombstones rather than their equivalent (as usual with Merrill, alternatives aren't opposites but aspects). Shifting terms a little, I suggest that composting might be an apt metaphor for this and related procedures defining Merrill's practice. Received or otherwise, versions of things in his work decay but aren't discarded; they fertilize revisions. An oracular voice in *Sandover* intones, "MAN WANTS IMMORTALITY & NATURE WANTS MANURE." Merrill might agree. The insistent human urge to monumental permanence is out of phase with nature's endless, submissive recyclings. But capitalized pronouncements have monumental aspects, too, and Merrill typically amends them. For instance, he adjusts the one just mentioned when another of his voices from beyond classifies human language as our "TERMITE PALACE BEEHIVE ANTHILL PYRAMID." This restores human desires for monumental structures (pyramid, palace) to their place within the natural; at the same time, by relating human constructs to the collective, instinctual work of social insects, it shrinks exaggerated pride in the presumed superiority of a particular self or system, whether language, culture, state, or species—while also encouraging esteem of other kinds.[17]

It comes to this: like Balanchine's artist-gardener, Merrill wastes nothing. Here and elsewhere in his work, his aim—without idealizing nature or prophesying redemption—is better to align the patterns of art, politics, and culture with nature's patterns. One result is that Merrill typically treats monuments not as permanent or eternal structures but as fertilizer for current and future plantings, things to be altered and reused, not worshipped or thrown away. He anticipates that his own crops—fed by the decaying structures of the past and grown for present nourishment (although—as if—to last)—will flourish and fruit for a while themselves and then decay and be ploughed under in their turn, neither immortal nor obsolete but part of an open-ended generative process, like compost or manure. Renewing recent and ancient monuments for human use, "Bronze" is a strenuous example. It shits on the idea of the work of art to nurture art's reworkings.

Bronze, that monumental stuff, is an alloy of tin and copper. The word *alloy* itself is an amalgamation, of Latin *ad* and *ligare*. It means to bind together, implying substances mixed or conjoined, hinting sometimes that added material debases something purer, but suggesting, too, that impurities fortify. As for Merrill, it might be said that he distrusts the unalloyed as he does the monumental. His "Bronze" is an alloy of alloys. One of the poem's crucial terms is *liaison,* also formed from *ligare* and meaning intercommunication, between the separated units of a military force, for instance, as well as a sexual encounter, usually illicit. Those related but asymmetrical meanings begin to suggest what "Bronze" obliquely brings together and separates, as if to recall that wax is lost when a bronze is cast and that, feet aside, clay is at its core. A list of the components of Merrill's poem might start like this (and in its own excesses begin to hint at how the overwrought performs compensatory, comic work within the poem's apparently severe specifics): autobiography, history, and myth (those narrative kinds); the self at its own throat; lovers estranged and intertwined; a pair of monumental statues, not quite matched; varieties of the domestic, heroic, and erotic that compete and overlap. All of these are bundled and wrapped in a crusted-cleansed anatomy of representation as it operates in works of art and other cultural systems.

At the beginning of this chapter, I used the phrase "elaborating constants" to indicate Merrill's memoiristic interest in the ways variety inhabits sameness—and likeness, difference—within an emerging self that's partially determined and somewhat free to choose. It's a quality he finds in life and language, too: the imperfect reversibility with which multiplicities exfoliate from and fold back toward the singularities that propagate them. Here's an example from Merrill's prose. He writes, "The first verb to learn in Ancient Greek was παιδευω. Pronounced pie-dew-o, it meant 'I teach.' In Modern Greek the same verb, spelt as before, is pronounced pe-dhe-vo, and means 'I torment.' The old word αγαθος [agathos] (good) has come to mean 'simpleminded.' " Then he adds, "These shifts are revealing, and their slightness reassures."[18] This sprightly passage illuminates the borders (dividing lines and regions of contact both) between the revealed torments and reassuring teachings that Merrill's "Bronze" alloys. Still, to start, some simpleminded background might be good. (Meanwhile, I hope the reasons for my own approach to Merrill's poem by so much detour, feint, and hesitation eventually will be apparent.)

In mid-August 1972, a vacationing chemist, scuba diving in relatively shallow water in the Ionian Sea near Riace on Italy's southeast coast, discovered two monumental Greek bronzes, larger-than-life-size nude statues of glorious, alarmingly powerful warriors. Restored, they stand at momentary rest—and seem ready at need to wreak havoc again. Perhaps while being transported the recovered figures had been heaved overboard in a storm to lighten an ancient vessel and fend off shipwreck. When found, the bronzes were heavily encrusted and somewhat corroded, but they had been brilliantly rendered and were remarkably preserved. They caused a sensation—and eventually occasioned Merrill's poem. The people of the nearby town, with that Mediterranean blend of things pagan and Christian, demanded that the statues be set up on site as types of the local saints.

But conservatorship (and state and museum control) prevailed, for while debates on the statues' provenance continue, they are generally thought to be masterworks of the fifth century B.C.E., the peak of classical Greek achievement in sculpture. Therefore they are enormously important to art history in particular and, more generally, to Western myths of the origins of culture. The monumental bronze statuary of classical Greece has been exemplary for Western civilization since Rome and the Renaissance; yet classical Greek bronzes are known almost entirely from literary testimony, drab Roman copies, and a very few extant originals. The Riace find greatly increased the available store of apparently authentic objects. This further swelled the statues' significance. (Meanwhile, *original* is a tricky word with regard to bronzes, as is *artist*. The Riace statues were cast in pieces in a process requiring the collaborative efforts of a workshop of artists and artisans; they are not the product of a single genius laboring alone, the typical Western model of artistic creation. Nor are the bronzes originals in the usual sense. They were clearly cast from the same molds, represent an identical heroic type, and were probably part of a larger monument comprising additional similar figures. At the same time, however, the workers' handling of detail prior to casting made these two figures distinctly individual, and remarkably different from one another.)

In any case, over local protests, the bronzes were soon removed to the national museum in nearby Reggio Calabria. There, they received three years of intensive study and were cleaned and restored. The conservators' work revealed still more dramatically the warriors' amalgamation of threateningly savage force with civilized and civilizing craftsmanship (an alloy Merrill makes much of). To critics who read the history of ancient sculpture as a formal progress from stylization to increasing naturalism, the realism of the statues' postures and marvelously accurate muscular anatomy was especially telling—as were the artistic skills lavished on their impressively detailed heads, whose verisimilitude was considerably heightened by the addition of naturalistic inlaid eyes and copper eyelashes and lips. (One of the figures retains a set of silver teeth; both have copper nipples. Joseph Alsop admired the treatment of each statue's scrotum, which was "carefully striated to suggest the crepe-like texture of the skin itself—an extra-realistic touch otherwise unknown in Greek and Western sculpture.")

In 1975, the statues were sent to the Restoration Center of the Archaeological Museum in Florence for further conservation. That painstaking task required five more years. Evidence for fifth-century B.C.E. dates for the statues mounted. (Those dates are contemporary with the time of Phidias, *the* artist-hero traditionally associated with classical statuary. However inappropriate the identification of a single artist-genius with commissioned sculptures based on regulated types and carried out by collaborative workshops may be, the mention of that legendary name magnified the excitement surrounding the re-covered sculptures.) When the figures were finally put on display, the scholarly and public reactions were intense. The bronzes were first shown in Florence, between January and June of 1981. Six hundred thousand people saw them. When they were briefly exhibited next in Rome, 300,000 persons viewed them in two or three weeks. (That the Rome exhibition was held at the Quirinal Palace, the home of the prime minister, is a nice reminder of the many ways art devel-ops associations with national identity and political power; Merrill reflects the fact when he has Greek bronzes found in Italian waters speak entirely in italics.)

After the Rome exhibit, the statues were returned to Reggio Cala-bria. There, crowds demanding access to *i bronzi* threatened to over-whelm the small museum, and police were called in to disperse them. Describing the exhibit there, the *New York Times* called the statues "presences of extraordinary power" and said the crowds moved "as if magnetized by a supernatural force," crying out in admiration, awe, and even terror. Italian reports described viewers attempting to place their children under the statues' protection, as though the artworks partook of the divine. The bronzes received 700,000 visitors during their first year on display in Calabria. (By 1992, annual attendance had dropped to 80,000, but in that year the statues received renewed attention when, with a major grant from Finmeccanica, the museum undertook a much-publicized project to prevent possible further corrosion and kept the bronzes on display during the preservation process. From a platform, viewers looked down into a kind of oper-ating theater-altar where, laid flat on tables, the monumental statues were attended to by white-coated acolyte-technicians; removing the bronzes' clay cores, they wielded endoscopes and television monitors to read their entrails.)[19]

Not all of this information is directly relevant to Merrill's poem, which was published in book form in 1985 and recalls a visit to the statues when they were on display in Florence in 1981, before the later events described here had occurred. But all of the information bears on attitudes and issues "Bronze" implicitly and otherwise ad-dresses. I've already mentioned how the statues' discovery raised familiar contemporary issues about originality and collaboration in artistic production, matters Merrill touched on often, most especially in *Sandover,* where the characters JM and DJ are (unequal) partners in the poem's creation. Meanwhile, debates about the Riace statues' provenance are often inflected by national pride, and arguments and decisions about where and how the statues should be displayed indicate some of the ways in which art objects are related to commercial and political considerations as well as to myths of cultural origin and continuity. (Along with their sheer artistic quality, this "heritage" aspect of the bronzes is the most frequent basis for assertions of their cultural worth; on such grounds scaled-down collectible reproductions were offered for sale by the Hamilton Collection and the Franklin Mint.) Those, too, are matters Merrill's poem takes up.

The voluminous scholarship on the Riace bronzes reflects both the sort of formalist narrative mentioned above and alternatives to it: for example, many scholars attempt to recover the statues' likely setting, context, and function, and remind us that the bronzes were most probably monumental public works of art commemorating a military victory (Marathon, perhaps). It's likely they were prominently displayed in a public place (Delphi is often named) where they were elements within an elaborate cultural apparatus consciously or otherwise intent on naturalizing and perpetuating an existing political and social power system. (In a somewhat extreme example, one critic, reflecting contemporary interest in how artistic representations underwrite cultures' encodings of particular versions of gender and the body as inevitable and natural, places the Riace bronzes within an Athenian "muscular diktat of the fine male nude," a sort of "'body fascism.'" It's an intriguing point, although it confuses ideals with norms. Meanwhile, Merrill's "Bronze" has its own interest in competing codes of masculinity and sexuality.)

In literary terms the division between formalist and contextualist approaches to the bronzes might be thought of as analogous to the shift from the New Critical emphasis on textual autonomy to the new historicist or cultural studies stress on placing works within social, political, economic, and other matrices. At least as atmosphere, that shift is one of the contexts of Merrill's career; he performs it in ways of his own, as we'll see. Meanwhile, all of these matters indicate the involvement of the Riace bronzes in long-standing and contemporary arguments that urge the veneration or dismissal of monuments and what they stand for. That involvement is part of their attraction for Merrill; it's further reflected by the statues' place within the changing culture of museums. Recently much concerned about what, how, and for whom they exhibit, museums are desirous to blur divisions between high and popular culture (now seen as elitist and in any case artificial); to contextualize displays in order to show works' engagements with assumptions or debates about the politics of, say, gender, class, and race; and to mount blockbuster shows attractive to large and varied audiences—and preferably underwritten by government or corporate sponsors (Finmeccanica, for instance).

This catalogue can conclude with mention of a few additional issues condensed by the Riace statues and bearing on Merrill's poem. The restoration of ancient objects is a vexed subject, since the choices it involves are based on limited knowledge and skewed by contemporary assumptions, desires, and needs. For instance, Carol Mattusch reports that recent studies show the Riace statues—now "restored" to gleaming bronze—were once black (a patina that may have been deliberately achieved by the application of sulfur). Until very recently the process available for cleaning bronzes removed surface color along with corrosion. Mattusch calls such cleaning "invasive." As we've seen, Merrill was unlikely to be anxious about such matters; he assumed that recovery includes additions and subtractions, invention and alteration. He had mixed feelings about the "modern" impulse accurately to know and recover the past, preferring Proust's convalescent reconstructions to Freudian and other redemptive archaeologies, and feeling neither distressed nor superior about such matters as the fate of originals and copies in the age of mechanical reproduction. He assumed the textuality of the archive. A final observation in this regard: on the evidence of "Losing the Marbles," although he might not have approved, Merrill would have been unalarmed to learn that the Riace bronzes may have been looted or stolen in ancient times, or removed from their original monumental context in order to be recycled as decorations or signs of status.[20]

I've run the risk of making Merrill's "Bronze" appear a kind of (meta) art historical study of specific monumental objects—the Riace bronzes—and of the cultural issues they and their recovery, restoration, display, and reception raise. It is that, but "Bronze" is several other (related) things as well. For instance, while the Riace sculptures and their exhibition in Florence provide the impetus for Merrill's eight-part poem (like a bronze, the text itself seems cast in sections, then welded together into a monumental structure), and while the statues occupy a climactic place at or near the poem's physical center, they do so within an elaborate set of interrelated historical and autobiographical frameworks. Those frameworks long postpone the statues' appearance in the poem—and then append to it an expansive aftermath. This challenges the statues' centrality, and it signals the porosity of "Bronze" to things, events, and contextual relations beyond its immediate object and occasion. To put crudely for now what I hope to refine, postponement and aftermath decenter the bronzes they bracket—and subvert the climax they also enable. The effect is to keep the poem's monumental objects in touch with historical change and private contingencies (those transient matters that traditional monuments claim to fix forever or transcend)—and in ways that displace the apocalyptic implications of narrative (and monumental) climax and closure in favor of antiapocalyptic open-endedness. It's entirely characteristic of Merrill's sort of complication that when the Riace bronzes do appear at the poem's center, the monuments use their privileged position at least in part for similarly decentering, not quite monumental ends—although *ends* isn't the aptest word.

Neither is *appear,* for when the Riace statues are finally reached in "Bronze," they're not so much seen as heard. In fact, the monumental presences of Merrill's poem are never directly described by the poet-viewer, the standard procedure in ecphrastic poems. Instead, the bronzes speak (so to speak) for themselves, addressing—in a single, plural voice—both Merrill and his companion David Jackson (as well as the poem's readers). This slightly skewed device is not unprecedented within ecphrastic texts, of course: the statues themselves cite Rilke's well-known "Archaic Torso of Apollo," where the bronze *kouros* the poem addresses seems also to address the poet (and bluntly decrees that he must change his life). But it is unusual: as John Hollander says, ecphrastic poems typically speak to silent works of art. It's typical of Merrill to use a received convention in ways that both polish and craze the glaze of precedent. In "Bronze," he does this to subvert *and* confirm the value of monuments—and to reconceive them for current use. (The poem's doubling of the usually single—and singular—ecphrastic object contributes to those effects as well.)

When the Riace warriors finally do speak in Merrill's poem (section four of "Bronze" is entirely theirs), they convey the immense impersonal authority and power typical of monuments. Their universalizing judgments, assertions, and instructions exude self-confidence and certitude; their assessment of contemporary nuclear and ecological threats is chillingly precise and charged with prophetic weight; and their sometimes near-dactylic speech invokes their Homeric, heroic, and classical pedigrees with nobility and strength. At other times, however, the bronzes slip into less dignified anapestic grumbling, and the grandeur of their speech is often alloyed with the coarser accents of cruelty and intimidation—and with a sneering sense of personal and cultural superiority backed by the threat of force. The bronze warriors boast of their own death-dealing "carnivorous" manliness, for instance, and they disparage other kinds, dismissively addressing their "boyish" contemporary auditors as pathetic "babies" given to nostalgia and illusion and weak with a "pitiful / Wish not to harm." This recalls the hegemony and violence within the Homeric and heroic, and within monumental structures more generally: their tendency to judge alternative arrangements as madness or folly and to depict cultural "others" as less than human barbarians to be ignored, demeaned, or destroyed. The statues' proclivity for force (which we, of course, inherit) makes them complicitous with the perils for which they blame us. At the same time, they also (more generously) warn us against those perils. Meanwhile, there are other complications.

The monumental statues not only judge the contemporary situation perilous and its people weak and wanting, but they also recognize that their own "heroic" time has passed and that the "virile" abilities and assumptions sufficient to it—and "willed" or "left" by them to us—are insufficient to the current moment. The Herculean tasks of the present involve responding to nuclear and ecological threats, and to the "hot" "Rhetorical / Postures" that intensify them. (Those dangerous attitudes appear in current as well as ancient monumental politics and art. Here, the Kremlin and Hart Crane are mentioned in terms that encode and dissolve both cold war binaries and the dividing lines between political and aesthetic categories—one more way Merrill's oblique approach to the topical turns formidably frontal.) The bronzes crisply assign the daunting task of dealing with current threats to their contemporary audience: "It's for you to defuse them." This suggests some (if rather desperate) confidence in the present. At one point, the statues actually praise contemporary courage (if that's what it is, and not evasion): they call their "old heroics" "child's play" alongside current nonchalance in the face of threatened "meltdown"—a particularly fearsome prospect for bronzes, no doubt, and the daffy sort of pun that at darker moments lightens the tone of "Bronze." In any event, these intricate features of the statues' speech are among the ways "Bronze" at once commends and disparages monuments. Merrill's poem falsifies monumental claims to time- and place-transcending permanence; it also affirms that the monumental past can helpfully address the present if we recognize its flaws *and* virtues (after all, they're ours as well), and revise the past's pronouncements to serve the vital needs of our own day without presuming that present contingent matters are monumental.

One more strategy by which Merrill keeps varied attitudes toward monuments in view—or audible—in "Bronze" is his characteristic method of baring the device. As I've said, Merrill's speaking statues both burnish and crack ecphrastic custom, encouraging us to accept his fiction and see right through it, to suspend disbelief while also disbelieving. Similarly, Merrill's poem plays on the common awareness in ecphrastic verse that its subject—a sculpture or painting—is a transparent representation of something "beyond" itself as well as an opaque object independent of representation and with a potent presence of its own. Merrill's loquacious bronzes shift so rapidly between seeing themselves as warriors and seeing themselves as works of art that they both blur and emphasize the distinction. They insist they're "men in their prime . . . with endocrine clout," for instance, but they also compare themselves to other sculptures and describe themselves in terms especially appropriate to bronzes: "the articulate shell / Of a vacuum roughly man-sized." When the statues complain that falsely prettified or sensational versions of the past are projected upon them by present styles in exhibition, scholarship, and promotion ("vistas of shimmering / Water red roses rope off" frame the statues in the museum; "much-touted terribilità" hypes them—as they see it—in brochures, the press, or scholarly journals), they're enraged at being misrepresented both as men *and* as artifacts removed from their original cultural contexts. (As we'll see later on, they also distrust contemporary efforts to recover those contexts.) To repeat, this confusion of the Riace figures' dual status as transparent representations (warriors) and opaque objects (bronze statues) exposes without disabling the fictions the poem deploys. It permits and requires us to be of many minds at once about the presumed capacity of ancient monuments to instruct and admonish us, and about our capacity to recover earlier works in terms that allow them to speak for themselves as well as to us.

And, of course, to speak *for* us. Another device Merrill exposes as it's used is the well-worn fiction that the statues' speech is their own. This is one function of the anachronisms that riddle their remarks. Perhaps those sleights of time are explained by the monumental bronzes having persisted for 2,500 years; still, for objects lost for centuries under water and sand, they're remarkably up to date. In addition to Rilke and Crane, they've apparently read Nietzsche and Mary McCarthy, and they're aware of computers and feminism as well as of pollution and nuclear weapons. That is, their reading habits and knowledge are transparently Merrill's, a fact underlined when, with warrior machismo, the statues mock as a "tea-gowned ephebe" the Charioteer of Delphi, the sculptural subject and title of an early Merrill poem (one much more like Rilke's than "Bronze" is).

As do other cracks in a poem's or persona's mask, intertextuality disturbs illusions of presence; it does so here as well, but without causing presence to vanish. Of course, nearly every work of art features some self-interrogating revelation of its own devices, but ecphrastic works in general, and particularly Merrill's revised ecphrasis in "Bronze," emphasize it strongly. It's especially palpable when the bronzes comment on contemporary efforts to restore their former glory. Disgusted by the accretions they've gathered through their long experience in time, they also distrust the modern "sonar probe and / Restorative poultice" that renews their original "high finish." Considering Mattusch's view that the Riace finds were originally black, this reference to highly polished bronze might be meant as comic, but whether it is or not, the statues see restoration as a dubious process fabricating a contemporary, nostalgic illusion rather than recovering the past. And like these current-sounding art-historical ruminations, the bronzes' insistence that even painful experience is heuristic ("taken / How deeply to heart") and scoured away at the expense of the desirable Proustian accretions of a lifetime's remembering and remaking, seems patently Merrill's, a signal theme of his revisionary (not visionary) art.

In a wide variety of ways, then, Merrill exposes, decenters, and disables fictions he also uses with confidence in "Bronze." His largest aim in doing so, I think, is to amend the apocalyptic, whether in monuments, literary and political plots, or the culture at large. As I said earlier, Merrill typically interrogates and seeks to limit epistemic power without presuming to escape it. One fundamental Western episteme is apocalyptic thinking, with its fearful imaginings of violent total destruction and its ferocious faith that holocaust can cleanse and transform the world, permitting radically new beginnings. "Bronze" everywhere subverts such faith in ends and origins (as my extended discussion of its attitudes toward monumental persistence, restoration, and revision is partly meant to show). Merrill's articulate bronzes do exploit the monitory value and force of apocalyptic language; it gives their warnings about the dangers of large-scale nuclear and ecological destruction contemporary urgency and meaning. Meanwhile, however, Merrill calibrates their speech to reveal the peril within such language: it can tempt us to welcome cataclysm as purgation, a universal cleansing that restores ideal origins or delivers final perfection. In a world where the power of total destruction is reserved for the gods, surrender to such temptation might be only locally catastrophic, but when humans have the weapons and tools to damage genetic material and poison or destroy the earth, the risk may seem too great—and epistemic revision may seem called for.

When the speaking statues of Merrill's "Bronze" explain their presence in the waters off Riace, they brag that they escaped the craft transporting them by throwing their weight around and going "overboard." This admits to willfully violent, apocalyptic excesses, but the effect is mostly a joke, as the contemporary, colloquial, punning tone implies; after all, they—and the world—survived. But further on in their speech, when they assign to their present auditors the heroic task of disarming current threats, they explicitly warn against apocalyptic methods. "Expect no epiphany," they say, citing the transcendent moment the archaic torso provided Rilke; "Quit dreaming of change." The word *epiphany* adds Christian springs of apocalyptic thought to other ancient sources; the imperative not to expect or project it warns against apocalyptic practices of several kinds.

A religious and literary term, *epiphany* recalls once more art's complicity with culture: here, its complicity with apocalyptic epistemes, as when, in ecphrastic poems, monuments deliver supposedly timeless wisdom about totalizing acts of transformation. *Epiphany* names the sort of "high," visionary, transfiguring seeing characteristic of apocalyptic thought and action. Merrill's statues prefer the more modest act their own instructions call for: "It's for you to defuse them." To defuse is a potent form of intervention, but it doesn't depend on radical transformation. Requiring skill and courage, it's unexplosive, potentially clarifying, less than apocalyptic. Somehow, these long-persisting monumental ancient statues have retained their original attitudes and aspects while also learning lessons from and for the present. It's *that* and not some transcendent, unalterable truth they carry forward from the past that permits them to speak to us usefully here and now. Obviously, they've learned those lessons from Merrill; among other things, the title "Bronze" names the poem itself as a monument. Its details defuse transcendent, potentially apocalyptic conceptions—they remake the monumental as a provisional matter, subject to reinterpretation.

Of course, to aim to alter a culture's epistemes involves immense ambition, with apocalyptic dangers of its own. As I tried to say before, Merrill tempers that risk by placing the bronzes' somewhat decentered but still central and monumentally authoritative speech within historical and autobiographical frameworks that long postpone the statues' appearance and append to it an expansive aftermath. To repeat, this placement defines but also challenges the statues' privileged position. It signals the porosity of "Bronze" to contingencies, contexts, and relations beyond its immediate object and occasion, and it collaborates with the poem's antiapocalyptic preference for ongoing revision over myths of ends and origins. One more way "Bronze" ties down the potentially "overboard" implications of its own devices (as in the links among centrality, climax, and apocalypse, for instance) is by mixing together narrative, dramatic, and lyric kinds and by weaving tales of erotic love with stories of domesticity and warfare. Like the bronzes themselves, those alloyed matters require extensive consideration.

"Bronze" begins with stage directions: "Birdsong. May. . . . Sunset." Merrill and David Jackson, his longtime lover and companion, are visiting in Tuscany, at the home of their old, now elderly, friend, Umberto, Count Morra (Merrill and Jackson are middle-aged). The restored Riace bronzes have been put on display in Florence. They're in easy reach by train but will remain there only briefly, giving the visitors their single chance to see them. The count unfolds a railway timetable (it's "Dense as himself with station and connection"), and characters' outlines begin to emerge. David and Umberto (the poem employs first names) are likened to bronzes. David (who is referred to in terms that recall his roles in other Merrill poems, a gesture that blurs the line between actual person and textual representation) is described as still "Marvelously young" and "gentle," but as having "lost" a "certain eager bloom . . . like wax, / To earn a new inexorable glint" ("lost . . . wax" and *glint* are brazen hints; mixed judgments appear in the pairing of *lost* with *earn*). Meanwhile, "like a local clay," the remembered life "inside" abstemious Umberto is "Gritty with names." (Art historians probe the clay cores of bronzes to recover their origins or sources; Umberto's core is a many-layered record of time and change: as we'll see, his origins remain a mystery.)

As for the trip to Florence, Umberto suggests that the morning train would give Merrill and Jackson forty minutes with the statues ("'all one needs'") and that the next train would have them back in time for lunch. Umberto's ease in balancing the respective claims of life and art is instructive, but David rejects the plan. He says that "'Close connections . . . / Harm the soul.'" Merrill is "Half resigned" to this. Mustering self-control, he checks "a groan" and recalls that David's "been unwell." But Merrill is also "Half fuming," enraged to have his passion thwarted (and not only his art lover's passion to see the monumental bronzes. There's emotional and erotic trouble between himself and Jackson, and David's distaste for close connections signals sexual and other sorts of "resistance" to Merrill as well as to tightly scheduled railway travel).

Merrill is torn between anger and acceptance ("Bronze" manufactures and welds divisions everywhere, not least in making this trivial spat recall Achilles' epic struggles with rage and empathic pity), and he steps out into the garden to let the dueling pair within him "settle their affair." (The phrase alloys love and combat, as the garden setting puts agony and agon in liaison.) Then, in an intricate lyric passage, Merrill ponders his own role in the lovers' quarrel and considers how writing and remembering might revise and undo or recast it, taming its destructive intensity. At the end of section one, those matters are left suspended. That evening at dinner, while his butler, Mario, serves, Umberto tells Merrill and Jackson a story of his service in World War II. It's a tale they've long been aware of, but the count's own telling has been deferred for years, one more in a series of delays that gather resonance and weight as the poem progresses.

Umberto diverts and entertains his friends and graciously relieves what might have been (in private and social terms at least) an apocalyptically fraught occasion. Perhaps his tale of a particularly humble sort of not quite military heroism offers them an example to try in their own time of strife (stiff with age, clay-cored and patinated, Umberto, too, seems like a speaking statue, delivering modest wisdom to adults who are still—as who is not—in some ways ephebes or students). In any event, revealing his emotional distress,

Merrill says he washed down Umberto's story "a shade too greedily" (perhaps with gullibility as well as wine). As a result, he claims, his own retelling is imprecise, not so much a chronicle or history as a "blurred" impression in chalk. We've seen in several ways already that "Bronze" consistently foregrounds its representational strategies. Here, it does so both in the emphasis on medium (chalk) and in the contrast between silent statues that seem to speak for themselves and Merrill's speaking for the living and articulate Umberto. This foregrounding instructs us, in the phrase from "Yánnina" discussed above, to "see through" such strategies both by piercing their illusions and by accepting them as means to understanding. Meanwhile, chalk is a modester, less monumental vehicle than bronze.

Vehicles (train, bus, jeep, a peasant's cart, shank's mare) prove important to Count Morra's story: they might be said to bring him by stages down to earth, leaving him (nobly) pedestrian before he's restored to a balcony's pedestal. In early September of 1943, the Allied invasion of Italy was about to succeed, a turning point in the war. The Italian government had accepted defeat, but it was imperative that the main Allied force come ashore and make liaison with the Italian resistance before the agreement to surrender was announced. A five-day delay was engineered to permit this. Count Morra's part was to make the perilous journey from Rome to Naples through territory still occupied by the Germans, then to join General Mark Clark on the Prefettura balcony and translate to the crowd the terms of surrender. Merrill leaves the specifics slightly "blurred," but he implies that the dangers and especially the detours and deferrals Count Morra experienced (and produced) in "haltingly advancing" toward Naples helped to create the delay that allowed the situation's vital political and military requirements to be met. Merrill applies Homeric epithets worthy of bronze-age warriors to his friend ("Skewfoot, fleet of spirit"), but he also keeps the tone of admiration light and not too monumental: this mild warrior doesn't speak for himself, he wears the "city clothes" of a civilian, and his most powerful weapons are his ties to the "social fabric." (As an heroic type, like General Clark, Umberto is more civic and Roman than individualistic and Greek.)

The ground Count Morra haltingly covered is gauged in, of all things, parasangs, a Persian unit of distance. The term seems comically forced on the poem by rigid rules of rhyme, yet its antique cachet connects Umberto's adventure with those of ancient heroes. Meanwhile, the parasang's a weirdly flexible, funny sort of measure;

its blurred chalk varies from two to four miles. At the section's end, David's response to Umberto's exploit is reverential awe, the sort of thing supposedly appropriate to monuments and heroes. But that attitude is partly undercut by Merrill's term for it—*wowed*—and by the lighter, comic gestures just described. Merrill admires Umberto's necessary bravery; he served sociably during World War II himself. But he refuses to render it in monumental bronze, avoiding the idolatry that enforces repetition and emphasizing instead the modest heroic potential of flexibility and deferral: qualities that keep precedents—and apocalyptic epistemes—amenable to translation.

Section three of "Bronze" returns to the issue put off by Merrill's retelling of Umberto's story, the vexing question of whether, when, and how Merrill and Jackson might overcome their estrangement and visit the bronzes in Florence. It returns, too, to the subject of how writing and other activities involving self-reflective deferral and translation might subdue anger and prevent violence (in individuals and perhaps in cultures). These are matters of form as well as content. Thus far, Merrill's poem has alternated between fifteen- and thirteen-line stanzas: these suggest (without quite being) sonnets, and they employ rhyme schemes that hint at well-established patterns without completing them. Now "Bronze" tightens to six-line tetrameter stanzas with truncated final lines and a not quite symmetrical, nearly mirroring rhyme scheme (abcbca). Those imperfect reflections are formal equivalents for the poem's stories and ideas, additional ways in which Merrill's revisionary "Bronze" honors its monumental inheritances without being overawed by them. Alternating fifteen- and thirteen-line stanzas reappear briefly in sections five and seven; section six is an all but perfect couplet sonnet; the eighth and final section veers off on a formal journey of its own.

At the narrative level, section three approaches Florence by yet another series of deferrals. Merrill and Jackson rent a car and head for the city and museum. They're soon diverted. A landscape depicted in terms of sexual enticement ("Bared shoulder and come-hither shrug / Of hill, the spread of golden thighs") lures them to the Adriatic and a picnic. This suggests a loving recovery from their estrangement, and it recalls the restorative banquet scenes common at the close of comedies of erotic and social reconciliation: there are even "two ecstatic / *Oh*'s." But the comic celebration of nurturing cultural institutions ("vineyard, castle") is chastened by the more nearly tragicomic awareness that those institutions also nourish, in

addition to love and intellect and art, "let's face it, grief, / Decep-
tion, strife." Meanwhile, in passages more lyric than narrative and
dramatic, other matters arise. The words *inky, desk,* and *stanzas* imply
the act of writing. *Blue-penciled* indicates revision. And images of
psychoanalysis as scuba diving mark other sorts of delving reconsideration. (The references to diving recall the way the Riace bronzes
were discovered; among other things, this locates the monumental
statues in the atavistic background of private consciousness as well
as collective culture.) Meanwhile, in addition to their other roles,
these details are all delaying tactics, and their most important effect
in the poem is strategic. As Merrill says at the end of section three,
"detour" (is he punning on the name of Doctor Detre, his one-time
psychoanalyst?) "Had to be structural before / Heroes tomorrow
stripped of threat / Could rise from it." As I hope the discussion of
the bronzes' speech has shown already, literal and structural detour
and delay have helped make the encounter with them relatively
safe, so that their influence can be accepted, resisted, and revised as
needed. It's at this point in the poem, in any case, that the bronzes
appear to speak.

Because I've approached "Bronze" through an interest in monuments, I've characterized its statues' central position as being framed
—and somewhat stripped of threat—by delay and aftermath. But
since the side trip to view the bronzes is itself a detour, the description might be reversed, with the encounter in Florence functioning
as a necessary delay in the course of a quite different plot, resumed
after interruption. In any case, section four (and perhaps the whole
of "Bronze") can be seen as a *nekuia,* the name given detours to visit
the dead in myths and epics. In such episodes, a questing hero nearing exhaustion undergoes a ritual death in the form of a dangerous
but reinvigorating encounter with dead ancestors whose wisdom
and encouragement produce a ritual rebirth and restore him to his
task refreshed. *The Odyssey* provides an illustration (there, tasting
blood enables the shades to speak); other examples include such
monuments of Western culture as Virgil's *Aeneid* and Dante's *Divine
Comedy,* as well as the divine comedies of Merrill's *Sandover.* (In the
last two instances, encounters with the dead as instructive detours
take up the entire works.)

"Bronze" directly invokes these traditions (its speaking statues
declare that blood is the fee to "fictive environments"), and Merrill
(as "artist-hero") encounters shades throughout the poem: not only

his (and our) bronze ancestors, but also Count Morra and David Jackson. (Umberto is dead when the poem is written; David isn't, but his and Merrill's relationship has died.) All this suggests additional strategies by which Merrill's poem revisits and revises the heroic world and its monumental statues, and with public *and* private aims: say, taming apocalyptic and redemptive visions and accepting without grievance the grievous loss of loved ones to indifference or death. Meanwhile, whether we refer to the three sections of the poem following its central encounter with the Riace statues as aftermath or resumption doesn't much matter. In either case, the effect keeps artworks modestly in touch with life in ways that revise art's "heroic" labor, shifting it away from tragic or comic transcendence and toward tragicomic accommodation and acceptance, mending and repair.

In section five of "Bronze," Merrill and Jackson obey the statues' parting instruction to get on with their lives. But despite the supposedly reviving *nekuia,* and despite the promise of erotic and social reconciliation implied by comedic banqueting, things don't work out (at least not in conventional romantic or resurrective terms). Florence proves exhausting. Spun outward through smoke rings and infernal traffic circles (Florence *is* Dante's city), the lovers split up, and Merrill and Jackson go their separate ways. David returns to the American southwest. (His house there is called a "fortress," indicating his besieged isolation and his buttressed resistance to Merrill.) Umberto weakens and dies. In the meantime, Merrill continues his journey, a warrior in what Marianne Moore called the "fight to be affectionate," and a writer-hero striving to revise the toxic epistemes that monuments bequeath.

Of course, saying it that way hopelessly overstates it. "Bronze" survives its heroic ambitions precisely by subverting them: it's only within its "fictive environments" that art can defuse the dangers art itself underwrites. Much of section five interrogates conventional private and public versions of "heroic" political, erotic, and artistic power and persistence. At times, its tone is almost despairingly dark: ecstatically rendered hopes prove "fake," and images of "lost life," "skeletal belief," war-time carnage, and "run-down DNA" predominate. Yet while individual lives are destroyed by war, by the failure of love, and by age, nature and culture go on: people and states recover from battle, war babies are conceived and born, art treasures concealed during conflict are brought back to light. Despite disaster, life persists, and Merrill musters energy enough to revise the apocalyptic admonition "dust to dust" to the more generative and hopeful "clay to clay." In the meantime, the poem's narrative pace and inter- and intratextual intricacies accelerate, in ways I hope my own full-tilt and interrupted summaries will reflect.

Section five calls "attitudes assumed in love and war" "All fair." Section six makes the declaration interrogative: "All fair?" Returning to private subjects and occasions, it questions the fairness of Merrill's treatment of Jackson throughout their long affair (it's best to think of it, perhaps, as an open marriage). A writer and painter, David Jackson was an artist in his own right, but he is best known as a character in Merrill's poems. In *Sandover,* (another poem that exalts and undermines dangerous, inspiring wisdom delivered by the dead), for instance, he plays the rather mechanical role of "hand" to Merrill's loftier, translating poet or scribe. Some critics, Alison Lurie most stringent among them, have thought Merrill drained or overwhelmed Jackson's creativity by submerging it in his own. Here, Merrill admits that might be so, and he tries to make amends: he depicts Jackson as a sort of sculpturally grand and mountain-climbing painter, scaling experience heroically to canvas.

Meanwhile, as a couplet sonnet, this section of "Bronze" (the only one comprising a single stanza) creates the poem's most fully "composed" moment, bespeaking love, companionship, and reconciliation in form and content. (Merrill even reverses *Sandover*'s roles and offers himself as "hand.") But the sonnet isn't perfect; its terms are sometimes sharp as well as conciliatory and praiseful, and its closing rhyme is interrupted or divorced (although the effect involves embracing). The upshot is that the relationship can't be recovered, but its sad decline and irreversible conclusion can be accepted without (too much) recrimination and with continuing warmth and affection. That's one of the modest heroic acts achieved in "Bronze." By means of revisionist making, it defuses violence and anger (the fuming Merrill of section one; the thwarted and sorrowing lover). It can't redeem the past or make it monumentally permanent and perfect. It does amend it, in ways that are neither comically redemptive nor tragically apocalyptic.

The seventh section of "Bronze" returns to Umberto—and reveals Merrill's revisionist attitudes toward monuments and the monumental in additional ways. Merrill recalls the history (or rumor) of Umberto's paternity (or origins). Supposedly, the count was not his father's son but the son of his father's friend, the king, also named Umberto. In any event, uncertain whether this is a well-known truth or fascinating gossip, Merrill remembers seeing a bust of the king in Umberto's house. This statue joins the many others "Bronze" collects in a sort of sculpture museum: in addition to the Riace figures and the king's bust, "Bronze" contains the Charioteer of Delphi, the bronze Zeus in Athens, David and Umberto depicted *as* bronzes, Rilke's torso of Apollo, and, at least by implication, Donatello's boyish, unwarlike, even foppish bronze of the biblical warrior David, along with, I suppose, in this poem of not quite symmetrical pairings, Michelangelo's more "manly" and "standard"—although mannerist—marble version, also housed in Florence. Like the poem's doubled ecphrastic audience and object, and like its multiple plot patterns and many literary kinds and designs, all this statuary functions as one more mode of revision. Rather than concentrate on a single exemplary monument—and monologue—"Bronze" puts several different sorts of monument in mutually modifying dialogue.[21]

As proof of parentage, the presence of the king's bust in Umberto's house isn't especially convincing. Neither is the other "evidence" offered, a description of competing past conventions in interior decorating. Umberto's mother died young; as a monument to her demise (and perhaps to kingly or imperial affairs), one room in the house she came to as a bride (the house Umberto eventually inherited) remained unused throughout Umberto's life, perfectly preserved "in prelapsarian Empire" ("gilt horrors, plush, veneers"). The rest of the house is furnished with "enchanting" Biedermeier, frayed by use. Loved, but not an object of veneration, it's more or less cared for, even repaired, but neither replaced nor restored. Standards of evidence (and taste in furnishings) aside, these details are another way "Bronze" addresses monumental matters. Merrill's poem undoes the conventional hierarchy ranking sculptural arts above "mere" domestic arrangements (again alloying consideration of grand and public works of art with attention to more ordinary sculptural objects and to private combats, love affairs, and friendships), and it chooses the wear and tear—and repair—of active living over deathlike preservation. In "Bronze," as in "Losing the Marbles," the past wears rather well as it's wearing away or wearing out.

Among many other things, "Bronze" is an array of unmournfully elegiac gestures. (For Merrill, losses and endings are less occasions for grief than painful but welcome spurs to compensatory recon-figuration.) In one such gesture, the poem's section seven considers Umberto's disposition of his estate. (Bequeathed and received inheri-tances are another interest of "Bronze," whether in the form of pa-rental models, sculptural and literary prototypes, or houses.) Count Morra's house "had entertained the subtler / Forms of discourse and behavior," and Umberto had planned to leave it as a " 'retreat for scholars.' " Instead, he leaves it to Mario the butler and his needy, lively family. On hearing the will, the house, as it were, seems to sigh, but this is more nearly the sound of amused (if exasperated) tolera-tion and acceptance than an expression of grief. It says something like this: however trying, only the alloyed "groan" and "laugh" and "tantrum" of life itself can pay the fee of blood that keeps a fictive environment (house, or poem, or monument) from being grimly untenanted, an empty memorial or tomb, a "cenotaph."

The closing section of "Bronze" returns Merrill from Europe to the home he shared for years with David Jackson in the United States. Set on a deck in Connecticut, the scene is aptly "democratic": the dress of the day is T-shirts; beer's the common drink. But it also recalls the poem's previous, more aristocratic and cultured Tuscan setting. Like Umberto, Merrill entertains a group of younger friends; perhaps the deck is a minor version of the balcony from which the count delivered his translation. The form of the section does simi-lar comparative work. Its near free verse stanzas contrast with the sonnetlike (European) patterns of earlier segments, but they occa-sionally tighten toward the meter and rhyme that are more typical there. Similarly, the colloquial syntax and diction that dominate part eight now and then intensify toward the inspired speech and epigrammatic density frequent in prior sections. As usual in Mer-rill, difference is a matter of alloy, overlap, and relation; earlier por-tions of the poem have their own more casual or demotic (perhaps American) relaxations.

Meanwhile, the deck is home to yet another monument in bronze. One of the "summer friends" (unlike David and Umberto, perhaps they're present only in fair weather) asks about the statue. Merrill is startled (his portrait bust had become almost invisible to him, as "things we live with do"), and he has, as it were, to be forced to see himself in this sculpted "sentinel / On the domestic ramparts." (Earnestly, mockingly, the passage invokes once more the concerns of "Bronze" with warrior heroes and representation; it also reunites

Merrill with David Jackson, although only in divorce: Merrill's East
Coast "domestic ramparts" echo his former lover's adobe "fortress" in
the west.) When Merrill finally answers his guest's question (he's careful not to claim for himself, as a character in the poem, Umberto's
teaching function, although in its halting ways "Bronze" is certainly
didactic), he says the bust is the "famous, cold, unblinking / Me at
six." He then stands beside the bronze to be identified (and self-
accused, at least, of failures of sympathy and responsiveness). This
sets off a troubled reverie of sorts; it ends in a pained but bearable
accommodation that accomplishes the poem's revised heroic task.

Although he's at home among familiar (if not quite intimate)
companions in section eight of "Bronze," Merrill is lonely and dis-
affected, removed and emotionally absent. Failed love and the reality of death—the losses of David and Umberto, perhaps his own
aging—cast shadows everywhere: they protect against the despair
they might encourage. Pondering (in "Bronze") his representation
in bronze, Merrill considers the bust's patination. Like the thrill-
ingly real, artificial, and ultimately unsatisfying erotic reincarnation
provided by a hormone injection described earlier in the poem, the
statue's patina was chemically induced. Time has coarsened and paled
what time is expected to nourish. Still, the effect of aging is actual,
and any temptation to distinguish here between the artificial and the
authentic might be tempered—for instance, by Mattusch's research
on ancient forms of chemical patination. Sad, or "deeply-bored"
(like the bronze bust's eyes), Merrill says his head is an unfit perch
for either the owl of wisdom or the nightingale of poetic inspiration.
This might seem self-pitying were it not for Merrill's regular twittings
of owlishness and of Yeatsian forms of stimulation (a matter given a
further comic twist in "Bronze" by Merrill's sharing there of Yeats's
notorious recourse to injections).

In any case, Merrill's bust does have its attendant bird: not Poe's
emphatically hopeless raven (perched on the bust of an aptly Greek
and probably helmeted Athena), but instead the "local braggart
gull" (one more warrior, *miles gloriosus,* hints we're all being gulled).
Frightened from its perch on some vaguely remembered occasion,
the gull in taking flight evacuated and whitened the statue's fore-
lock as it went (the manuring detail I had in mind when I coarsely
claimed that "Bronze" shits on the work of art to nourish art's reworkings). Recalling the man who sculpted the bust, Merrill recollects a headline associated with him: "QUEENS MAN AXED BY

SONS." This Aeschylean sounding caption might mean murder, or only someone fired from a job in a family enterprise. Perhaps it connects with other pairs of fathers and sons (and instructors and ephebes) in Merrill's poem. One certain effect, however, is to interrogate art's power, for Merrill now says bluntly that art is "helpless to forestall / The molten, grown-up scenes" where "ire and yearning, / Most potent of alloys / Within us" come to grips.

As it has all along, "Bronze" brings longing and rage to grips, and comes to grips with them, here by rhyming *Seek* with *shriek.* The inextricable interpenetration of anger and desire in the making of war and love and art is this poem's surest knowledge. It's dramatized in multiple, mutually confirming and contesting narratives, forms, and genres as "Bronze" exposes and tries to revise the ways statues, epics, and monumental public and private structures perpetrate and perpetuate the ire and yearning they seek (and shriek—more "hot" lines) to pacify, satisfy, eliminate, or transcend. The sad and quiet, funny final scene of "Bronze" is the sort of "safer" revision of the monumental Merrill offers. He doesn't "correct" inherited traditions (since standard measures, like parasangs, are shifting). Instead, using "molten" "alloys," he modifies conventions (the way artists and artisans rework identical molds to manufacture subtly different bronzes—like the older and younger, more serene and more menacing individuals of the warrior pair discovered at Riace).

Seeing Merrill "absent" (the word implies both Merrill's unhappiness or distraction and the dangerously acute and cold remove that permits the artist's vision), one of his guests (Augie, a summer friend whose name diminishes august and Augustan monumentalism of aesthetic and political sorts) carelessly leans his arms on the bust's "unruffled" hair. Augie spills a little beer, staining the statue's cheek. (The poem, by the way, like its other speaking statues, says "my cheek," and throughout this passage, self and statue merge and separate, keeping art warmly in touch with and frigidly distinct from life.) Augie's refreshing, accidental libation restores to Merrill's bronze (for the moment at least) a natural—no, natural-looking—"bluegreen" patination. Meanwhile, Augie's T-shirt reprises alarms the Riace bronzes sounded in section four. It warns the world of ecological disaster: its chapter and verse is "*Clean Air / Or Else.*" This trivializes, confirms, domesticates, and publicizes the danger it portrays—and (since the terms "or else" threaten punishment as well as consequence) it exposes once more the threat of apocalyptic and vengeful violence lurking within even honorable monumental admonitions. While these rather intricate matters are being conveyed, the face of the child-statue is pressed against the young man's chest. There's a good deal to say about this nourishing and distant moment, in which art represents recoveries only life can deliver (or prevent): it signals Merrill's mature and childish ire and yearning with regard to erotic and paternal love, for instance. But at the cost of simplification, I return to my narrower interest in "Bronze" as a monument to monuments and let its slant and all but final rhyme speak for itself about art's mixed capacities for catastrophe and comfort: in it, "the Work of Art" (including the Riace sculptures, Rilke's poem, Merrill's bust, and "Bronze" itself) alloys with "help and hurt."

J. D. McClatchy described Merrill as working with "dissolves." I close this lengthy consideration of Merrill and monuments with several of them, citing three characteristic images in which Merrill mends and amends the monumental urge to permanence. In "The Friend of the Fourth Decade," Merrill receives instruction in lifting burdens the past inscribes (it involves dipping postcards in water to liquefy their messages). He tries it on writing from his mother. Her inks prove indelible, but they fade a little, which lightens a cargo that full erasure might have overloaded. "The Book of Ephraim" describes a heart composed of white meal and lit rum and made by Maya Deren as a blessing for the threshold of Merrill and Jackson's home. "Hardened on the spot" but pared to smatterings by "come-and-go," it promises to persist for a time that the poem's own measures estimate as long enough. In "Prose of Departure," Merrill finds Japanese incense sticks that trace, as they burn, a line of characters in ash so delicate the "pious formula" the flame inscribes is "scattered by a touch." Marble and bronze are heavier stuff; Merrill's respectful revisions buoyantly heft their weight.

4

Derek Walcott
"The Sea Is History,"
Omeros, *and Others*

"Where are *your* monuments, *your* battles, . . . *your* tribal memory?"
Those colonial insults open Derek Walcott's poem "The Sea Is History." I've sharpened their edge with italics, but antagonism cuts
through Walcott's more neutral inflections. Those allow for a range
of tones and of possible speakers: representatives of a current or
former colonizing power, tourists or other presumptive "masters," a
colonial subject who believes an empire's teachings. But no matter
who asks the questions, and however bluntly or sharply they're put,
the poem's initiating queries are at least partially rhetorical. In that
sense, they're aggressive even if polite. Implied declarations solicit
no answers; speechless surrender to the inquisitor's values is the only
response they require or allow.

Posed in rapid sequence, the poem's questions conduct a rough
interrogation. It aims to dominate, enforcing the law it lays down.
That law's prime tenets go something like this: monuments (whether
artistic or institutional) are the visible proof of a culture's military,
religious, civic, and other achievements and traditions, that is, of
its very existence; therefore, a culture rich in monuments (as the
questioner assumes his own is) is superior, and a culture with few
or no monuments (as the questioned party's is presumed to be) is
inferior—or isn't a culture at all. (The last rule stands whether the
monuments are actually missing or are present in forms that the
dominant culture can't perceive or refuses to credit—judging them
derivative, inept, or otherwise illicit.) Additional statutes are implied:
inhabitants of superior cultures speak—they question, command,
and evaluate; inferior peoples are silent—they listen and obey: their

measure is taken by others. This précis of (racist) colonial logic is accomplished in less than two lines of verse. The brevity displays Walcott's skill as a poet-dramatist; it also recalls that within the hierarchy of imperial formulations there's nothing left to say.

Here, however (in a postcolonial context), questions meant to stifle response provoke one instead. It begins this way: "Sirs, / in that grey vault. The sea." At first, those broken phrases might seem more like an apology than a retort; they appear to reinforce rather than to rebut the interrogator's assumptions. Perhaps they suggest linguistic incompetence—and (since they're courteously introduced) a servile respect for the master's voice. The impressions are quickly dispelled. The poem's reply goes on for several pages; its volubility in the face of a rhetorical strategy designed to compel silence signals vigorous resistance, not surrender. Perhaps the formulaic courtesy of *Sirs*—borrowed from the schoolroom or from slave or military barracks—conveys sarcastic subversion, as excessive servility may. Perhaps in the many-tongued Caribbean where the poem's exchange takes place, the sentence fragments challenge the presumed superiority of any single set of grammatical, syntactical, and other cultural conventions. Elsewhere in the poem, local idioms depart from "standard" grammar in ways that suggest heightened rather than diminished linguistic craft: for instance, the word *strop* in the phrase "strop on these goggles" hones what the lenses promise to deliver: sharpened insight into "subtle and submarine" conditions.

Unfortunately, the antagonistic emphasis of my own discussion partly betrays the poem's reply. "The Sea Is History" does sometimes compete within the constraints of the "superior" culture's assumptions (thus its concern to demonstrate that the Caribbean *has* monuments—and therefore possesses the history, culture, and cultural worth that monuments are said to certify). But Walcott knows those same assumptions can permanently rig the competition, since—if the past is precedent, for instance—European priority means primacy forever over more recently emerged Caribbean and other cultures. At the same time, however, he also knows that a revolution making newness preside would only reverse the fix, for in Walcott's analysis, judgments that privilege either antiquity *or* currency are structurally identical; each makes the imperial mistake of reading history as sequential, fixed, and fatal.[1] That analysis is crucial to the several imbricated positions Walcott lays down and laminates as his poem both follows *and* rewrites (but doesn't simply invert) the rules of the game it inherits. In the process, "The Sea Is History" revises—and creolizes—the meaning of culture, disables simple notions of cultural comparison and competition, and recalibrates the nature and value of monuments, of the history monuments perpetuate, and of perpetuity itself.

The procedures by which Walcott achieves those multiple, asymmetrical ends are complicated, logically messy, and brilliantly contrived. Perhaps they begin with the pun on *vault* in the passage quoted above. As a banker's term, *vault* implies a safe full of monuments held in opulent reserve; as a mortician's word, it intones their final interment in an unmarked and watery (if monumental) grave. Or perhaps the intricate layering of Walcott's poem begins even earlier: in the deliberate elision of punctuation that could clarify (and oversimplify) whether its exchange takes place between a European master and an obedient, if rebellious colonial student or servant, or occurs within an independent postcolonial citizen who (under duress, but gratefully as well) has internalized certain colonialist cultural assumptions that he also resists.

"The Sea Is History" has two major strategies for refuting charges of Caribbean inferiority: each considers the nature and worth of monuments, and each explores the political, artistic, and cultural issues monuments concentrate. One strategy the poem deploys is descriptive; it pictures local monuments in glowing terms, and the simple facts of their beauty and presence combine to rebut the questioner's crude or naïve assumptions about West Indian culture (such as the idea that the islands have either no culture or an inferior one, since they supposedly lack or offer only impoverished examples of the conventional monuments presumably required to express and record a society and its people). Meanwhile, the condition of these indigenous monuments (they're "submarine" and require the assistance of a local guide in order to be seen) conducts its own subversive transfer of knowledge and authority.

The monumental structures the poem describes are "colonnades of coral," "the gothic windows of sea-fans," and "groined caves" like stone "cathedrals." This is the language of the natural sublime, of course, and, as we'll see, Walcott uses it for several conflicting purposes. The *natural sublime* refers to a set of ideas that invert standard codes for deciding cultural supremacy. Rooted in romantic European and New World rejections of classical values, it operates like this. In the traditional view, civilization shapes and restrains dangerously formless and wild nature, wresting elegant monuments from natural and human barbarity. This helps guarantee the superiority of older cultures to young ones; they've been at their culturally fundamental civilizing business longer, and monuments mark their history of virtuous successes. From the perspective of the natural sublime, however, civilization barbarically tames and taints nature, breaking its ancient bonds to creation and divinity; the refinements of monuments merely record the rupture. That view permits the removal of monumentality from its traditional locus within aesthetic and institutional forms (which "rawer," more recent cultures inevitably lack) and its relocation within the grander (now monumental) objects and processes of nature (which newer—especially New World—cultures often possess in abundance). By this means, the undeniable cultural priority and profusion of older civilizations becomes a liability, while the absence of conventional monuments and the presence of natural ones within newer civilizations becomes an advantage.

In part, Walcott's poem straightforwardly applies this logic. To repeat, "The Sea Is History" rebuts the imputation of inferiority in its opening lines by describing distinctive Caribbean nature in sublimely monumental terms that confirm the existence and value of local realities. One response to the question "Where are your monuments . . . ?" then, is not the expected speechless admission of cultural deficiency but a proud assertion saying something like this: *Our* monuments are in the sea, and the natural grandeur of corals, reefs, and caves equals or surpasses your more conventional artistic and architectural splendors, so that if monuments verify cultures, we surely have one, and our natural monuments do the work of validation as well as or better than your manufactured contraptions can. But Walcott's argument from the natural sublime is considerably more subtle in its analysis and effects than this rather crude reversal. (To say it again, Walcott rewrites or revises but doesn't invert the codes he's heir to.)

Irony is part of Walcott's basic equipment (his well-stropped goggles, if you will), and he subjects his strategy of rebuttal as fully to irony's lens as he does the interrogator's pretentiousness. To put it another way, Walcott's ironies are inherited from literary modernism as well as from factors usually associated with postmodernism (his racially mixed colonial background, island picong and calypso traditions, and his postcolonial and internationalist contexts). Ironies in Walcott's work not only mock and puncture received colonial pieties in both righteous anger and knowing pastiche, but they also address the sanctities of postcolonial resistance (whether in affectionate parody or aggrieved attack). They insist that multiple and conflicting meanings (including competing definitions of monuments, history, culture, and cultural worth) are apt to coexist—uneasily perhaps, but also firmly, and in elaborate, mutually qualifying relational patterns that abrade and reconfigure one another without attaining complete erasure or inscription, final victory or defeat.

"The Sea Is History" reflects all this, and, among other things, the effectiveness of its arguments from the natural sublime is both reinforced and partly compromised by the way they're applied. For example, Walcott's frank borrowing of Old World architectural descriptors for his Caribbean "monuments" (groined cathedrals, gothic windows, colonnades) implies derivation and belatedness, a circumstance that partly undercuts the cultural equivalence or precedence the descriptions assert. At the same time, however, the condition of belatedness also confirms what the poem's rebuttal claims, for Walcott is confident that *all* cultural activity is derivative by definition, a form of creative, or, better, re-creative mimicry: in short, a creole.[2]

Meanwhile, the matter has other facets. At the same time that "The Sea Is History" depicts the Caribbean natural world as sublimely monumental: awesome, beautiful, and sacred, it also recognizes nature's potential as an indifferent and overwhelming destructive force. Predatory sharks, hellish heat, home-wrecking hurricanes, and city-devouring tidal waves are as much a part of local nature and of Walcott's poem as undersea cathedrals are. Those natural threats to civilization cramp the logic of the natural sublime as a response to the colonialist equation of monuments with cultural presence and permanence. But they don't wholly crush it—after all, the sublimity of nature depends in part upon its being unconstrained, and Walcott's admission recalls that conventional monuments, for all their immortalizing pretensions, are also subject to the eroding and corroding powers of nature and time. (Barnacles on underwater structures reflect the "pitted" surfaces of stone cathedrals; the image implies that organic growth trumps inorganic decay, challenging traditional views of monumental persistence.)

The implications of these mutually entangling and entangled positions become especially acute elsewhere in the poem, when Walcott demonstrates that the powers of conventionally recognized civilization and culture can be as dangerous and destructive as natural forces sometimes are. But for now my point is this: the argument from the natural sublime in "The Sea Is History" not only undercuts the demeaning charge of its opening voice but also qualifies its own responses to it. Meanwhile, qualification isn't cancellation, and here, as more generally in Walcott's work, complexities ramify as he presents the politically and aesthetically charged categories of colony and empire, nature and culture, and transience and persistence in terms that are interdependent or relational rather than hierarchically discrete. The flexibility of the poem's responding voice is symptomatic: it coolly admits limitations within arguments it strenuously advocates. Strongly at odds with the more or less pretentious certitude of its opening interrogation, the poem's response unsettles the standard meanings of *monument, culture,* and *cultural worth.* That should upset the inquisitor's confidence (tip it over as well as disturb it).

"The Sea Is History" employs a second tactic for defending the Caribbean against the charge of cultural deficiency. This device also responds to equations of monumental presence and cultural merit, although now from a slightly different angle. Among the implications of the poem's opening queries is the notion that conventional monuments certify the existence in a place of what the poem calls "tribal memory," a history worthy of remembrance and commemoration. They further imply that the Caribbean lacks such monuments and therefore lacks a proper past (one more version of the historian A. J. Froude's notorious accusation that the West Indies has "no people in the true sense of the word"). Most of "The Sea Is History" is given over to refuting that indictment. It does so by offering a convincingly monumental version of West Indian history (thus proving that the Caribbean has one). But it also does so by casting doubt upon "history" as an authoritative source of evidence and judgment (so that history is appealed to in order to substantiate a claim of cultural worth but also partially discredited as a witness and arbiter). In much the same way, elsewhere in the poem arguments from the natural sublime are both upheld and cross-examined: once more, Walcott responds to slurs he deprecates by using *and* revising but not simply repeating or inverting the terms that underlie them.

Those already dauntingly intricate matters are further complicated by the poem's admitting (as monumental history usually does not) that Caribbean history (like history everywhere) includes corruption and failure alongside nobler events and achievements. In a further revision of standard monumental commemoration, the Caribbean's glory is represented here as having more to do with its people's endurance and survival than with military, political, or artistic triumphs; this further undermines the grounds upon which cultures traditionally stake imperial claims. Meanwhile, Walcott now draws his parallels not from sculptural and architectural monuments but from the Bible, that monumental (but borrowed) "Western" text in which history surely appears, but in combination with literary, legendary, and mythic versions of cultural experience and knowledge. Those categories (and their kinds and degrees of credibility) intersect, compete, and overlap.

In all of this, Walcott's method combines catalogue with analogy. In a series of parallels with biblical incidents, he shows that West Indian history has monumental scope and scale. Beginning with the islands' creation, Walcott includes the European discovery and invasion, considers colonial warfare and piracy, covers colonization, the Middle Passage, slavery, and emancipation, and concludes with independence and federation, the federation's breakup into individual nations, and some recent government chicanery. Meanwhile, he implies that while those historical events and experiences are important, none of them is final or fatal (I mean deterministic, a matter I'll return to). One effect of Walcott's biblical parallels is to put Caribbean history on the same level as events in the Bible. For instance, the islands' creation and their European "discovery" echo Genesis. (They involve a glorious transformation of chaos and a devastating fall from paradise.) Similarly, the Middle Passage and slavery are connected to elements in Exodus and the Babylonian captivity; emancipation recalls the resurrection; and government corruption recollects Egyptian plagues of animals and insects. Those pairings give Caribbean history monumental status, but that status isn't borrowed; it's presented as a matter of observation, not elevation or ennoblement.

In his poem "Roots," Walcott notes a blunt colonial fact: "When they conquer you, you have to read their books." But Walcott typically sees this imposition as a privilege or gift as well: you *get* to read their books—*and* to rewrite them, so that if a cultural inheritance prevails upon and shapes you, you reconfigure it, and influence flows both ways. For Walcott, this is true even of the Bible, *the* book. Biblical parallels in "The Sea Is History" not only reveal the past's imperial reinscriptions in (and on) the present; they also revise the past for current use. This is partly an effect of Walcott's way with comparisons. Timothy Hofmeister calls Walcott's analogies "discursive." The adjective stresses Walcott's unusual emphasis on analogy's characteristic consideration of affinities *and* disparities. One frequent result of that practice in Walcott's work is to put related but competing cultural discourses into complicated conversations in which likenesses across cultures are asserted, cancelled, revised, and reconfirmed. Here's a prose example. In the essay "The Muse of History," Walcott recalls analogies conventionally drawn between New World slavery and the book of Exodus. Traditionally, those parallels interpret the suffering, migration, and eventual liberation of ancient Hebrews enslaved in Egypt as a painful but also promising precedent for Africans more recently enslaved in the Americas. Walcott writes, "There was this difference, that the passage over our Red Sea was not from bondage to freedom but its opposite, so that the tribes arrived at their New Canaan chained. There is this residual feeling in much of our literature, the wailing by strange waters for a lost home."[3]

There's much to remark on here. From an American and specifically West Indian perspective, calling the Atlantic "our Red Sea" both reinforces and corrects a structural parallel between biblical and Caribbean histories, since unlike the Hebrews' Red Sea, the Atlantic of the Middle Passage was not divided by God (or the gods) for an enslaved people's safe passage; it was made "Red" by the blood of their suffering and death. Similarly, the Africans' Caribbean-Canaan was not a lost homeland restored along with their liberty but a place of deracination and enslavement—although also of eventual settlement, freedom, and national identity. Walcott's term "New Canaan" sharply recalls the triangle trade and New England's role in slavery; it also suggests his fundamental conviction that uprooted people in the West Indies, African and otherwise, must make a new home in the Caribbean, and do so in ways that neither forget what they've lost and how they lost it nor yield to either nostalgic dreams of a return to origins or bitter dreams of revenge. For Walcott, "wailing by strange waters for a lost home" is a vital strain in Caribbean psalms but not their entire music. Meanwhile, in more general terms, Walcott's combined recollection and revision of biblical precedents invokes the real comfort provided by a religion forced upon the slaves but also adopted and creatively adapted by them. It exposes the role of comforting religious stories within a "Christian" disciplinary system that justified slavery, helped dismantle the slaves' own cultural faiths and forms, prompted quietist passivity rather than rebellion, and safely displaced the promise of liberation from this world to the next. Those are tight knots; they model Walcott's many-stranded response to his inheritance, including the burden and blessing of monumental traditions.

To return to "The Sea Is History," analogies there between biblical and Caribbean matters knot affinity and disparity as well. Walcott again relates the Middle Passage to Exodus, for instance. Once more, the former tale is no triumphal journey from bondage to liberation: slave voyages are characterized by "packed cries," "moaning," and "shit," not manna and other miraculous manifestations; horrific conditions make the shark's shadow seem a "benediction" and drowning a relief. Those descriptions recall degradation, abuse, and desperation; they also indicate the courage of slaves who chose death rather than captivity. Walcott's tactics restore the biblical parallels they dismantle. He combines those parallels with local conditions in order to construct unpretentious monuments to resistance and persistence. West Indian coral solders the bones of dead slaves into "mosaics" that quietly name the Hebrew leader and become a Caribbean Ark of the Covenant, a repository of shared experience and knowledge defining a culture and people. Sunlight filtered through Caribbean waters in "plucked wires" echoes the psalms and harps that eased and memorialized captivity in Babylon. Caribbean cowries convert the manacles of drowned African women into the ivory bracelets of the sensuous Song of Solomon. (The mixture of texts recalls that the Bible is a book made out of books. For Walcott, who sees all writing as rewriting, this is so of every book, just as every culture is a mélange.)

Walcott's poem records in revised but still elevated (although not elevating) biblical terms a rich Caribbean history that's impressive in scope and scale and thereby rebuts the charge that his native place lacks a meaningful past. Meanwhile, it doesn't idealize that past. Alongside the achievements of emancipation and independence, Walcott describes wretched suffering and contemporary political corruption ("furred caterpillars of judges," mantislike police, "bullfrogs bellowing" for votes). Similarly, while Walcott appears to accept his inquisitor's view that a monumental history verifies the existence and value of a people (although perhaps he accepts it only for so long as it takes to refute indictments based upon it), he also brusquely rejects that view, along with the imperial version of history it represents. In one sense, he does this by implication, exposing a tart irony about the cultures whose grand (or grandiose) histories have given them the power to establish monuments, define their civilizations as exemplary, and rule on the claims of others. Those same cultures practiced the brutalities of colonization, genocide, and slavery. Meanwhile, Walcott also subverts history as witness and jury in more focused ways in "The Sea Is History."

Walcott's poem treats history as myth, so that historical moments separated by gulfs of time are presented as simultaneous rather than sequential. As Walcott says in "The Muse of History," "the death of a gaucho does not merely repeat, but is, the death of Caesar." That assertion undoes conventional beliefs in precedent as privilege; it also subverts the privileges of class and political positions. Biblical and Caribbean relations in "The Sea Is History" are similarly nonhierarchical. That allows Walcott to tap authoritative historical (and monumental) precedent without making authority monolithic and without permitting priority in time to indicate priority in value (since that would diminish or marginalize more recent events). It's this that underlies the poem's intricate strategy of appealing to history by pairing West Indian events with biblical precedents while both revising those precedents *and* denying that "History" (capitalized) exists. The poem puts it this way, "the ocean kept turning blank pages / looking for History"; it never finds it. By such means Walcott rejects ideas of history as objective and fixed: a complete set of facts with inevitable consequences and a single meaning. For him, lowercase history is the only sort there is. Like ocean waves, it is endlessly iterated, erased, and repeated, but repeated always with a difference: revised, for instance, by the addition to the archive of previously unknown or suppressed perspectives, voices, and facts. This keeps history (like monuments) open-ended, what Walcott says culture in the Americas is: a matter "of references, not of certainties."[4] And this is so whether we look forward or look back. The past affects the present, yes, but not deterministically, since the present can always reinterpret and revise the past—thus the aptness of the Bible as Walcott's source of parallels in "The Sea Is History." Its mixture of history with literature, legend, and myth tells a firmly patterned tale but invites interpretation; in it, as in the poem, history is a system of stories, and monuments are textual mosaics.

"The Sea Is History" keeps monuments in view, but Walcott's treatment of them there all but sinks their traditional forms and functions. The poem associates conventional monuments with imperial arrogance, cruelty, and oppression. It recasts them in natural and textual versions that are more flexible, more vulnerable, and less committed to claims of supposedly superior and permanent cultural achievement than are standard objects in stone or bronze. Conventional monuments, especially architectural and sculptural ones, come under repeated attack in Walcott's writing. He corrosively applies postmodern, postcolonial, and more traditional critiques of monumentality to them and their pretensions. But as the word *recasts* implies, Walcott's rejection of monuments is never final or complete. Like Bishop, Lowell, and Merrill, Walcott addresses monuments to examine the aesthetic, political, and more broadly cultural matters they condense. Urged by his artist's vocation and by a passionate desire to commemorate his people and his place, Walcott frequently salvages monuments for contemporary use. Demolition and damage accompany his retrievals, but they prepare for the reconstruction of monuments in renewed and less rigid or pompous forms in several of his poems, in images, in essays, and especially in *Omeros,* Walcott's memorable reimagining of epic, literature's most monumental genre.

Meanwhile, Walcott frequently assails monuments, for their complicity with hierarchical and oppressive master narratives and for their claims to an immortality that falsifies the fluid and fragile nature of things. The early poem "Ruins of a Great House" eventually turns its heated rage at colonial tyranny toward tempered compassion. Encouraged by literary works that subvert imperial hierarchies and replace fantasies of permanence, power, and revenge with a vision of shared humanity, Walcott finds reasons for empathy even in the decaying monumental house of colonial slave masters; he responds to signs of our common fate in the eventual surrender to "the worm's rent" of every person, cultural pattern, and artifact. Nonetheless, "Ruins of a Great House" involves a frontal assault on monumental arrogance. The poem associates the mansion of a British plantation in Jamaica with the imperial monuments of Greece and Rome, with the stench of Caribbean and U.S. slavery, and even with supposedly benevolent literary works, which are sometimes used to underwrite a sense of cultural hegemony and justify oppression. In an act of forceful literal and literary trespass (it proves his deed of ownership), Walcott angrily, even exultantly, catalogues the details of the house's rot; he makes it a metonym for the "leprosy of empire," the sick cruelty and inevitable decline and death of civilizations that imagine their provisional arrangements are absolute and eternal.

Perhaps it could be said that the complicity of monuments with imperial power and pretentiousness incites a Juvenalian strain in Walcott's work, while their resistance to the inevitable wearing out of every human self and structure (a resistance perversely at odds with natural cycles of growth and decay but also a time-honored, understandable, and potentially moving reaction to the brevity of life) prompts a tone more tenderly Horatian. Both responses are satiric, and like other mixed feelings in Walcott, they tend to coexist, whether in tense or relaxed relations. Mixed feelings are Walcott's birthright. Heir to black grandmothers and Dutch and English grandfathers, he was born on St. Lucia, where his middle-class standard English was enriched by an English patois and a predominant French Creole. His family's Methodism encountered French and Irish Catholicism as well as something pagan, and his rigorous classic (and classical) British colonial education was supported, challenged, and revised by the interest of family and friends in local and European art and by the presence of lively African- and French-inflected folk traditions. Walcott's reaction to those inheritances and influences shifts in emphasis over time, as does his reaction to literary and other sources, but perhaps those reactions are best characterized by the word *hybridity*—and by Walcott's famous assertion in "The Muse of History" that "maturity is the assimilation of the features of every ancestor." The term and the definition both stress composite and unresolved inclusive amalgamations rather than a choice from among alternatives or the dissolution of differences in one or another synthesis. For Walcott, assimilation is the reverse of being assimilated: it's a creative borrowing (or theft) that recognizes even the most painful indebtedness as the ground of renewal rather than a mark of abject derivation or belatedness.[5]

In any case, whether because they're aligned with colonial exploitation or are relatively rare and alien in the Caribbean (where "shipped" statues are "dead on arrival"), conventional monuments play more marginal than central roles in Walcott's work. Paintings (and painting) figure prominently in his life and writing, but unlike Bishop, Lowell, and Merrill, Walcott never addresses a monument directly as the focus or subject of a major poem. Nevertheless, architectural and sculptural monuments appear frequently in his verse, most often as negative examples, illustrations of aesthetic as well as cultural and political values he diagnoses as malignant. For instance, it's a common antimonumental charge in literature and elsewhere that monuments elevate dead objects over eventful life, and Walcott regularly states his preference for living things over monumental works of art, routinely associating monuments and their attendant attitudes with exhaustion, inertia, and death.

Sometimes, the choice to be made is relatively simple, as when warm flesh outscores cold stone in erotic diversions. In "The Schooner *Flight,*" for instance, the voyager-poet Shabine reverses Prufrock's prudish desire for sculptural rather than human arms: he wants no "sexless" seraph but the marmoset "round brown eyes" and tickling claws of an agile, earthy lover. In "A Propertius Quartet," a living Cynthia's breasts outshine the "marble busts" of Rome's St. Peter's. And in "The Villa Restaurant," Walcott prefers a "terra-cotta waitress" to a "Greek urn or amphora." (*Its* artful curves are preserved in a museum case, frustratingly in sight but perpetually out of reach.) Each of those examples renews a classic trope, like Cummings's naked girl who's worth a million statues, and Walcott sometimes extends the valuation to the literary monuments of books. In "The Gulf," the works of the "great dead" are "gilded gravestones" on a shelf. In *Omeros,* narrator and muse shelve immortality itself when they agree that "A girl smells better than a book" or the world's libraries. Still, assertions stress aspects; they're subject to change. Walcott says elsewhere that poets "work for the immortality of the poem" because "literature is stronger than life" "for them." Of course, the bookishly cautious final phrase tweaks the alternative judgment it asserts.[6]

Walcott often contrasts inanimate monuments with living things to focus on aesthetic as well as erotic complications. In "Tarpon," for example, a painterly approach taps some of the ambiguities of artistic representation caught in the aptly inert and mobile term *still life.* The great migratory fish Walcott's poem describes "grows beautiful" only as it is dying. A tense shift underlines the point: only the tarpon's demise permitted its depiction; it was only when dead that it "sought design" and turned from flesh to "silk" to "lead" then "bronze" and "stone." The identification of increasingly monumental materials and forms with advancing rigor mortis abuses art in general and monumental art in particular. It doesn't quite discard them, though; like paint, words bring the smothered fish to life and then preserve it. Throughout his career, Walcott worries the contradictions framing the relationship of art to life (or reality, or nature). Each category violates and depends upon the other; as Oscar Wilde implied, they overlap, and the unresolved tension between them proves a major source of power in Walcott's writing. It generates considerations of apprenticeship, influence, intertextuality, and artistic reputation that strongly inflect how monuments and monumentality are treated in his work (all matters I'll return to).

Meanwhile, as complications in some of the relatively simple examples discussed above suggest (for instance, like Shabine, the terracotta colored waitress is hyphenated, a mixed-race "red"), Walcott's fear that a cult of monuments disparages life often mixes aesthetic, political, and cultural critiques together in his writing. In "The Fortunate Traveller," for instance, Walcott expresses dismay at the brutality of contemporary global economics, where famine perversely accompanies surplus food supplies and there's less sympathy for a living "human face" than for the ancient scrolls long since consumed in Alexandria's monumental library. This is perfectly straightforward, but in many of Walcott's poems, the association of monuments with political, cultural, and artistic issues creates more tightly woven tangles. For example, aesthetic admiration for attractive monumental objects and values can be both fully felt and especially problematic for colonial or postcolonial subjects whose monuments are likely to be foreign: it can sap their love of local things and drain their respect for themselves and their homeland's culture.

In "A Change of Skin," "arrogant" English "stone" menaces living (and implicitly Caribbean) flesh and bone as they shudder before it in "deep-tutored awe." The quoted phrase is exact. Being too well schooled in awe of another's monuments threatens profound, even fatal personal, political, and cultural wounds. In *Another Life,* Walcott describes his colonial education. It was generous and gave him a language and models of artistic excellence, but it also tutored him to believe that his native palms were less noble trees than imagined elms, the foliage of breadfruit plants more coarse than the leaves of iconically English oaks, black skin inferior to white. Those dismal instructions teach fundamental errors, and it's a foundational effort and effect of Walcott's writing to expose and correct them. Celebrations of Caribbean landscapes, seascapes, and people are essential features of his work. And although the rich poverties of those places and people are neither conventionally magnificent nor monumental, their beauty and value are intensely real. Walcott describes them clearly, lovingly, sometimes fiercely—and in ways that redefine what magnificence and monuments might be and mean. (The paradox of apparent deprivation as privilege or wealth in the phrase "rich poverties" is Walcott's own, a compliment to his native place and a cure for metropolitan materialism, whether imitated or imposed.)[7]

Nonetheless, as in "The Sea Is History," Walcott avoids the self-regarding vice of flattery even when praising his immediate surroundings. Monumental errors occur where they occur, and in a rare instance when he addresses a specifically Caribbean monument (in the eight-part "Tropic Zone," poem XLIII of *Midsummer*), Walcott attacks it equally with European examples for establishing feudal hierarchies it hopes to enforce forever. The poem is set on an island where all the graffiti agree with the government, where hotels are the only temples, and a "new ogre / erects his bronzes over the parks." The speaker is a visitor (West Indian, but from a different island). He "doubts the murals and trusts the beer." His ironies unhorse the local equestrian statue. Imported or imitated, the bronze can't take the heat: the rider's sword arm tires; he'd like to dismount his stallion, curl up in the shade, and sleep. In a final twist, the tropical climate that the now-departed colonizers complained of as being "enervating" suggests a possible line of defense against the active "northern" busyness that can oppress or kill, against imperial stances not every West Indian has managed to resist.[8]

These antimonumental strains in Walcott's work are thoroughgoing, if incomplete. One form they take reflects his faith that power is "unstable" and "ephemeral," that "who rules" is the "least important aspect of any culture."[9] This might come as a surprise to people being badly ruled at any given moment, but Walcott takes the long view, and to make his case he often tolls the list of once great, now fallen or faded civilizations. "Ruins of a Great House," for instance, recalls that the vanished Roman Empire colonized Britain before Britain's empire colonized parts of the Caribbean and much of the wider world before vanishing itself. *Omeros* affords similar treatment to Portuguese, Spanish, and other empires. Again, the theme is partly conventional; it echoes "Ozymandias," where time brings monarchs and monuments low. But the matter has special weight in Walcott's colonial, then postcolonial West Indies. The sun sets ironically on empires often in his poems, especially on the British Empire some once described as vast enough to be exempt from sunsets. As he puts it elsewhere, presumptions of cultural permanence are vanities presumed in vain: Carthage, Atlantis, and Alexandria all "can go," and went.[10]

For supposedly subaltern peoples, such depositions liberate, and Walcott shares their elation. Still, his reactions to the depredations of time and fortune on empires, monuments, and other human structures vary. Erasures leave palimpsestic traces; they don't obliterate, and that keeps ruins and other records available for admonition, study, and revision. Walcott is especially subtle in this regard. He recommends a willed and "responsible" amnesia in reaction to the Caribbean experience of slavery and colonization, for instance. It's a version of forgetting that remembers the awful facts but doesn't allow them to restrict ideas and feelings to the cripplingly narrow range of victim's shame or victimizer's guilt, desires for revenge or punishment. Perhaps only incidentally (like the way his definitions of the self and language as "hybrid" mimic but don't quite repeat postmodern views of the self as "dispersed" and language as an affliction), Walcott's "restorative" amnesia reflects the postmodern interest in absence as presence. Amnesia's erasure is trauma's ineradicable mark, a special sort of scar recording psychic wounds it doesn't wholly heal or keeps too painfully open. An endlessly unsettled and self-revising formulation, it hints at Walcott's literary stances, too, where every language, trope, and technique that's gratefully learned and independently handled proves to be a creole, a convention we re-form and reform as it forms us, so that what's called old or new is always already a hybrid: already was, will be, and is a matter of renovation. That logic constructively subverts the comparative categories of relative purity and impurity so often applied to languages, literatures, cultures, and peoples, sometimes with murderous results. It does so in a way that praises Caribbean and other creoles, but only while paying every language, literature, culture, and people the expansively friendly compliment of being designated one as well. It begins to define the sort of monumental art Walcott finds he can bear to make.[11]

Meanwhile, time's devastation of monuments and empires has other outcomes in Walcott's thinking. It instructs us in humility, for instance, as does the Caribbean's (and nature's) vastness of water and light. The sea and sky are truly monumental; beside them human constructions are tiny, trivial, and transient. As Walcott says in an interview, this is partially a commonplace: on islands as elsewhere, the "immensity" of nature gives human beings a "sense of insignificance." He intensifies the diminishing effect. "Nothing can be put down in the sea. You can't plant on it, you can't live on it, you can't walk on it." It shrinks mere human achievement to a "bubble" or a "speck." Yet the lesson Walcott takes from this doesn't teach him to despair or relax; the ultimate irrelevance of human effort neither absolves him from application nor counsels him to abandon his tasks. It makes him more, not less ambitious. Walcott is among the most aspiring of poets, and his ambition is never greater than when it struggles modestly to keep his largest, most lasting labors in scale with the "humiliating," that is, humbling nature of things.

One hinge that articulates connections among those incongruently congruous matters is the sea's effect on history (that is, on "History," the supposedly authoritative "progressive and linear" version of events Walcott regularly debunks). He says the "strength of the sea"—like light, the sea has "never had epochs"—"gives you an idea of time that makes history absurd." Still, the resulting deprivation doesn't generate constrained surrender but an expansive enlargement of endurance instead. It does so because it makes the past a common resource, not a walled-off site some set of "superior" others owns or controls forever. It's entirely characteristic that Walcott's clearest attacks on monumental excesses (attacks in which the facts of natural grandeur and human weakness expose the fraud in hierarchical claims to power, permanence, and privilege) turn out unexpectedly and firmly to encourage the construction of monuments, although not, of course, the usual kind. Like its companion "survival," endurance is a monumental value. As we'll see, it plays a major role in Walcott's revision of commemorative practices and poetics. In the meantime, his paradoxical linking of human constraints to expansive endurance has another hinge as well, this one vocational and religious: Walcott's unshakeable faith that artists and others are obliged to magnify the greatness of God or the creation, even though the effort, at least in ultimate terms, is unnecessary and unavailing. In "A Village Life," he writes, "Nothing endures. Even in his cities / man's life is grass." The sentiment echoes Isaiah ("all flesh is grass"); it prophesies the decay of every human creation and of every human self. (The village, by the way, is Greenwich Village; its association with the proudly monumental skyline of Manhattan sharpens the lesson, as does its pairing with grassier villages in the Caribbean, where the adage is accurate as well.) Again, the effect is antimonumental, but the position is often qualified in Walcott's work, where "statues themselves would choose life over Art." That brief statement from "A Propertius Quartet" suggestively recalls that "Art" (recast, perhaps, as "art") has the power to chastise and correct itself. For now, I'll let it stand as warrant for the multiple, masterful ways in which Walcott conceives and makes a revised and lowercase commemorative art adjusted to human, natural, and supernatural scales. His more humble, provisional monuments memorably stake their claims—but in a register where the truth is multiple and varies, and permanence is temporary.[12]

Walcott likes the figure of the rower, who moves on while facing back, and as I move on, I want to look back at Walcott's suspicions of monumentality once more. In remarks on literary reputation, Walcott suggests that he not only dislikes conventional monuments but also fears he might become one. Fame immortalizes poets by turning them into statues. The transformation might be welcome after death, but Walcott thinks the change is disastrous if courted too self-consciously in life. For living poets, fame is like being turned to stone or buried alive; the poems go morbidly stiff alongside. That's why Walcott praises minor poets; we love them "mainly because they're not posing for their busts." By contrast, poets too sure they're major writers have "edges of hardening marble," the "immortalized lineaments" of bards. Walcott commends Frost for fighting off his "petrifaction into a monument." He compliments Lowell and his deliberately broken, self-disruptive work for refusing "to be embalmed by fame."

But Walcott uses sculptural terms in praise as well as condemnation; here, statues are modeled, carved, and damaged as they're named. Lowell doesn't "sweep the fragments off the floor . . . and show you only the finished sculpture," Walcott writes; "you see the armature, the failed fragments, the revisions, the compulsions," the "deliberate, wide cracks in his technique." Walcott fractures his own techniques as well, along with the sculptural or monumental forms and functions his poetry sometimes undertakes. His aim is to forestall their calcification and his own. (No wonder the tutelary visitor in Walcott's poem "The Hotel Normandie Pool" is Ovid: the exiled Roman master of metamorphosis—from flesh to stone, from stone to flesh—teaches his craft to an apt apprentice in a scene of instruction only an already masterful initiate could represent.) Walcott can treat his fear of fame lightly. Speaking at the University of Milan not long after being awarded the Nobel Prize and pictured on a postage stamp, he described with mock horror the experience of "turning into a very minor monument" and feeling the "concrete" creep over his flesh. I suppose the joke's diminishments ("minor," "concrete") reveal and exorcise desire as well as dread, and express the proper modesty of well-earned pride, but even in jest Walcott won't risk a claim to marble or bronze. (However, in Castries, on St. Lucia, they did rename Columbus Square for him.)

Meanwhile, Walcott's strategies for avoiding the hardened postures of fame no more limit him to minor efforts than they limit Lowell or Frost. I've called Walcott ambitious. He is, but there's a fairer way to put it: Walcott's greatness, as he said of Frost's, is a matter "not of ambition but vocation." He eventually reaches high and far enough to dismantle and remodel the monument of epic, but (as the paired infinitives convey) that doesn't sentence him to petrifaction. He affirmed that Lowell, in taking on and rewriting the voices of poets "he loved and unashamedly envied," could "inhabit each statue down the pantheon of the dead and move his hand in theirs." Walcott's hand moves warmly in cold, "already statued" hands as well, including Homer's and Dante's. Perhaps in the end, terms like *minor* and *major, modest* and *ambitious,* even *living* and *dead* dissolve and run together. As Walcott says, "Poetry is a narrow spring, the mountain-cold brook of Helicon, and it is not its narrowness that matters but the crystalline, tongue-numbing cold of its freshness, which in the largest works still glitters like an unpolluted spring."[13] Walcott's own large work both taps and freshens the flow.

Before I consider the epic recastings of Walcott's *Omeros* and the reworking of monumental images in some of his essays, I need to explore at some length two overlapping matters that contribute to those revisions. One is Walcott's thinking about literary influence and its companion categories: apprenticeship, imitation, originality, and intertextuality. The other is the treatment of the art-reality relationship in his work (where, since the supposedly sealed compartments leak, their interplay turns out to be both juicily indeterminate and a citric spurt—I mean spur—to composition). Both matters help to define and redefine Walcott's most major and monumental vocational aspiration: accurately to record and commemorate Caribbean people and places.

As most of his many fine critics observe, Walcott's Caribbean context gives the always vexed question of artistic influence unusually intense political and cultural importance in his work. At the same time, the poet's struggle to find a voice while going to school to potent ancestral voices (Yeats called their monuments the only singing school there is) is strenuous everywhere, and Walcott takes up the issue of influence in general as well as "local" terms. Precedent and inheritance affect every aspect of writing, from diction and rhythm to figure and trope, subject and theme, genre and form. And every literary decision involves negotiations between linked acts of affiliation and defection, neither of which can ever be pure or complete. As Walcott said in an interview, "there's nothing without a predecessor in literature, no matter how minimal." Walcott thinks this situation makes imitation inevitable for writers and other artists, and as much a resource as a hindrance. He comments on the circumstances often: sometimes in the form of description ("the more you imitate when you're young, the more original you become"), sometimes as advice ("Young poets should have no individuality. They should be total imitators, if they want to be masters"), and sometimes as diatribe ("Fear of imitation obsesses minor poets"; "Originality is the obsession of ambitious talent. Contemptible from early on and insufferable in the young"). Walcott was quietly scathing about the student who seemed sure that poetry "progresses" by junking its inheritance and therefore expressed surprise that Walcott sometimes uses rhyme. Walcott's dry dismissal: "It's like saying, 'By the way, your piano has eighty-eight keys.'"

Those sometimes cantankerous remarks imply conservative respect for the monuments of inherited traditions, although their emphasis on youthful imitation as a stage on the way to achieving mastery complicates their stance. As to stances, Walcott chided critics who condemned Ted Hughes's "mineral strength" as "posturing"; he said, "one might as well accuse Stonehenge of having a stance." But accusations aside, monuments do take positions, and Walcott thinks strong artists continue to imitate throughout their careers. Meanwhile, Walcott often draws his imitative model of artistic apprenticeship from the history of painting, and from his own experience of being taught to paint by his St. Lucian mentor Harold Simmons: "you copy the great draughtsmen because they themselves did . . .

The old masters made new masters by the discipline of severity." At times, Walcott thinks of painters and poets as members of guilds, praising a medieval (and in some ways postmodern) ideal of communitarian artistic anonymity over more romantic and modern emphases on individual and "idiosyncratic genius." But Walcott's version of imitation is never a matter of copying alone, much less an end in itself. As with assimilation in Walcott's definition, for him, imitation always involves invention and disruption as well as obedience. It can be individualistic and assertive, even rebellious, especially in the context of Caribbean political and cultural situations. I'll turn to that cluster of connections shortly. First, though, I want to notice Walcott's paradoxical aesthetic sense that imitation better obeys tradition by renovation than replication.

In a 1990 interview, Walcott recalled his earliest attempts to write, when he filled his exercise book with imitations of modern poets. He says of those apprentice verses, "because I treated them as poems I was recreating, I never felt that they were anything else but original. I knew they were imitations, but I had a sense of original excitement in the imitation." In just such ways, the usually opposed categories of originality and imitation or innovation and tradition interpenetrate in Walcott's commentary and conversation. For instance, he writes that, for Philip Larkin, artistic development "lay not in metrical experiment, or varieties of stanzaic design . . . but in concentration on the shifts and pauses possible within the pentameter." Larkin's achievement was not to break the pentameter (as the rebellious Pound had tyrannically commanded) nor to condemn its "melody as archaic," but rather to explore "the possibility of its defiant consistency, until technical mastery became freshness." Walcott's acknowledgment that Pound constitutes an alternative tradition against which Larkin rebels adds its own consistency-defying complication here, but Walcott typically prefers developments that refresh tradition from within to the violent breaks from continuity that avant-gardes promote. For him, works of art create their meanings—and give pleasure—precisely by combining endorsement with upheaval, the looked for with the unforeseen. He remarks on the satisfactions of formal verse: "Stanzaic structure creates anticipation; and the verbal music, by its chords, its elisions, its caesuras, delights the ear when expectation is confirmed, but with additional surprise."[14]

As I've said before, Walcott's ideas about artistic influence and imitation take on special political and cultural resonance in the contexts of the Caribbean and of postmodern and postcolonial situations. That resonance is particularly audible in Walcott's understanding and practice of intertextuality, to use the critical jargon he sidesteps nimbly. In the chapter on Bishop, I quote Barbara Johnson's definition of the term. She calls it one of the many ways a text has of being "traversed by otherness." That's well phrased and clearly describes literary works that use textual references to complicate, chasten, and decenter their presumptions to originality, authority, and authorship. But it's vital to emphasize that in Walcott's case (as in much of the best postcolonial writing), intertextual traversing or transgression moves both ways, with later texts boldly appropriating, correcting, and renovating earlier ones as well as modestly or otherwise admitting to reliance on or relationship with them. As a result, conventional ideas of artistic originality and imitation—and political and cultural notions of priority, privilege, proprietorship, and debt along with them—are reconsidered, queried, and revised in Walcott's work rather than either "conservatively" enforced or "radically" reversed. Meanwhile, by whatever name we choose—echo, quotation, or paraphrase; intertextuality, allusion, or appropriation—Walcott's writing is unusually dense with explicit, even insistent references to other writing (including his own), as well as to painting and film, and, as we've seen, to sculptural and architectural monuments.

Walcott's early poems frequently recall and refigure Defoe's *Robinson Crusoe,* for instance, making much of the bereft and burdened state its hero suffers both because and although he carries the cargo (that is, the baggage) of his wrecked but well-stocked ship—and of his British and European heritage, including slavery. References to the Bible and Shakespeare (*The Tempest* and *Othello,* but many other plays and poems as well), and to writing from many periods, cultures, and canons appear remarkably often in Walcott's verse, as indicated by this long but hardly exhaustive list of writers he cites: Sophocles, Horace, Virgil, and Catullus; Langland, Marlowe, and Nashe; Milton, Browne, and Donne; Blake, Byron, Wordsworth, and Keats; Melville and Whitman; Tennyson and Arnold; Yeats, Joyce, and Synge; Pasternak and Brodsky; Eliot, Auden, and Lowell; Guillén, Césaire, Carpentier, Naipaul, and Perse; the Mighty Spoiler, the Mighty Sparrow, Bob Marley, and the Beatles. Walcott's plays are similarly referential; in them, to take only a very few examples, Aristophanes and Aeschylus encounter "conteur" tricks and West

Indian and African myths, Tirso de Molina's Spanish Don Juan finds himself translated to the Caribbean, and Homer's *Odyssey* is brilliantly staged as a partly creole story. Revised Odysseus figures are a staple of Walcott's later work (in "The Schooner *Flight*," for instance), and *Omeros* appropriates, pays homage to, abuses, and revises Homer and Dante.

Particular "intertexts" in Walcott's work, as well as the frequency, extent, and explicitness of textual references there, both honor indebtedness and claim originality and ownership, while they also redefine those terms as relational and interdependent rather than self-contained. The implications for Walcott's Caribbean political and cultural situation are many and intense. Meanwhile, perhaps this is the place to hazard yet another digression, in hopes the impertinence will prove to be pertinent. The male cast of Walcott's references may say as much about the canon presented to his generation as it does about him: he was born in 1930 and completed graduate work at the University of the West Indies in 1954. However, episodes reflecting women's wrongful subjugation and their cultural value appear forcefully in *Omeros* and in Walcott's stage version of *The Odyssey*. The latter is especially notable for its multicultural transformations ("Blind" Billy Blue is a black storyteller; Eurycleia is a patois-speaking Egyptian; Odysseus' descent into the underworld is enabled by an Afro-Caribbean Shango rite; and Penelope's fidelity is Rastafarian "rock-steady") as well as for its de-emphasis of the original epic's stress on violent revenge in favor of the arguably more "feminine" virtues of peace and reconciliation.

Similarly, Achille's dream-journey to Africa in *Omeros* celebrates an Afrocentric element often downplayed in Walcott's earlier work. It respects the longing in the Caribbean and elsewhere to recover roots brutally severed by slavery's forced migration. At the same time, though, because Achille's encounter with his African past both revives him *and* sends him back to his actual home in the Caribbean, his journey honors the desire to restore black heritage without wholly reversing Walcott's distrust in myths of return to origins. Walcott thinks origins are always multiple and never, as it were, "original." Moreover, a purely black version of West Indian identity would violate Walcott's own racial inheritance and the racial reality of many island people, as well as his hopes for what he considers the noble West Indian "experiment of multi-national concentration in small spaces"—as on Trinidad, for instance, with its black, East Indian,

Chinese, and other populations: Walcott mainly lived there from 1959 through the mid-1970s. Such matters reflect Walcott's idealistic sense that hybridity is congruent with a common humanity underlying undeniable differences. He told Anthony Milne, "I don't think anyone is going to keep the artist from having a universal type of mind." Writers and critics wholly convinced of the values of identity politics will disagree. Meanwhile, Walcott called the African experience "historically remote, but spiritually ineradicable."[15]

In his Nobel lecture, Walcott framed the cultural plight of the West Indian artist and of any artist who belongs to an allegedly "marginal" people, group, or place: no matter how monumental the work, his or her every "endeavor is belittled as imitation" by literal or metaphorical colonizers or by the "metropolis" in general. Add to that the real or apparent complicity of much of the islands' cultural inheritance with colonialism, slavery, and other degrading systems that assign and police inferior status, and artistic imitation can seem an unbearable activity for artists in the Caribbean. Yet as we've seen, Walcott is sure that imitation is art's foundation; he thinks there can be no art without it. Walcott can't refute the libel of belittlement by claiming not to imitate at all, then, and he believes self-conscious decisions to follow real or cobbled alternative traditions are much too narrowly defined: they fail his test for maturity (absorbing the features of *every* ancestor) and, in his view, therefore produce sentimental and artificial work. Walcott's solution is characteristic (although *solution* isn't quite the word, since the dilemma doesn't disappear but stays in place as a factor in a newly formed equation). He recalibrates the meaning and value of imitation so that instead of insuring belittlement it warrants pride. This involves what Walcott calls "cunning assimilation," the ability of "the tribe in bondage" to imitate the monuments of imposed traditions in ways that simultaneously borrow, challenge, and change their values. The result is transfiguration, as the tribe renews received traditions to make them its own (in a creole process without any visible origin or end).

Cunning assimilation is a frequent feature of Walcott's verse. In the early poem "Origins," for instance, he appropriates Old World myths and converts them to New World terms: Hermes' snake-wound staff is "rechristened" as a constrictor coiled around a mangrove trunk, Arion's dolphin becomes a tropical dorade, and the Mediterranean sibyl is transformed into a black Caribbean woman, with frangipani as her sign of prophetic power. Those imitative relocations "naturalize" myth without stilling its resonance; they use likeness against belittlement without eliding difference. Something similar is at work in the later poem "Names." European colonizers in the West Indies used the word *bays,* which came into English from the Old French term for a partly enclosed space. In the French patois of St. Lucia, bay became *baie-la.* Those facts have ironic implications for ideas about linguistic purity and priority (and for politics, given French and English battles in the Caribbean). Walcott sums up the matter this way: "the names held," but the "African acquiesced, / repeated, and changed them." The intertwining in all of this of obedience with rebellion, similarity with difference, and continuity with alteration is Walcott's affirmative version of linguistic, cultural, and poetic assimilation: a re-creation that embraces the monumental past but isn't engulfed by it. As he says, "you cannot embrace without imitation." Imitation alters what it holds.

Of course, the political realities of Caribbean life in Walcott's time make his strategy of revaluing imitation in order to defend West Indian art and artists against belittlement less comfortable and less comfortably acquiescent than I may have made it sound. This is so in terms of the former colonial's relation to the former colonizer *and* in terms of internal postcolonial Caribbean cultural debates. I begin with the first. Having said that embrace requires imitation, Walcott adds: "The trouble with that is that when the empire does it, it is known as acquisition and when it is done by colonials it is know as imitation [in the belittling sense]. The amorality of that is absurd." Walcott frequently uses the vocabulary of theft to describe the Caribbean artist's situation. It expresses his anger at the irrational injustice of imperial claims to exclusive rights to own and evaluate; it also becomes a weapon or (better) tool in his armory-workshop of insurgence by artistic means: "Empires are smart enough to steal from the people they conquer. They steal the best things. And the people who have been conquered should have enough sense to steal back." Walcott thinks rebellions begin with "forged or stolen" implements, and he often depicts his taking and taking back of what's already his as piracy, a tactic neatly aligned with the history of buccaneers in the Caribbean and, in natural history, the presence there of frigate birds, those magnificent aerial marauders Walcott much admires.

In *Another Life,* his West Indian imitation and revision of Wordsworth's *Prelude,* Walcott records his call to poetic vocation. An act of theft is central: again, it sharply accuses colonial and other masters of using power, position, and wealth to deprive their fellows of things (including art) that everyone ought to share; again, it acquits itself by converting poverty to wealth and reinterpreting appropriation as the restoration of rightful inheritance. "I had entered the house of literature as a houseboy, / filched as the slum child stole, as the young slave appropriated / those heirlooms temptingly left / with the Victorian homilies of *Noli tangere*." Ecstasy and communion accompany the burglary—although (and this is typical of Walcott's way of handling crucial moments in his work) their nature and meaning vary between the extremes of ridiculousness and sublimity. When he describes himself and his partner in the righteous "crime" of stealing back as being "lit" (his companion, by the way, is his boyhood friend, the painter Dunstan St. Omer, called Gregorias in the poem), he represents them as both the exalted light of their world and merely drunk, although (and, yes, it takes several "althoughs" to swallow the many intoxicating rounds Walcott puts down) they're drunk on the liquor of inspiration and craft as well as rum.

The language of theft concentrates Walcott's several strategies for transforming rage at colonial insult and deprivation into recovered pride and ownership, and for doing so without abandoning or destroying "heirlooms" (or monuments) in revenge, since, to repeat, in Walcott's view inheritance is the ground of imitation, and imitation (including revision) is the place where art and culture begin and the method by which they persist (that is, it's no just cause for belittlement). In the sometimes heated context of postcolonial Caribbean cultural politics, some have judged those strategies insufficient or merely wrong, and Walcott has sometimes been accused of not being radical enough. He's firm in response. I can't adjudicate the issues: I share Walcott's perspective on them, but what matters here is the additional light his responses shed on why and how he dismantles and rebuilds both conventional monuments and monumental conventions. Walcott suspects that much of what's called radical in art (and sometimes in politics as well) is a form of obedience or complicity. He says that "those who break a tradition first hold it in awe," that those who openly fight tradition "perpetuate it," that "revolution is a filial impulse." He thinks radical rejections can make colonial or postcolonial literature pietistic, ready to "accuse great art of feudalism and excuse poor art as suffering." As we've seen in many other forms, Walcott rejects simple repetitions of the past. (Imitation without revision is feudal: slavery at worst, at best a juvenile phase of apprenticeship.) He rejects radical breaks from the past as well. (Although founded on suffering, those breaks are variously impossible, naïve, or violent and vengeful.) Walcott is attracted to visions of the Americas as a brave New World free of the European past, for instance, but his American novelty is the already inscribed one of a "second Eden." The figure who connects his early revisions of Crusoe to his later versions of Odysseus is a specifically postlapsarian Adam, wiser as well as fallen. In Walcott's view, the art of the New World doesn't pretend to "innocence." Like Caribbean fruits, its savor is acid and sweet; "the tartness of experience" flavors it. These opinions and assertions are articles of faith. They underlie Walcott's bracing definition of poetry as more a matter of "remaking" than making: as "perfection's sweat . . . fresh as the raindrops on a statue's brow." In that sculptural figure, monuments are demoted but refreshed and not discarded. Meanwhile, as to Walcott's radicalism, perhaps the artistic revolution he successfully exports to the empire and beyond should qualify. Walcott redefines every culture, language, and art as a continuous activity of grateful imitation, creative invention, and rebellious revision; this makes the entire human enterprise a creole; it gives pride of place to island practices previously condescended to or despised as derivative, impoverished, and corrupt. (Although, at the same time, the transformation Walcott offers is nonhierarchical, shifting, and never permanent, since creoles are always being creolized.) I'd call the revolution quiet, except, as Walcott says, "We like we noise."[16]

Another matter important to Walcott's revisions of monuments and monumentality is his persistent worrying of the congruities, conflicts, and contradictions involved in the relationship of art works to reality. Beginning with his earliest work and continuing throughout his career, Walcott explores (as in "Tarpon," for instance) how art's desire for permanence falsifies the world it represents by substituting synthetic forms for natural, living ones that endlessly change in continuous cycles of growth and decay (of growth as decay as growth). For example, the image of amber appears repeatedly in *Another Life*. At times, it celebrates the innovative varnish used by Italian Renaissance masters to heighten and conserve their paintings' colors. But the same image recalls the fossilized resin that kills the insects it preserves. (Amber keeps them looking as if they were alive. I suppose my phrasing it that way is pedantic, but the echo of Browning's "My Last Duchess," where art and permanence and murder unite, and where painting and bronze combine, seems right.)

A youthful romance is idealized elsewhere in *Another Life*. Walcott recalls a particularly intense moment when the beauty of his lover's "sunburnt nape" and laughing voice seemed to transform their entire world into a timeless monumental frieze: "stone hands, stone air, / stone eyes, from which, // irisless, we stare, / wishing the sea were stone, / motion we could not hear." This is a classic rendition of action experienced as stasis, but by turning sound and sight and touch to stone, it chillingly betrays the warmth of voice and flesh it means to praise. Of course, Walcott sometimes attacks architecture and sculpture precisely to protect poetry and painting from the charge of petrifaction he often levels at the former and arguably more monumental pair, but it's a distinction he typically can't maintain, and the desire to depict in stone or words or paint, to make of two living bodies "one body of immortal metaphor" typically comes to this: "The hand she held already had betrayed / them by its longing for describing her." The epigraph to Book One of *Another Life* (borrowed from Malraux) makes a similar point about the "noble treachery of art"; it says artists are more moved by works of art than by the people, objects, and events they portray—as least at first.

On the other hand, while it divorces art from life, *Another Life* also affirms that it was exactly when Walcott "fell in love with art" that "life began"—including a broader, deeper (livelier) access to island places and people beyond somewhat cloistered Castries and the "standard" English-speaking middle class to which Walcott was born. I'll return to this matter in its own terms soon. First, I want to mention the effect of Walcott's response to the art-reality relationship on his view of poetic style. At the levels of subject, theme, and technique, debates about the respective values of baroque and plain styles appear often in his verse (perhaps mirroring his eventual decision to paint in watercolor rather than more "rhetorical" oil). In "Islands," for example, he describes his desire to write verse "crisp as sand, clear as sunlight, / Cold as the curled wave, ordinary / As a tumbler of island water." Elsewhere he hopes for "a style past metaphor," for pages "plain as a bleaching bedsheet under a gutter- / ing rainspout," for a carpentered craft shaping strokes of sound as clean as wood coils scrolling off a shaving plane. Those sensuously chaste descriptions nearly beget what they conjure, but they remain in the optative mood, more wished for than achieved, and their compilation of detail and ornament keeps the baroque in play.

A passage in "The Gulf" captures the complications: "All styles yearn to be plain / as life," it says, and the deftly managed enjambment implies how intricate a plainness that yearning might demand. As with the terms of the art-reality relationship, Walcott can't or won't (and shouldn't dare) resolve those matters. Like the antimonumental views that cross his impulse to commemorate, they're the springs that generate his work, his fundamental resource—as are two other categories where he doesn't choose from competing possibilities but uses any and all of them as needed: the many registers of English and other languages available in the Caribbean, and the oral and scribal emphases to which poetry has access. (Of those, Walcott says in an essay, "Poetry is speech, but it is also writing"; these vital lines from "The Schooner *Flight*" confirm their oneness and their difference: "I am satisfied / if my hand gave voice to one people's grief.") A final point about the art-reality relationship in Walcott's work: not only do art works lovingly falsify the world in the always somewhat monumental act of trying to make it permanent, but the world itself never comes to us naked to be known; it's always seen through veils, the filters, for instance (are they philters, too?), of works of art. For Walcott, the sky is always Canaletto's sky, or someone else's; "that empty bench Van Gogh's."[17]

The strands I've been fingering are knotted in Walcott's work. As he writes in *Midsummer,* "the lines I love have all their knots left in." Still, some lines bind without too much entanglement. For Walcott, poetry is a profoundly spiritual calling. He said once, "I have never separated the writing of poetry from prayer. I have grown up believing it is a vocation, a religious vocation." In *Another Life,* Walcott's election of poetry (or its election of him) is presented as a conversion. A solemn vow designates his (and St. Omer's) vocational duty: "we would never leave the island / until we had put down in paint, in words," its "neglected" landscape and people. But even untangled lines have twists and turns. The word *neglected* implies a people and place not yet properly recorded in language or paint, and the Caribbean's relative freedom from artistic representation at the time of Walcott's youth is an important aspect of the elation he feels in taking up his life's work: the powerfully felt obligation and privilege to create a Caribbean art to commemorate West Indian natural and human beauty. Walcott's entire career reflects that commitment. To take a single instance, it appears in his cautious but passionate answer to an interviewer's question. Asked to define his "major theme," Walcott said, "When you talk like that, you talk in capital letters, right? But this thought here is in lowercase, and it's true. The Caribbean people have a dignity, a suppleness and a beauty that I would like to articulate."

On the other hand, as I hope I've made clear, Walcott's conception of the West Indies' "newness" to representation has a special cast: it's less a matter of being wholly without depiction than of being always already inscribed yet open to revision. Walcott speaks of Caribbean literature's "great joy in making a world which so far, up to then, had been undefined," but he also sees the Caribbean as simultaneously "old" and "new." Part of what he means is expressed in this remark: "My generation of West Indian writers has felt such a powerful elation at having the privilege of writing about places and people for the first time and, simultaneously, having behind them the tradition of knowing how well it can be done." Newness, then, involves indebtedness (and its companions, gratitude and grievance, since some inherited patterns of excellence also carry with them imperial, colonial, and racist assumptions). For Walcott, the Caribbean's relative "unwrittenness" is accompanied by pre-texts and pretexts, models to be followed, refuted, and rewritten. His inspired excitement in his island situation comes in part from the fact that old and new can be reversed and intertwined there: "We were blest with a virginal, unpainted world / with Adam's task of giving things their names, / . . . with nothing so old / that it could not be reinvented." Adam's presence in the formulation anchors novelty in precedent; reinvention means the anchor can be weighed.

Caribbean freshness is thrilling, and Walcott sometimes debases monuments to praise it: "I didn't want to be in Europe and write poems about magnificent monuments. I just felt that you had to find not magnificence, but the reality of the beauty of your immediate surroundings." He adds elsewhere, "I think it has to do with the sensation of freshness . . . [Y]ou're stepping outside into the streets without monuments, without cathedrals, and museums." The effect of this, however, is not (or not only) to abuse the forms and institutions that contain and conserve the past. When read in the Caribbean, Walcott says, a page of Shakespeare (the most magnificent and monumental bequest the English literary canon

preserves) becomes as fresh as a mango leaf. What this tricky collocation means, I think, is that when Walcott completes his dismantling of monuments something monumental still remains: his
desire to record, articulate, and commemorate his place and people
in the renewed inherited forms of works of art. Meanwhile, given his
deep and abiding distrust of monuments and their artistic, political,
and cultural implications, those works of art encounter extremely
strict regulations. For instance, they have to repay their debts to the
past in a coinage minted from its worn and tarnished metals, yet at
once a counterfeit and perfectly legal tender. Moreover, they have
to commemorate while avoiding monumental falsifications, among
them, the assumption that permanence or perfection exists or can
be attained, the idea that art should master rather than honor life,
and the fallacy that the islands, seas, and people whose endurance,
survival, and grace Walcott loves either need or want his ennoblement and commemoration (especially in the form of monumental
literary works that venerate and immortalize their prideful authors
as much or more than they do their subjects).

Fears that he'll fail to meet such self-imposed restrictions are a
constant feature of Walcott's work and one way he insures his compliance with them. In poem XVI of *Midsummer,* for instance, he
batters the impulse to commemorate by reminding himself that the
dead have "no urge / to be ever-remembered." (Although, in lines
that connect the Caribbean practice of using conch shells to outline graves with the more ancient and monumental-sounding rite
of erecting burial mounds or tumuli, he continues to ponder how
to serve the dead: "our life-long attraction is drawn" to their graves,
he writes, and the mutual adductions in the quoted phrase join the
pairing of antique rituals with new ones to keep the quick in contact
with the dead.) Self-accusations in *Omeros* are harsher, as in this example, where Walcott worries that his literary urge to memorialize is
antiquated—and complicitous both with older imperial politics and
with the neo-imperialism of tourism, which threatens to turn poor
and beautiful places into theme parks or museums that treat inhabitants like exhibits (or insects): "Didn't I want the poor / to stay in the
same light so that I could transfix / them in amber, the afterglow of
an empire, // preferring a shed of palm-thatch with tilted sticks / to
that blue bus-stop?" Even on the celebratory occasion of his Nobel
lecture, Walcott bruised his affectionate recollections of the Antilles
by expressing dread that his words of praise threaten the places he

cares for as much as any bulldozer, "surveyor's string," or blight does, and by insisting that the goal of praise or love or art "is not to hallow or invest the place with anything, not even memory."[18]

Still, however chided and chastened the monumental impulse to remember memorably is in Walcott's work, and despite his many vigorous attacks on monuments, his urge to commemorate persists. We've seen examples already, but Walcott's most convinced and convincing reconception of conventional monuments and monumental conventions appears in *Omeros,* his reimagined epic. Revisions of monumental figures in Walcott's essays forecast and confirm *Omeros's* methods. Revision requires breakage, and the repair of precious objects turns out to be both less and more than perfect restoration. Walcott puts it this way in "The Antilles: Fragments of Epic Memory," his Nobel lecture. "Break a vase," he writes. That makes the damage sound deliberate; let me begin again: "Break a vase, and the love that reassembles the fragments is stronger than that love which took its symmetry for granted when it was whole." This contentedly cracks a range of monumental values, including conventional preferences for originality and wholeness, but it doesn't make a fetish of fragments, and the original object isn't abandoned; it's respected and transformed. Like grout lines in mosaics, glue lines keep the broken parts in view without obscuring the larger picture. The vase remains, but it's altered and improved, more able, it might be said, to encompass breakage as a concomitant of flawed perfection (for Walcott, the only kind there is): "The glue that fits the pieces is the sealing of its original shape. It is such a love that reassembles our African and Asiatic fragments, the cracked heirlooms whose restoration shows its white scars." Like amnesia (the indelible record of the trauma it forgets), those "white" scars heal without erasing the wounding racial history of Caribbean slavery and colonization. (Meanwhile, the plural of *heirlooms* multiplies possible objects and occasions, and the references to Africa and Asia reflect West Indian racial and cultural mosaics.) The passage continues: "This gathering of broken pieces is the care and pain of the Antilles, and if the pieces are disparate, ill-fitting, they contain more pain than their original sculpture, those icons and sacred vessels taken for granted in their ancestral places." The vase is still sacred, an icon (or a monument), but—revised, that is, both damaged and repaired—it accommodates more pain, is more loved (rather than taken for granted or worshipped), and is less hierarchical, less sure of its permanence, and less triumphal than the original sculpture it supplants but doesn't replace. Walcott makes the procedures he's described a model for poetic creation: "Antillean art is this restoration of our shattered histories, our shards of vocabulary, our archipelago . . . And this is the exact process of the making of poetry, or what should be called not its 'making' but its remaking."

This is brilliant writing, in which description does argument's work; it illuminates strategies used throughout *Omeros*. Similar passages elsewhere in Walcott's prose do the same. In the relatively brief but major essay called "The Caribbean: Culture or Mimicry?" for instance (where the subtitle might equally well have been culture *and* mimicry, or culture *as* mimicry), Walcott defends the West Indies against the slander of being cultureless. Some colonial or metropolitan critics assume that because Caribbean culture mimics prior ones it isn't a culture at all. Walcott shows that culture *is* mimicry: a natural act of imagination and design that's endlessly repeated everywhere with always different, always indebted results. Mimicry isn't exact repetition or complete invention; it recalls and renews what it borrows, steals, and inherits. Like imitation properly understood, it shouldn't warrant belittlement, any more than creoles or so-called illegitimacy should. Having affirmed such propositions, Walcott goes on to show, to anyone who still requires proof, how "mimicked" Caribbean achievements in calypso, steel-band music, and Carnival costumes demonstrate the existence and value of West Indian culture.

The discussion of Carnival costumes bears particularly on Walcott's revision of monuments and the monumental. He writes, the "intricate, massive and delicate sculpture" of Carnival costumes is "improvised" without "self-conscious awe" of precedent, "for the simple duplication of ancient sculptures is not enough to make a true Carnival costume." These extravagant homemade costumes sever the conventional connection between monuments and hierarchical ideals of permanence in conflict with life's endless, leveling, generative flow. Not made to last, they're defined instead by "the concept of waste, ephemera," and "built-in obsolescence"—"not the built-in obsolescence of manufacture but of art." These "intricate sculptures" don't seek to conquer time by setting up themselves and their temporary (although also cyclical) values as unalterable and eternal. They respond to natural and ritualistic rhythms connected to the seasons, religion, and art. They create objects that encourage renewed creation through their own eventual displacement. Last year's costumes or sculptures "are discarded as immediately valueless" when Carnival ends at midnight on Shrove Tuesday: "last year's songs cannot be sung this year, nor last year's tunes, and so an entire population of craftsmen and spectators compel themselves to this regeneration."

A similar model for Walcott's revision of monuments (his crafting of forms that include their own decay and disfigurement and undermine the memorial impulse without destroying or giving it up) appears in his Nobel lecture. Like Carnival costumes, the bamboo "sculptures" depicted there aren't the creations of artists in the usual sense; they're crafted by the ordinary extraordinary people Walcott wants to commemorate in art while avoiding the falsifications to which art is heir, especially monumental art. His decision to describe these "ephemeral" objects, and to do so on the exalted (noble) occasion of the Nobel lecture, itself revises conventional monuments, which are usually commissioned from professionals, made of "permanent" materials (bamboo is a grass), and erected by elites to commemorate remarkable individuals or events. The roughly woven sculptures represented here are being prepared for a community reenactment of "Ramleela," a drama based on the Hindu epic, *Ramayana*. More ritual than theater, a fresh expression of persistent faith rather than a self-conscious act of cultural "recovery," "Ramleela" is to be performed on Trinidad by East Indian descendents of people who migrated there to work the cane fields and factories as indentured servants after the emancipation of the slaves. "Under an open shed on the edge of the field, there were two huge armatures of bamboo that looked like immense cages. They were parts of the body of a god, his calves or thighs, which, fitted and reared, would make a gigantic effigy. This effigy would be burnt as a conclusion to the epic." Here again is the "built-in obsolescence not of manufacture but of art," especially of art connected with "ordinary" and communal life and with seasonal and religious rituals maintained through time precisely because they leave room for destruction and rebuilding. It remembers as well as it can (or chooses to), but it also inevitably alters and invents. The Trinidadians performing "Ramleela" don't know India directly; their performance is probably an amalgam, as Walcott's response to it certainly is. Meanwhile, for him this creole mimicry is less at odds with authenticity than it is its properly wobbly signature. A bamboo monument just might serve Walcott's mixed purposes, his wish to monumentalize without being too monumental. Bamboo is a grass, but it's firm enough to last for quite some time. Still, it doesn't presume to be permanent; the present structure is built to be burnt.[19]

The Trinidadian "Ramleela" revises epic and keeps it living; the St. Lucian *Omeros* does likewise. Walcott shares the genius of major artists for parsing and transforming inherited genres. For instance, distressed by the conventions of the "standard elegiac" (which can make solace seem too easy or, much worse, treat deaths as convenient occasions for advancing a poet's career), Walcott vilifies the "neat gravestone elegies / that rhyme our end." But although he compounds the insult (rhyming *end* with *offend*), his aim is to learn a "mocking tolerance" for the mode he abuses but still wants to use. His method (it's a convention itself, a version of "recusatio," the ancient trope of avowal by disavowal Gregson Davis detects in Walcott's work) is to incorporate his objections to the genre in a way that tempers but doesn't silence his doubts—and thereby keeps the elegy a usable poetic kind. In poems for his mother and for Auden, Brodsky, and others, Walcott revises elegies ("our solemn rubbish") in ways that let him go on writing them. In *Omeros,* he does something similar with epic. The poem rejects many of the genre's defining conventions in ways that revile, remember, and rewrite them while revising their values.

For instance, *Omeros* follows the epic requirement to begin dramatically in medias res, but rather than present heroic warrior-kings in glorious and devastating battle it describes ordinary St. Lucian fishermen felling trees to build canoes. This subversively democratizes the aristocratic hierarchies of character and action associated with epic, but it also respectfully borrows (and cunningly filches) some portion of epic grandeur for transferal to its own activities, people, and scenes. At the same time, the splendor of Walcott's St. Lucian characters, events, and settings is clearly their own and needs no imported enhancement or refinement. Such intricacies abound in *Omeros.* Here's another example. Traditional epics are said to subordinate their details to a single, all-important central focus. *Omeros* multiplies subplots and develops them extensively. It moves Philoctetes, a marginal character forgotten in Homer, toward its center, renaming him Philoctete. This is a fundamentally postcolonial maneuver, as the categories "margin" and "center" and the linguistic shift imply, but it's also one with vital precedents in Greek legend and in Sophocles, if not in Homer (the wounded, abandoned Philoctetes must be recovered and recover before the Trojan War can end).

Walcott employs nearly every variety of Caribbean English and St. Lucian French in *Omeros,* thereby challenging the recourse of conventional epic to a single exalted register. It proves that vernaculars (the word has roots in the Latin *verna,* meaning a home-born or native slave) are fully capable of monumental epic sweep; it also shows that dignity is no more the province of a particular vocabulary or set of tropes (formal speeches, catalogues, Homeric similes and epithets—although, of course, Walcott renovates each one of those) than it is the exclusive possession of a few special persons or cultures. On the other hand, as will be obvious, such demonstrations are hardly unprecedented in the history of epic as a genre. Dante's *Comedy,* another refigured resource in Walcott's poem, is written in ordinary Italian and generally thought divine enough, and Walcott's supposedly antiepic use of personal (rather than impersonal) narration, like his inclusion of extensive autobiographical material, has ample epic antecedents, in Wordsworth as well as Dante, for instance. All of this recalls that once-standard versions of epic as a monolithic genre (including Bakhtin's libel of the epic as "monologic") are simply wrong, as recent work on the epic powerfully argues. Walcott's epic revision tells an old story about old stories, then. Revision is itself an epic tradition, and epic, like elegy and every other genre, is malleable and fluid. It creates meaning not by following rigid regulations but by continuing and altering inherited conventions, in the creole pattern of mimicry that characterizes art and culture in general, as Walcott's essays, plays, and poems all show, and as recent postcolonial and other adjustments to canons emphasize.

Walcott's brilliant and extensive imitation of epic in *Omeros* (remembering that, for Walcott, to imitate means to recall, reject, confirm, and refute, to honor, revile, and revalue) has been well and widely studied. Interpretations of the poem by Rei Terada, Robert D. Hamner, Paula Burnett, Paul Breslin, and Jahan Ramazani can all be recommended, along with the special issue of *South Atlantic Quarterly* dedicated to intertextual perspectives on Walcott's work; I'm indebted to their arguments. But for present purposes I want to concentrate on how the strenuously antimonumental attitudes of Walcott's great poem turn out to serve a forcefully revised but still monumental commemorative impulse. Bishop revises monuments and monumentality by fashioning a virtual artifact of wood; Lowell recasts Saint-Gaudens's famous relief; and Merrill gives voice to ancient bronzes. The revised monument of Walcott's *Omeros* is not a specific object, however; it's *Omeros* itself and the poem's revaluing of epic, literature's most monumental genre and the literary kind most intimately tied to Walcott's monumental task of commemorating his Caribbean people, place, and culture. (The result is also international, of course, and one of the pleasures of Walcott's work is the nonimperial global reach of its creole response to empires of every sort.)

As we've seen, raids on sculptural and architectural monuments and their related institutions (cathedrals, museums) are a staple of Walcott's verse. He dislikes, even detests their pretensions to perfection and permanence, their smugly hierarchical and elitist implications, and their complicity with imperial and colonial attitudes, ideas, and actions. Those attacks are particularly virulent in *Omeros* (although, as usual, they're sometimes tempered by admiration for excellence). They dominate several angry episodes near the center of the book. One, set in a museum that seems to conflate Boston's Museum of Fine Arts with New York's Metropolitan, exhibits several of Walcott's familiar themes. In museums, "Art has surrendered / to History with its whiff of formaldehyde," statues' subjects have suffered "death / by marble," and the statues themselves, like fame, invite the artist-viewer to die. "Art is immortal and weighs heavily on us" not only because it freezes living things in friezes but also because we inevitably see the world through the illuminating *and* distorting lenses it provides. (There's a sense in which nothing is "outside" the museum; every view "is a postcard signed by great names"). Furthermore, those lenses, whether they come from books or paintings, are apt to convey, say, racist attitudes as well as a sense of human dignity (as references to Melville and Winslow Homer in the passage attest.)

Related episodes set in the once imperial capitols of Lisbon, London, and Venice reinforce such matters; they also emphasize art's complicity with empire, as fountains, equestrian bronzes, and marble statues repeat the ancient lie that "power and art" are one and the same. Walcott's correction is scatologically harsh. Preferring the Caribbean (which manages by willed amnesia's remembrance to think of the past "as better forgotten than fixed with stony regret"), he depicts a dirty Old World "permanence." It's deeply cut in stone that slow decay is nonetheless and surely wearing out, as witnessed by the "dreck" under "the scrolled skirts of statues," the "grit" in "stone lions' eyes," the "grime" "in the balls of rearing bronze stallions." (Meanwhile, in London a church-warden in "polished pumps" perversely illustrates a sermon on charity by kicking off the church's steps a ragged poet-beggar who seems to have wandered there from the former Commonwealth; elsewhere in the poem, the U.S. imperial practice of exterminating native peoples is exposed in an extended treatment of the story of Catherine Weldon and the Sioux Ghost Dance.)

One seemingly minor result of all of this is Walcott's announcement of a preference not for statues but for "the bird in the statue's hair." I stress it to recall once more that when monumental art is dismantled in Walcott's work something of monumental art remains: the statue isn't razed; it stands, if only as a roosting place for the living bird. Similarly, Walcott cracks but doesn't topple epic; his revised version commemorates St. Lucia and St. Lucians (and does so humbly, without claiming to ennoble them or, by doing that, to elevate its author or itself). As I've said before, this is an effect of the entire book as it strikes and furls, patches, bends, shakes out, and then sheets-in the genre's sail. I'll mention a very few of its myriad invigorating details to illustrate. One of the larger strategies of *Omeros* involves two of its ancillary but important characters: the expatriate British former sergeant-major called Major Plunkett and the version of Derek Walcott who participates in the poem but (like Dante in the *Comedy*) is slightly less savvy than its author. Both admire their St. Lucian neighborhood and neighbors, especially as represented in the person of the beautiful Helen (who is splendidly herself and also a kind of stand-in for the island sometimes known as the Helen of the Antilles because of its natural beauty and its role as occasion and prize in epic battles fought for her by the "thousand ships" of French and British colonial navies). Plunkett and Walcott seek to honor and commemorate St. Lucia and its people, Plunkett by discovering and inventing a history worthy of the island and of Helen and her companions, Walcott by writing a relatively conventional epic filled with Homeric parallels. The poem lets those projects go forward at length and then sharply cuts them off because they're based on "forged" coincidences inappropriate to Helen's "ebony" head; she, like all the island's people, has no need for the historian's or the poet's remorse or elevation. The alternative Walcott imagines and pleads for is beautiful and moving. He asks, "Why not see Helen /

as the sun saw her," "swinging her plastic sandals on that beach alone, / as fresh as the sea wind?" He prays to enter the "light beyond metaphor." But those ideals aren't possible in an actual poem, or in human experience. The obstacle can cause disgust—anger at "All that Greek manure under the green bananas." Still, manure nourishes roots as it rots, and having raised a stink is one more way Walcott's epic restrains pretension and excess while doing epic's noble commemorative work. In the words of "The Spoiler's Return," "I decompose, but I composing still."

Similar effects occur in Walcott's treatment of the Hector-Achille agon in *Omeros*. The convincing use of these ordinary St. Lucian men as heroes domesticates and pastoralizes epic without yielding any of epic's capacity both to resolve the most dreadful disputes and to show that no resolution is ever perfect or lasts for very long. (Think of the *Iliad,* where Achilles eventually yields his maniacal rage to pity and takes in his hands the hands of Hector's father, the grieving enemy who's son he's killed, but where both the continuing Trojan War and Achilles' emblematic shield demonstrate that the battle between chaos and order is beyond any human control and goes on forever.) In *Omeros,* Hector takes Helen from Achille. The two friends are estranged, and Hector dies when his taxi crashes, leaving Helen pregnant with his child. In a poignant scene near the poem's conclusion, Achille puts a wedge of dolphin fish "he's saved for Helen in Hector's rusty tin," showing his healing acceptance of her and his dead friend's baby as his own. Nonetheless, as the poem ends, the sea is "still going on," as are the world and its quarrels, including the sorrows awaiting St. Lucia. The forces of tourism and capitalist economics are changing the island: Hector is killed because he's speeding to make more cash; international factory trawlers are depleting the stocks of fish Achille's traditional ways depend on. Meanwhile, by means of a potion and ritual derived from African roots and mimicked by St. Lucian creole-speakers on this one-time French and British, now independent, island, Philoctete's dreadful wound is healed. It leaves a vivid scar.

Perhaps Walcott would accept these words as an all but final comment on his accomplishment in *Omeros;* they're his own, from near the end of *Tiepolo's Hound:* "There is another book . . . , the one / I have tried hard to write, but let this do; / let gratitude redeem what lies undone." Whatever is undone in *Omeros,* gratitude redeems it. The cracked and chastened epic monument the poem so gingerly erects (it might be crafted of bamboo; it certainly reflects art's built-in and therefore nourishing obsolescence—more manure to nurture other, and different, works of art) firmly commemorates Walcott's place and people and will stand for quite a while. I hope those slightly muted words respect the yearning in Walcott's later poems for humble anonymity and the disappearance of the too-insistent self. Less fatalistic than anything in Homer, *Omeros* ends in neither triumph nor despair. It has balance without contentment, if balance is the word for something that shifts so restlessly back and forth. Its beauty is "deciduous"; its leaves or pages fall, but (this is the Caribbean) they don't go all at once and can be cyclically replaced, in the sort of repetition with difference Walcott dramatizes everywhere. In the essay "What the Twilight Says," Walcott describes "the always surprisingly stale smell of the sea." Conventional monuments seem stale in the West Indies, but in the same way that Walcott's magical phrase converts staleness to freshness by means of repeated surprise, *Omeros* refreshes literature's monumental epics for Caribbean and contemporary use.[20]

5

Seamus Heaney
"The Grauballe Man," "In Memoriam Francis Ledwidge," and Others

Conventional monuments are rare in Seamus Heaney's poems, but memorial objects and processes crowd them. Those statements criss-cross. I'll try three takes to explain them. First: Heaney founds his surest, sweetest trust on commemorative footings he jackhammers out and then repours in alternate forms he's scoured, flushed, and refurbished. Second: When Paul Muldoon classed poets as cheeses, he named Heaney a "monumental / Emmenthal." Nourishing and ordinary, good Swiss, like the monuments Heaney savors, is firm but not hard, full of holes yet still substantial. Third: When Henri Cole plied Heaney with an interviewer's ploy, asking what building he'd be if he could be one, Heaney played along and named Rome's Pantheon. That nearly two-thousand-year-old structure is sturdily monumental, but it has a fluid history. There's a hole in it, as well.

Heaney approaches commemorative procedures as a builder, wrecker, and renovator all at once, since in his eyes commemorations comprise conflicting meanings. They're associated with his warmest memorial urges, for instance: impulses to cherish, preserve, and venerate. But they're also associated with threatening aspects of his local and larger culture: with the occluded history of British imperialism in Ireland, say, or with republican and loyalist foundation myths, penitential practices within the church, and cults of suffering and sacrifice at the root of civilization. They're associated, too, with what Heaney sometimes thinks of as facile or evasive rites of consolation in his verse—and in art in general. Those intersections school Heaney to cast a cold eye on commemorations, exposing them as half-truths at best, at worst as frauds that incite or connive with violence. Still, just as a warm eye needn't be wet, a cold one needn't freeze. Heaney responds to chilling revelations about memorial processes by revising their objects, activities, and terms and warming to them once again. His choice of the Pantheon as architectural totem can indicate how monuments are placed (and displaced) in his work—especially because the Pantheon's long survival as a monument has involved outlasting, altering, and multiplying rather than repeating or otherwise confirming its original significance.

Massive and ancient, the Pantheon was built to perform the sort of culture-defining, culture-perpetuating work traditional monuments exemplify (and Heaney razes and reconstructs). It commemorates an earlier temple erected on the site but destroyed by fire; its mutually reinforcing architectural, religious, and political statements proclaim the empire's world view (or used to). But other features of the Pantheon (quirks in its original design, perhaps, but especially its history after Rome's decline) undermine and reconfigure monumental conventions. The Pantheon was erected early in the second century, when the empire's wealth and physical extent were greatest. Its decorations displayed Rome's riches; its outsized symmetrical grandeur asserted her power and scope. The Pantheon also depicted an imperial vision of reality. As Spiro Kostof explains, images of the gods and of deified Roman rulers shared the Pantheon's rotunda; Hadrian, its builder, delivered judgments there. Those features presented the state, the building, and the cosmos as mutually reinforcing analogues. Each had varying parts but functioned harmoniously under the aegis of a single unifying power: the emperor, the building's ingenious statics, and the heavens' firm design. By such means, the Pantheon expressed an immutable closed system.

The Pantheon was sited to face the coastal highway and to captivate visitors as well as the local population. Originally, its vast, unprecedented dome—unique for centuries and a metonym of sorts for the empire's broad umbrella—was concealed behind a conventional temple front and porch. (Street level then was considerably lower; when the building was approached, the dome's exterior curve was out of sight.) A first-time viewer's expectation of something familiar, even commonplace, was deliberately aroused by the standard facade, then shattered, then replaced by the elegant interior (which, like a gloved fist, concealed in its turn the massive supporting walls). The whole experience might have felt like an idealized version of conquest by Rome: the shock of being overwhelmed by superior size and force undergoing a gradual conversion from awe to acceptance as the rights and virtues of an irresistible order (backed by military power) sunk in. It's the sort of sweetened strong-arm tactic at which monuments and empires excel—and that Heaney, steeped in Irish colonial history and Ulster's "postcolonial" troubles, sees through, subverts, and revises (altering means and ends).

Of course, Heaney might well admire the Pantheon despite its original message: the building's adequacy to its cultural moment, its brilliant design and craftsmanship, its interplay of bulk and airiness certainly recommend it. But I think the Pantheon draws Heaney especially because by now it tells not one but so many competing stories, and particularly because it tells them in spite of its seemingly monologic monumental and imperial intentions. Some of those stories might go back to Hadrian himself. It's tempting to interpret the Pantheon's oculus (its light-giving, weight-bearing eye—the hole in its dome) as puncturing the monolithic structure it illuminates, or to observe that the temple's trick facade expresses disruptive wit and whimsy as well as immovable weight. We might read the building's odd quotation as an intertextual gesture teasing as it honors Roman love for ancestral precedent and mocking the monumental claim to permanence it also extends: the Pantheon's pediment cites the maker's inscription carved on its burned-out predecessor; credit for Hadrian's building seems transferred to or borrowed from Marcus Agrippa, whose earlier temple had failed. Those interpretations might jostle the Pantheon's stability, but it's likely they're too contemporary. The ancient experience probably differed. The oculus and facade are clearly functional; the bow to Agrippa may have seemed modest—or a politically adroit move to fend off charges of excessive pride or to invoke the great Augustus (Agrippa was his minister and son-in-law). The cultural relativism of those remarks makes a point of its own, I suppose, but however such matters are judged, changes in the use and meaning of the Pantheon since the fall of imperial Rome refute its monumental claims to singularity and permanence in ways amenable to Heaney, as a simple list can show.

In 609, Pope Boniface IV consecrated the polytheistic Pantheon as a Roman Catholic church devoted to a single (triune) god. In 663, the Byzantine emperor stripped the gilded tiles from the church's roof. In 735, Pope Gregory III reroofed it in lead. In the fourteenth century, with the papacy in Avignon, the temple became a fortress—and a market for poultry or fish. In 1524, at his own request, the

Renaissance master Raphael was interred there. In 1632, Pope Urban VIII melted down the bronze from the Pantheon's portico to make the Bernini baldacchino in St. Peter's, along with eighty cannon for the Castel' Sant'Angelo. (He also had Bernini top the Pantheon with turrets; those were later judged absurd and taken down.) In the nineteenth century, the Pantheon became the tomb of the newly united Italian state's first kings. And, of course, it remains an architectural marvel, an imperial relic, a consecrated church, and a secular tourist attraction. Those varied uses tell conflicting stories about a number of things: shifting political, religious, and aesthetic codes, for instance; desecration, revision, and restoration as competing responses to cultural heritage; rival public demands for exalted and ordinary structures; the artist's varying role as culture-hero, saint, and patronized servant. Together, they suggest that, whatever its original meaning and purpose, the Pantheon has persisted precisely by being receptive to varied interpretations and by serving multiple, competing, and changing needs. As we'll see, Heaney's flexible poems inherit, dismantle, modify, and reconfigure memorial objects and actions in similar ways.[1]

Homelier structures than the Pantheon are much more common than monuments in Heaney's verse; however obliquely, they also indicate his characteristic attitudes toward commemorative objects and procedures. I'll pursue those indications before discussing Heaney's memorial poems more directly; I'll introduce some of his characteristic methods, contexts, and predilections along the way. Monuments can be viewed either as traps (so that escapes to openness are desired) or as shelters (so that repairs to enclosure are preferred). Openness and enclosure conspire and contend all through Heaney's work. Their encounters are particularly dramatic in the descriptions of roofed and roofless structures in poems in *Seeing Things*. (They quietly recall the Pantheon and its perforated dome.) In the sonnet "The Skylight," for instance, a cozy liking for the nested feel of a tight-roofed upstairs room ("all hutch and hatch" and "tongue-and-groove") is startled by surprise itself: renovation's "held . . . wide open" when the sky is let down through the house's slates. A similar engagement shapes the initial poems of "Squarings." There, too, enclosure is a comfort and a constraint, and openness is fraught with risk but also liberates. The stern command to "Roof it again" is both endorsed *and* challenged by the airy scope of the unroofed walls it wants closed in; stresses (or emphases) slip into and out of formation as demolition and construction variously endanger or exhilarate, sustain or restrict. Similar crossings strain and take the strain in Heaney's commemorative verse.

Roof work plays a role in the radio talk Heaney titled "Something to Write Home About" (so the scribal "marches" the oral). There, he describes how the image of the minor god Terminus was housed in ancient Rome. It was kept on the Capitoline Hill, in Jupiter's Temple. But "the roof above the place where the image sat was open to the sky, as if to say that the god of . . . boundaries . . . needed . . . access to the boundless." Heaney's agile prose puts limitlessness and limits into modifying relationship. (The now-you-see-it-now-you-don't maneuver conveys an atrium's interplay of spaciousness and enclosure; it renders the roof both palpably there and buoyantly nonexistent.) This sleight of hand deftly stages Heaney's sense that contrasting terms retain their distinctness in one another's presence but also interpenetrate and overlap in reciprocally altering exchanges—whether in the roofed and unroofed habitation of Terminus in Rome, or in the region of boundaries everywhere and of every kind (since borders bring into contact the things they separate). Heaney was born and raised in troubled Northern Ireland, a fractured place that, during his lifetime, has often been at something close to war. He knows that commitments to definitive positions (the kind that monuments support) create and confirm communities but also disrupt and destroy them. He knows, too, that negotiations between such commitments can lead to resolution but also prompt or intensify struggle. Perhaps this helps to explain the contradictory, complementary maneuvers Heaney combines in his poems. He presents competing practices and beliefs as participant terms in mutually qualifying, potentially generative borderline relationships; he grants the constituent terms their durable, one-sided, culturally confirming but also destructive individual realities; and he creates and sustains a darkly hopeful imaginative space where the terms, their relationships, *and* the structures that underwrite both might all be scrutinized—a space where new configurations can be proposed and entertained.

Throughout his work (commemorative and otherwise), Heaney constellates autonomous elements in mutually contesting and qualifying patterns. Among those elements are Ireland and England; nature's unrestrained green *pagus* and civilization's lined-page *disciplina;* and (as we've seen) bare walls, tightly stapled roofs, and skylights either open or glassed in. Other important combinations in Heaney's work (they're variously arranged in binary pairs or in triangles and other polygons) include the Irish, English, and Irish-English languages (each of them confirmed and subverted by encounters with other tongues, regional variations, and variant etymological histories or myths)—as well as these competing but not entirely incompatible conjunctions: politics, ethics, and aesthetics; conceptions of poetry as responsible or free (unfettered, governing, or governed); and postures of faithful affiliation to and wayward defection from literary, religious, familial, community, and cultural traditions (or else some shifting stance of obedient rebellion or dissident fealty in between). Those lists could be greatly expanded: by adding the Irish state and the Ulster statelet, for instance, the latter with its unionist, Protestant, and British, and nationalist, Catholic, and Irish permutations. These and other elements bear significantly on Heaney's way with commemorative acts and occasions. For now I want to stress that Heaney gathers competitors and partners into mutually abrading, bracing, and embracing contact in his work, whether they assemble for combat or to dance. Typically, no single party comes away from such encounters wholly smitten or rejected, completely victorious or vanquished. Contrasting claims and categories meet and intersect in the process, but they're neither fully reconciled nor finally sorted out.

All that might seem a formula for stalemate, but Heaney isn't programmatic. He keeps things subject to change—and his attitudes towards things supple. He slips but doesn't destroy the loops and snares (and loopholes) he devises and inherits. His models are more like practices than molds. They include ancient Terminus enforcing private bounds at common borders with an eye on the boundless sky, and modern-day patients of Jung straining for new psychic levels where insoluble conflict can be borne without surrender to either exhaustion or destructive simplifications. Meanwhile, Heaney travels along and veers from the tracks he follows (just as he musters, dismisses, and reconvenes opposing parties and competing perspectives or judgments). He reconfigures elements and relationships he also honors, decries, and deploys. In the demolishing, constructive encounters of his poems, roofs are blown off, nailed down, and opened up as the "earthed and heady" come together and apart.[2]

Closed and open roofs, pierced domes, atriums, and skylights all suggest the sort of riddled commemorative gestures Heaney favors, gestures that revise the memorial patterns they inherit, interrogate as well as ratify their own revisions, and still leave space for reconsideration. Here's a prose example. A moment ago, I used the word *marches* in a way I assume sounds odd outside of Northern Ireland. The usage is borrowed from Heaney. In the radio talk already cited, he notes that Terminus reached Ireland in the word *tearmann* or *termon* (which, in Irish place-names, indicates land set apart for religious applications—say, pasturing the glebe cow or building a church). This seemingly indelible partition reminds Heaney of other divisions inscribed on Ulster soil: for example, the annual Ulster marching season.

Ulster's yearly unionist parades commemorate the 1690 Battle of the Boyne, in which British Protestant forces, led by William of Orange, defeated (also British) Catholic ones arrayed under James. This insured the long British and Protestant hegemony over Ireland that still continues in the north. Descendents of Protestant colonial settlers constitute the majority of Northern Ireland's population. Many are loyal to England; they fear that if Ulster's political affiliation with Britain were dissolved they'd be dominated by the Catholic majority in the south. Their Orange parades have monumental force: they memorialize a past event; they make its outcomes permanent by anchoring current conditions in a verifying precedent and projecting them into the future. The marches bolster unionist identity and foster community pride. Deliberately or not, they also drum ascendancy home in ways that taunt and bully other members of the Ulster populace: the North's minority Catholics. Many in that community are nationalists; they see the Battle of the Boyne as a disaster (the source of their own continuing oppression), and they want Ulster's six counties freed from England and (re)united with the independent Irish nation in the south. In and out of marching season, violence sometimes breaks out as factions on either side attempt to enforce their own assumptions, histories, and hopes.

Heaney (born a Catholic) invokes intractable views of the memorial marches in "Something to Write Home About" (Protestant glory, Catholic grievance), but his aims are antimonumental: he wants to reconfigure supposedly permanent attitudes and actions (and their allegedly unchangeable precedents) as amenable to alteration instead. Heaney's response to sectarian quarrels isn't to attack or defend a sectarian position. Elsewhere, Heaney defines the poet as a person "displaced from . . . confidence in a single position" by a "disposition to be affected by all positions." He also insists that "the idea of the poem as a symbolic resolution of opposing truths" doesn't "absolve . . . the poet from political responsibility." As a result, when Heaney encounters confidently believed-in certainties in conflict, he does (to say it again) several contradictory and complementary things at once. With regard to the commemorative marches, Heaney recognizes the historical depth and present intensity of commitments on both sides; he proposes an additional, alternative version that might connect the opposing parties without eliding or overriding their differences; and he suggests that both the alternative he offers and the conflicting meanings it partially disrupts are all better understood as malleable interpretations than as permanent truths with inevitable or "natural" consequences. It works like this: Heaney presents a supplementary tradition to counterweigh (and lighten) Protestant and Catholic versions of the marches. He recalls a meaning of *march* which the divided parties commonly inherit and therefore might accept without either party claiming victory or feeling routed. In rural Ulster, Heaney says, the verb *to march* meant for fields or farms to meet at a border. Lands that "marched" were "matched up to and yet marked off from" one another in a way that "acknowledged division" but "contained a definite suggestion of solidarity as well."

Of course, Heaney's "third term" isn't a directly practical solution to Northern Ireland's political divisions. But it isn't empty wordplay either. It posits a "marched" place where marches and the values they perpetuate on either side might be recognized as arbitrary constructions, like any cultural system, and much like words themselves—including the charged word *march*. It's a strategy that hopes to deter violence by making fixed or monumental interpretations more nearly fluid, by multiplying meanings, and by suggesting that the mind can manage several competing versions of things at once without resorting to defensiveness or assault. Meanwhile, Heaney is tough- as well as tender-minded. His semantic discussion grounds hope in an actual alternative prior practice, but the retrospective tense that outlines the precedent also questions its current force. It does similar constructively subversive work for the other versions of "marches" it encounters.

As the preceding discussion implies, competing cultural histories and discourses are the shifting ground of Heaney's personal-public writing. This gives his work a loosely poststructuralist dimension.

On the other hand, while Heaney's poetry regularly subverts conventions and "bares the device," and while his prose sometimes refers to current theorists, he resists theoretical labels. As he says in his Nobel lecture, "Crediting Poetry" (its verb intended in every sense), consciousness needn't be "theoretically instructed" to realize it's "the site of contending discourses." Even so, Terry Eagleton's observation that postcolonial peoples are "more hospitable" to the clash of cultural codes than to "doctrinal assurances" clearly applies to Heaney, who belongs to such a people, whatever Ulster's official status. Perhaps it could be said that Heaney's poetry arises where poststructuralist and humanist ideas about identity, culture, art, and language creatively intersect. For instance, Heaney acknowledges that selves and cultures are plural and shifting constructions, yet he maintains his faith that both can be made at least momentarily coherent—and he believes they develop and grow precisely by expanding to acknowledge and include whatever in and around them resists coherence (and without ever reaching some finally mature or steady state).

Similarly, Heaney sees art as complicit in civilization's self-interested perpetuation of established exclusionary or hierarchical structures, but he's also confident that art participates in what he calls civilization's "creative push," its establishment-disturbing, alternative-seeking, increasingly inclusive counterthrust. As to language, Heaney is alert to the arbitrariness of linguistic signs and systems, but he's apt to see this as a matter of efficiency (as Bernard O'Donoghue, citing Saussure, suggests) or else as his and everyone's natural working condition. For Heaney, the arbitrary or dissonant in language and other codes perturbs received arrangements in constructive as well as destabilizing ways. That keeps things open to revision—and it serves as a healthily chastening limit to the too-monumental entrenchment of any particular order, pattern, or interpretative system, including the renovations Heaney carries out himself.

Whatever its sources in humanist creeds and theoretical suspicions, Heaney's writing also participates in a homegrown Irish cultural critique which, since the late 1960s, has addressed the often violent troubles in the north through a rigorous effort to reframe sectarian cultural debates and prevent the battles and stalemates they perpetuate. That critique seeks to multiply and—without canceling or ignoring them—to disarm and detoxify warring memorial or monumental versions of the Irish past that condition the present and restrict the future. Visible in the work of many recent Northern Irish poets (and in cultural work of several kinds, including the nonsectarian revisions of local archaeology in Irish museums and the excavations of competing myths of Irish identity in the Dublin journal *The Crane Bag*), this critique may have helped create conditions for the current hopeful, if uncertain, cessation of hostilities in Ulster.

The question of contribution aside, Heaney's participation in this critique (particular to his native place but also connected with the international rise of multicultural, feminist, and postcolonial ideas) is audible in his strategic march on "marches." It echoes throughout his work—not least in his characteristic second thoughts on everything, including second thoughts themselves. In the aptly paired but unrhymed lines of "Terminus," Heaney calls second thoughts his birthright. Generated by the sorts of multiple and conflicting allegiances listed above (to Irish, English, and Irish-English languages and literatures, for instance), they come with the territory, whether of Ireland or Ulster or of Heaney's private life. (For example, his move from intimate family farm to boarding school and the wider world beyond strained his formative affiliations by adding to and confirming them as well as giving them the lie.)

To return to the point, in Heaney's early work, the partitioned loyalties and self-divisions of second thoughts are sometimes a source of fear, anxiety, and guilt. But as his career has developed, they've become something else (perhaps they always were). In the scripted radio talk I've been discussing, Heaney calls second thoughts "an acknowledgement that the truth is bounded by different *tearmanns*" (now understood less as ecclesiastical borders than as interpretations or epistemes of any kind). This definition makes differences bearable without requiring a final choice between them and without demanding they be synthesized, resolved, or otherwise denied. It sees truth as a unified yet varied and always shifting terrain bounded by many competing but not mutually exclusive sets of borders: bounded, that is, by rival systems that are variously roofed and open, divergently marched or matched, and diversely apt for different persons or groups on differing occasions. That position frames Heaney's characteristically commemorative verse—and the antimonumental means by which it wrecks and renovates memorial impulses and structures while attempting to restrain, revise, and redirect their cultural force. For although Heaney rarely considers conventional monuments in his verse, he regularly addresses memorial processes and objects there in order to consider the unsettled and unsettling political, aesthetic, and more broadly cultural issues monuments condense.[3]

Heaney's earliest commemorative acts are largely reverential, but they're rarely contented. For instance, the poems "Churning Day," "The Forge," and "Thatcher" lovingly record rural practices threatened by modernization: they consecrate (and imitate) forms of skilled labor that transform raw materials into food, tools, and shelter. Yet even those tender or awed memorials accept demise as their enabling occasion, something they can mark but can't prevent. Similarly, echoes of heroic or epic description in "Digging" indicate monumental respect for family traditions, but the poem's most vital power comes from its nostalgia-deflating rivalry between Heaney's desire to follow those traditions and his need to defect from them. In "Blackberry Picking," a summery effort to keep ripe fruit is sickened by decay (a "rat-grey fungus, glutting on our cache"), as if preservation violates natural processes and creates the rot it means to resist. In "Relic of Memory," fossil objects are a "lure": they attract *and* ensnare; they're associated with drowning and petrifaction as well as perpetuation.

Commemoration is purest in Heaney's early poems when matters of nationalist (and Catholic) politics are at stake. "Requiem for the Croppies," for instance, marks the anniversary of the Easter Rising of 1916 by granting resurrective persistence to the earlier, also defeated revolt of 1798: its memorial gestures keep the aims and energies of both rebellions alive. In "Bog Oak," a similar restorative contact with native roots (promised by the tannin-cured, recovered timber of the title) is nearly cut off by intervening memories of British imperial intrusion, represented here by Edmund Spenser, the eminent English poet. As a colonial planter in Ireland, Spenser libeled the Irish in racist terms and recommended a strategy of linguistic destruction to help subdue their resistance. Of course, Heaney's quiet indictment of Spenser is itself a form of resistance, especially for a poet writing in English. At times in his early work, Heaney responds to the complications of his political, literary, and linguistic inheritance with postcolonial commemorative maneuvers meant to assert or recover continuity with the Gaelic tongue (and therefore with Ireland in the time before England's invasions). He uses Irish *deibidhe* rhymes in English poems (as in "Follower"), extends the Gaelic *dinnseanchas* tradition in ways that challenge the official history and language by restoring connections between native names and places (as in "Toome" and "Anahorish"), and manipulates the cultural and political implications of vocabulary, etymology, and pronunciation (as in "A New Song" and "Broagh").

Commemoration is confident, even aggressive, in those poems of Irish (and Catholic or nationalist) retrieval and self-assertion. But Heaney's always astute political understanding sharpened and deepened as the situation in Northern Ireland deteriorated in the late-1960s and after, when increased Catholic pressure for civil rights met Protestant and British resistance, positions hardened, commemorations (Fenian anniversaries, say, or Orange marches) fomented violence, and something resembling civil war broke out. These developments led to changes in Heaney's writing, some of them forecast by the distrust of commemoration in the nonsectarian poems discussed above. "Bogland," the final poem of *Door into the Dark,* is especially prescient. Like the *deibidhe, dinnseanchas,* and etymological poems already mentioned, "Bogland" recovers and displays a buried Irish past, but it does so without the sense of achieved continuity or confidently grasped alternative that can ignite and fuel confrontation.

"Bogland" shares with other poems in *Door into the Dark* and *Wintering Out* a fascination with the capacity of peat bogs to preserve lost objects and deliver an Irish history different from the official (British-inflected) version. The entire process might be thought of as countermonumental, with a local set of memorial objects supplanting imposed and alien ones. But "Bogland" differs from more fully sectarian poems precisely because it conceives of alternative traditions as supplementing rather than supplanting competing patterns. ("Broagh" has similar nuances: there, strangers find local pronunciation "difficult" but not impossible "to manage." Perhaps all of Heaney's "language" poems are subtler than I've made them sound; multiple linguistic codes coexist as well as do battle within them.) In any case, "Bogland" sets Irish bogs against other national landscapes (English coal beds, American prairies), and it describes a specifically Irish terrain that is inward, "downwards," and soft rather than hard or horizontally expansive. The finds unearthed in the bogs affirm an indigenous Irish tradition and foster cultural pride. But whether they're astonishing or domestic (a skeleton of the Great Irish Elk, long-preserved butter), these finds aren't presented as entirely substantial: a skeleton isn't the living animal; the Irish elk is extinct and can't be fully recovered.

Furthermore, the bogs themselves dilute the solidity and permanence they also provide. In this poem, the bog melts and opens continuously underfoot; digging there is endless. The bog is a kind of palimpsest (Heaney associates it with "pulp" and therefore with paper and writing); every newly stripped layer seems "camped on before" (or previously inscribed). Additionally, the bog's "wet centre is bottomless"; its base is both palpably there and continuously receding, not yet but always about to be discovered. Manifold, and subject to endless change, it seems a vertical version of a landscape bordered by "different *tearmanns.*" Meaningful shapes or sets of shapes are present in the form of competing cultural traditions, but no single version of things is definitive or final. The political import of the strategy of centered decentering in "Bogland" is clearer in the densely brilliant poems of *North.*[4]

Catholic-Protestant (or republican-loyalist) violence returned to Northern Ireland in the late 1960s. British troops were deployed there in 1969, and internment without trial was introduced in 1971. Early in 1972, the events of "Bloody Sunday" led to a series of reprisal killings on both sides, and later that year, the government of Ulster (which had devolved to Stormont at the time of Ireland's partition in 1920) was returned to Westminster. The year 1972 also saw the appearance of Heaney's third book, *Wintering Out,* and his move with his family to the Irish state in the south. Nonetheless, as the title of Heaney's next book asserts, events in the north continued to define his writing. *North* (1975) is a remarkable attempt to practice political analysis and intervention in verse. The difficulties it confronts are clear from its mixed reception. Outside Ireland, *North* was praised for its tragic understanding of intractable divisions; inside, it was sometimes accused of mythologizing and (therefore) condoning violence.[5] Each judgment miscalculates the book's procedures. *North* seeks to render the intractable tractable by showing that myths, however fatal they seem and however ineluctable their power, are arbitrary constructions subject to revision.

Many poems in *North* are based on descriptions of remarkably preserved human bodies recovered from Scandinavian peat bogs: the remains of coerced or willing sacrificial victims slain in early Iron Age scapegoat rituals intended to cleanse communities, insure fertility, and prompt the return of spring. These bog bodies have special resonance for Heaney: deposits from Viking invasions constitute yet another layer of Ireland's stratified cultural history. Meanwhile, the recovered bodies serve several purposes in *North*. They distance the violence of then contemporary Ulster by providing a partially explanatory (and dangerous) mythic precedent at some remove, so that Heaney's poetry might represent and address brutality without being overwhelmed by it. At the same time, the slashed and strangled bodies (and the mysterious, even sexual glamour Heaney attributes to them) combine with the poems' percussive rhythms precisely in order to convey the current violence, its brute immediacy, and its appalling but real attractiveness. Furthermore, the bog bodies also communicate certain specific (if hardly exceptional) characteristics of Ulster's sectarian violence: its aura of atavism, ritual necessity, and abstraction. (People are killed because they've inherited and symbolically represent the political, religious, and cultural beliefs of a specific group. The repeated, nearly cyclical slayings imply that communal identity requires ritual murder—that being sacrificed and sacrificing others are vital strands in the weave of life, inevitable, natural, and beyond alteration.)

The functions I've just described as separate are an emotional, intellectual, and psychic snarl in the poems themselves, a tangle whose resistance to being unknotted transmits the feeling of impasse in then contemporary Ulster. Yet Heaney's strategy in *North* also offers a difficult alternative to impasse by suggesting that even the most ancient and obdurate myths can be challenged and revised. Because he finds explanatory precedents for the current Ulster killing in sacrificial rites at the root of Western culture, Heaney risks making violence seem commensurate with civilization itself and therefore fatal (and acceptable), even if (or especially because) it's tragic. Yet he also scrutinizes civilization's sacrificial patterns, whether they appear in ancient scapegoat killings, Ulster politics, Christianity, or art (including the ameliorative structures of his own poetics). This threatens conventional faith in culture, but because Heaney uses the tools of culture both to make and to resist that threat, he also verifies and demonstrates culture's "creative push," its capacity for imaginative reinvention as well as faithful and sometimes deranged and destructive repetition. All of those matters intersect in *North* with another aspect of the "bog people," the memorial and monumental qualities of their long-preserved and statue-like bodies. Heaney describes, interrogates, and revises those qualities, as he seeks to imagine alternative understandings, representations, and behaviors while also depicting a rigidly divided sectarian circumstance that seems to disallow them. This is especially so in one of *North*'s most effective poems, "The Grauballe Man."

"The Grauballe Man" is a representation of representations, like many poems in *North*. As Neil Corcoran points out, Heaney's fourth book is unusually dense with allusions to writing and to carving and sculpture. Borrowed passages of text are frequently placed as epigraphs or set in quotation marks or italics; the faces of the recent dead are "soapstone masks," and the bodies preserved for centuries by tannin-rich bogs resemble recovered monuments as much as human remains. That referential density foregrounds the self-conscious and skeptical nature of Heaney's interest in memorial processes in *North*. He evaluates and resists rather than records, reenacts, or otherwise confirms them; he interrogates the enduring cultural artifacts they produce, whether they're political faiths, works of art, or anthropological exhibits. This decenters the authority, naturalness, and necessity of inherited commemorative procedures and their sacrificial outcomes in religion, poetry, or politics. Without rejecting memorial rituals and objects, Heaney opens them (and their supposed consolations) to repeated weighing for aesthetic and ethical accuracy and adequacy, and therefore to reconsideration, choice, and alteration. Like the "bottomless" center of "Bogland," the repeated, never satisfied attempts of "The Grauballe Man" to find appropriate descriptive or comparative commemorative terms for its victimized subject subvert notions of a single, perfectly accurate interpretation without surrendering the search for useful ones.

"The Grauballe Man" describes an early Iron Age victim of scapegoat killing, his throat cut ear-to-ear in a midwinter rite intended to insure the return of spring. In the context of *North,* the victim's sacrifice to his community's ideas of necessity and the higher good is echoed in the ritualistic reprisal slayings of contemporary Ulster, which also seem rooted in unalterable myths of communal suffering, sacrifice, and redemption. The Grauballe Man's remains were found in a peat bog in Jutland in 1952, and carbon dating places his death in the late third or early fourth century. The body was carefully studied, then excavated and prepared for exhibition in the anthropology museum at Aarhus. Heaney's descriptions of it are based on textual and photographic depictions in P. V. Glob's *The Bog People* (one more way *North* implies that knowledge of origins or precedents is always filtered through received assumptions and interpretations and is thus more arbitrary than absolute—a condition Heaney finds hopeful as well as disruptive).

Glob's illustrations include a sequence showing the Grauballe Man's delivery from the matrix of the bog, his body coming gradually to light in a pictorial simulacrum of birth (or rebirth) that Heaney eventually takes up. But Heaney's poem begins by attempting a more than archeological resurrection—and by means of poetic figuration, not photographic reproduction. The six curt stanzas of the poem's first half posit a series of comparisons. As Helen Vendler shows in her remarkable discussion of Heaney's "grammatical" tropes, those comparisons begin with hesitant "as if"s, move to less hesitant similes, and culminate in still less hesitant metaphors, as though to imply intensifying confidence in poetry's power to transform differences into unifying resemblances or sameness. This combines with the sequential and declarative drive of the images themselves to announce a movement from description toward revelation, an unveiling of essence. When the opening image-sequence reaches fruition, a dramatic and even miraculous resurrection occurs. The long-dead Grauballe Man isn't merely exhumed and depicted; he's brought eerily to life. His "head lifts," and his "cured wound" (healed as well as tanned by the bog) "opens inwards" to reveal a ripe and nourishing "elderberry place." The poem's aesthetic progress from relatively inert comparative terms ("bog oak," "a basalt egg"), to more nearly animate if amputated ones ("a swan's foot," a "swamp root"), to ones both living and intact (mussel and eel) climaxes triumphantly in the unveiling of ripeness within the wound itself. This ripeness seals the act of aesthetic restoration with the kind of consoling, regenerative, perpetuating organic image earlier Heaney poems find so satisfying: the barley sprouting hopefully from the pockets of slaughtered Croppies, for example.

But by the time of *North,* Heaney's increased awareness that cultural myths of suffering, sacrifice, and redemption lead to violence in Jutland bogs and Ulster roads requires sterner satisfactions. The first half of "The Grauballe Man" enacts a triumphant resurrection, but that triumph is doubly qualified by the remainder of the poem, which ponders rather than confirms the earlier stanzas' aesthetic transformations, and by dissonant countermovements in the opening stanzas themselves. Heaney praises Yeats for confronting in his late poems what Heaney calls "despair at the very notion of art *as* triumph." "The Grauballe Man" confronts the same despair. (It's one of the ways Heaney obliquely assesses and assails the monumental in *North*. The volume's final poem is "Singing School"; its title echoes Yeats's "Sailing to Byzantium" and its famous instruction or command to study "monuments"—when Heaney obeys, he learns something other than rote repetition.) But to return to the poem at hand, countermovements in the first half of "The Grauballe Man" restrain, perhaps even block, its exultant resurrection.

For instance, the sequence of images in the opening stanzas is more a matter of serial displacement or disruption than of continuity or coherence. (Thomas Docherty likens it to a collision of independent shots: montage, in Eisenstein's definition) Similarly, while the compiled images do revive the sacrificial victim, they accumulate in ways that subvert recuperation—and expose its outcome as somewhat monstrous or perverse. Revivification involves restoring wholeness, as the progress of comparisons from dissociated swan's foot to integral eel implies. But that process is accompanied here by a contrary one. When the poem begins, the Grauballe Man is intact ("the black river of himself"). Subsequent images take him apart and deliver the pieces: wrists, heel, instep, hips, spine, chin, "slashed throat." In its final term, this progressive dismemberment reenacts the victim's ritual murder, and the entire sequence contradicts the miraculous *re*-membering it parallels: a freakish stitched-togetherness in the resurrected figure is implied, especially when the culminating image of the slit throat literally undercuts the heraldically triumphant chin-as-visor that precedes it. Meanwhile, the central "elderberry place" buries the elder it resurrects. The living, migratory eel is "arrested," cut off from its natural life-giving and reproductive motion.

Taken together, those details confuse resurrection with confinement, autopsy, and murder. They assert an intimate connection between the poem's recuperative procedures and death itself (just as, to save his people, the Grauballe man—or Jesus—had to be cruelly sacrificed; just as, to realize and preserve community ideals, Ulster citizens sometimes had to be slaughtered). This implies that culture's commemorative religious, political, and aesthetic operations contribute to or even cause the pain and death they soften, precisely *because* they soften them, because their soothing memorial transformations cover up and silence the suffering, pain, and death that sacrifice entails. Those operations enable and require suffering's endless repetition, whether in communal scapegoat rites, terrorism, or warfare. No wonder that at the moment of resurrection in the poem, the scarred throat (supposedly healed by a transforming verbal art founded on time-honored, comforting cultural precedents) gapes in a (silent) howl of grim rebuke, preserved, to be sure, but neither cured, convinced, nor converted. The sutured meaning of *cured* to which the early stanzas lead—tanned *and* healed—is violently severed as it's sewn; the cultural and linguistic resources that heal the wound open it again as they close it up.

All of this transmits the snarled no-exit feel of life in then contemporary Ulster, while it implicitly (and critically) relates that life to cults of violence at the core of pagan, Christian, and Irish cultures. But then, as though to acknowledge that evocation and implication aren't enough, "The Grauballe Man" turns toward explicit evaluation—in a stanza of starkly paired rhetorical questions that congratulate *and* condemn the poem's procedures. "Who will say 'corpse' / to his vivid cast? / Who will say 'body' / to his opaque repose?" This celebrates the poem's remarkable revival, accusing interpreters who see the Grauballe Man as merely dead of failing to appreciate the poem's restorative achievement in resurrecting his body or corpse. But it also accuses those (including some aspects of the poet himself) who admire the opening stanzas' consolatory achievement without perceiving its complicity in violence, its fatalistic and fatal commitment to repeated painful sacrifice. It condemns poetry's transcendent metaphors as much as politics and religion for faithfully rehearsing inherited rites that convert and conceal the reality of suffering and death and therefore make it bearable. By transforming a "twisted" corpse into the "opaque repose" of an ameliorative "cast," that is, into an effigy or monument, they compensate for pain but do so in ways that also obscure it and ensure its continued ritual infliction. Given such accusations, the certainty that usually accompanies rhetorical questions weakens and collapses: the poem's queries about who will call a cast a corpse might justifiably be answered either "I will" or "I won't," and with hovering accents.

At this point, "The Grauballe Man" seems stunned by its own self-brutalizing discoveries. (Heaney shares the thirst for accusation he noticed in Lowell.) Still, the poem isn't quite defeated; it has energy enough to react (or recoil): it attempts a return to description. A coordinating "And" tries to heal the breach that countermovements and questions have opened up. But the resurrective terms of the opening stanzas can't be recovered, or, better, the poet and poem (since both know what they're doing) refuse to be taken in by them again. Comparative forays continue, but they descend from difference-transcending metaphors to the plainer resemblance-with-difference of simile, and from images of death and resurrection to warmer ones of incarnation. Those shifts in emphasis record the poet's now chastened, perhaps saving sense of what's possible—saving because, since redemptive metaphors license the repeated infliction of pain, avoiding them might deter it. Of course, as implied both by my own language (the redemptively charged word *saving*) and by the involvement of incarnation in the Christian story of nativity, death, and resurrection, the structures we inherit aren't so easily avoided. Vendler observes that Heaney's treatment of the Grauballe Man as a newborn in the second half of the poem indicates an awakening in him of tenderness following reproach. It does. But tenderness, like the earlier and darker transformation, exacts a familiar cost. As occurs so often in iconography depicting the Christ child, images of the Grauballe Man as an infant forecast the suffering he has, as it were, already undergone. He's first described as a fetus (the clinical term suggesting abortion as much as birth, like his perversely grown-out mat of rusted hair); he's then portrayed as a bruised and twisted "forceps baby," damaged by the means supposed to deliver him safely (that is, to save him). This comes very near despair: all the poem's compensatory and commemorative gestures seem fated both to leave the sacrificial rites that require them in place and to encourage their painful rehearsal.

But Heaney's poem no more rests in despair than in its earlier triumphant application of pagan, Christian, and literary patterns of resurrection. The concluding stanzas return to evaluation. They involve a balance scale, that metonym for disinterested acts of ethical appraisal. Yet Heaney insists that even evaluative procedures are implicated in the violence they're meant to adjudicate. (The phrase "hung in the scales" makes the case, emphasizing Heaney's sense in this poem, as in *North* in general, that there's no privileged place from which objective cultural observation and judgment can be made. Culture has no "outside"; the terms we inherit from it inflect or infect us all and all we undertake.) The deliberate difficulties of the poem's conclusion make a related point. There, hard questions arise and accumulate. Given what's been said about art's complicity with pain, can beauty and atrocity be separated and weighed, or are they mutually implicated strands in the inextricable processes of sacrifice? If they are sorted out and measured, do they balance one another? Or does one (which one?) have greater weight? More specifically, are victims who've been beautified by art actually transformed (and their suffering redeemed), or are they additionally injured by the further atrocity of having their pain converted or ignored? On the other hand, would letting the victims stay "slashed and dumped," as they truly are, unbeautified, and without commemoration's relieving cure, be an act of authentic testimony or a callous atrocity of another kind? More generally, can weighing truly evaluate, or does it merely apply (and reify) preconceived and culturally embedded patterns? Those questions are urgently implied, and as urgently unanswered.

Yet, for all of that, and although their outcome can't be named, meaningful attempts to weigh and counterweigh occur in "The Grauballe Man"—the questions themselves confirm it. That's why a reading of the poem as condemning art (to death) for complicity in painful sacrifice convinces partly but doesn't convict. It's a work of art, the poem itself, that makes the prosecution's case, and it speaks for the defense as well, putting art's capacity (its ability to expose the cultural systems it also inhabits) into extenuating if not exculpatory evidence (in keeping, perhaps, with Heaney's modest precept that the "literary is one of the methods human beings have devised for getting at reality"). I suppose that implies a hung jury, a stalemate. Vendler concludes that the poem's descriptive endeavors end in impasse, suspended between faith in art, with its beautiful stylizations (the resurrected Grauballe Man, or the Dying Gaul, for instance), and the recognition that no religious, political, or aesthetic faith can redeem the victimized body. Perhaps that's so. I think the poem takes one more turn—and tips the balance slightly.

"The Grauballe Man" exposes cultural systems that perpetuate the pain they allay. It implicates itself within those systems. But it also resists them, by exposure and evaluation, as we've seen, and in another way, one that opens the possibility of changing what seems unalterable in our aesthetic and more broadly cultural and political inheritance (including the stark, sectarian politics of Ulster, rooted in commemoration). I've used the term *commemoration* (and its companions, *memorial* and *monument*) throughout my comments on Heaney's poem. This may seem like thesis grinding. It isn't only that. Throughout "The Grauballe Man," Heaney struggles to offer proper memorial tribute to the dead. The poem is rich in materials fit for carving: oak, basalt, swamp root, and horn. It represents its victim in commemorative terms: he's an effigy, for instance, with his head on a pillow of turf. By converting his chin to a visor, the poem provides him with a martial, heroic, monumental air. And, by using the words *cast* and "poured in tar," it suggests connections between the bog's preserving fluids and the casting of bronze.

Of course (and not surprisingly in a poem so at odds with itself), "The Grauballe Man" suggests such connections partly to reject them, marking Heaney's antimonumental refusal of a too-sculptural and "perfected" memorial transformation of his poem's unearthed and violated figure. Moreover, like Horace, Heaney prefers verbal processes to bronze; he prefers organic to aesthetic imagery, as well, perhaps in keeping with faith in seasonal cycles. On the other hand, it's clear in the poem that organic figuration is as complicit in cultural systems sustaining violence as more obviously aesthetic objects are. Even depicted as poured in tar or as the river of his tears, the Grauballe Man (and Heaney's poem) evokes literary and other artistic representations of pain: Dante's boiling pitch and Niobe's dissolving sorrows come to mind. Meanwhile, although the poem begins by distancing itself from conventional and monumental artistic representations, it ends by setting "hooded victims" (both ancient and contemporary ones) alongside and against a famous work of sculpture.

The statue, known as the Dying Gaul, is a Roman copy in marble of a lost Greek bronze. In it, an imperial victor memorializes a rebellious Celt fatally wounded in battle. Haltered and subdued, he's a captive in his death throes but superbly self-contained, artfully composed within the framing circumference of his shield, whether by virtue of his own stoic courage, the sculptor's potent arrangement, or both. It's precisely the statue's composure that Heaney distrusts. He suspects that the beautiful Gaul is "too strictly compassed," another aesthetic betrayal of actual torment. He associates him with other ancient and contemporary victims unceremoniously "slashed and dumped." Perhaps this fits the art-reality stalemate Vendler describes. But something else seems quietly at work. Heaney typically writes out of and against what he's written before. In earlier poems, I think, he would have yielded to the temptation to make the dying

Gaul—a fellow Celt—one more recovered forebear (like the Croppies) affirming resistance to wrongful domination (whether by the
imperial British or Ulster's majority Protestants). He doesn't do that
here. As sculpture, the Dying Gaul represents the implication in
atrocity of beautiful representations. As a victim, he is ancient and
contemporary. As a contemporary (Ulster) victim, he has no sectarian label; he represents Catholic and Protestant at once.

In this way Heaney refuses to allow inherited patterns of suffering and sacrifice to justify today's or the next day's killing, as they did
so often in early 1970s Ulster. By "marching" ancient and current,
real and sculptural victims and their different *tearmanns,* he suggests a way to break the seemingly indestructible pattern the poem
describes, despite how limited and even dangerous the recuperative
powers of monumental consolation are. The argument isn't stated,
and the tactic's enacted obliquely, but however much the poem is
tempted to cut its own throat in despair or sympathetic sacrifice,
it also demonstrates art's resilient capacity to comprehend, expose,
and resist the patterns it inherits. When Heaney praised Yeats for
confronting despair at the idea of art as triumph, he also praised
him for wresting out of the struggle a "margin of trust" that let him
contemplate renewed artistic effort. I think Heaney's quiet refusal
too narrowly to recover the Dying Gaul (or the Grauballe Man)
for present circumstances represents his own margin of trust, the
not-to-be-raveled selvage that permitted him to renew artistic effort
after the grievous experience of his native place and after the grave
revelations of art's complicity with violence in *North.*[6]

The case I've made for Heaney's margin of trust in commemoration rests on flimsy evidence. That's part of the point. Glimmers
of sunlight and (meager) sparks frame the darkness of *North.* In
the wake of its weightings and weighings, Heaney's poetry lightens
somewhat. In *Field Work* (1979), his lines unclench and lengthen;
sonnets return, and although there's no rest from political and ethical
assessment in them, they sometimes provide a deliberate and delib-
erated respite. Many of the volume's finest poems are personal and
domestic; they recover territory made marginal in *North.* But even
those poems arraign as well as defend poetry's compensatory tactics,
as in the ninth of the "Glanmore Sonnets," for example. Meanwhile,
Ulster's troubles persist ("field work" resonates with warfare as well as

the "calendar customs" of farming), and Heaney continues to record the killing and to offer—and measure—art and culture's real and insufficient consolations for it. He does so in "The Strand at Lough Beg" (where memorial anointing responds to random murder) and in the opening panel of "Triptych" (where, amid the title's commemorative and aesthetic associations, a basket of produce delivered by a girl precariously counterbalances the threat of armed young men on the hillside: it composes cabbages and carrots, nationalist green and unionist orange, with plainly Irish potatoes).

One poem in *Field Work,* "In Memoriam Francis Ledwidge," commemorates an Irish poet killed in the First World War. A rarity in Heaney's work, it explicitly addresses an actual monument. It considers an earlier phase of Ireland's troubles—and its continuing resonance for Ulster and for Heaney. It joins "The Grauballe Man" in courting the threat of stalemate to study what portion of trust in poetic commemoration might be retained, given art's complicity with violence. The terms of a later poem can hint at the result. Part ii of "*Lightenings,*" section one of "Squarings," offers the following zigzag advice about the straight and narrow: "Do not waver / Into language. Do not waver in it." This implies that to write at all is a betrayal; it also suggests that, however imperfectly, writing helps us understand and modify the cultural systems of which it partakes (including commemorations); both must be practiced—and vigilantly proofed and amended.

Francis Ledwidge was born in 1887, near the River Boyne. He worked as a road and mine laborer and in an insurance office, and he was involved with the defense force called the Irish Volunteers. Established in response to the formation of the Ulster Volunteers and with a Home Rule rather than Unionist bent, the Irish Volunteers were part of "the surge toward Irish independence" that swelled in the years before World War I and Ireland's subsequent partition. The words just quoted are Heaney's, from his introduction to a 1992 selection of Ledwidge's poems. Much of what follows also comes from there; it helps establish contexts for Heaney's earlier poetic commemoration. Ledwidge was taken up as a poet by the Unionist peer Lord Dunsany, who saw his books into print and provided him with financial support and introductions to other Irish writers (Thomas MacDonagh, AE, and Padraic Colum, for instance). Dunsany was generous but also condescending, dubbing his protégé a ploughboy or peasant poet. In 1914, the Irish Volunteers split when a faction calling itself the National Volunteers (and defined by its members' willingness to enlist and fight for Britain) broke away. Ledwidge took an active part in debates preceding the division. (In response to a colleague's claim that England's success would also be Ireland's, he said England's "uprise" had always been Ireland's downfall; when asked if he were an Irishman or pro-German, he answered that he was anti-German and an Irishman both). Ledwidge held out with more separatist members of the original group. Still, five days after those exchanges, he enlisted, saying that the British army stood between Ireland and a common enemy. The complexity of his position is conveyed in his stated unwillingness to let Britain claim that she defended Ireland while Ireland stood by (like a colonial dependent). Ledwidge survived Gallipoli and Salonika and was killed at Ypres in 1917, the victim, in some ways, of divisions in his own geography, inheritance, and personality.

As Heaney says in prose (echoing descriptions he's given elsewhere of his own split landscape), Ledwidge lived between a Catholic and pre-Christian, Celtic Ireland, on the one hand, and an anglicized Ireland, on the other. He played both Gaelic football and cricket; he modeled his Irish poems on patterns borrowed belatedly from Keats. The weave of those strained strands unraveled when Ledwidge was at home on convalescent leave in 1916. The Easter Rising had been suppressed. Then, as Heaney says, Ledwidge's "equanimity" was "shattered." For their part in the rising, MacDonagh and Joseph Plunkett were sentenced to death in the same barracks where Ledwidge had enlisted; they were executed "by soldiers in the uniform he had elected to wear." Those bitter ironies seem reflected in Ledwidge's subsequent, uncharacteristic behavior: he was court-martialed for insulting an officer, drank to excess, and reported late for duty. Still, despite his nationalist affiliations, and after composing a memorial poem for MacDonagh (using the Gaelic patterns of assonance and internal rhyme MacDonagh had recommended for Irish poetry in English), he returned to his unit in France where he was killed.

As to Ledwidge's poetry, although it improved after his contact with other Irish poets and took on bite in the few months left him after the events of 1916, it's largely conventional, pastoral, Georgian stuff. Nonetheless, it had a double afterlife that Heaney also mentions. On the one hand, those nostalgic for a demure and pious

Ireland "appropriated" Ledwidge's poetry as "a charm against all that modernity which threatened the traditional values of a country battening down for independence." It also became part of a minor republican myth. Based on the false notion that Dunsany, a pro-British aristocrat, had prevailed upon Ledwidge to enlist, it interpreted his death as a tragic silencing at just the moment when his poetic gift was finding its proper nationalistic political note. Heaney, who experienced his own versions of Ledwidge's divisions, and who had seen competing parties make claims on or lay claims to his writing, surely felt the resonance. Among other things, his poem on Ledwidge sets out to avoid such outcomes for himself—in part by revising memorial procedures.

Heaney's poem for Ledwidge is self-consciously concerned with monumental traditions. It describes a bronze memorial to Irish soldiers killed in World War I; its title and hic jacet subtitle place it within an elegiac, commemorative genre to which its formal *abab* iambic pentameter quatrains are properly suited. But the poem also challenges memorial conventions. Autobiographical emphases blur a standard memorial focus. The poem mocks the permanence of the bronze monument "forever craned" at a distance from fluid and fluent life (courting couples rising from sand dunes, boats on the move in the harbor). And it judges Ledwidge in terms more harsh and honest than conventionally eulogistic: "In you, our dead enigma, all the strains / Criss-cross in useless equilibrium." Nevertheless, as the warmth of "our" suggests, the aim here is to revise and revive commemoration, not to discard it. "In Memoriam Francis Ledwidge" looks for a way to allow competing strains to crisscross usefully within commemorative procedures. By increasing their accuracy and inclusiveness, Heaney disrupts their utility as propaganda (and extends the tempering of memorial art begun in "The Grauballe Man").

Heaney's poem begins with a description of the war memorial he saw with little interest as a child visiting Portstewart in the years just after World War II. (He depicts himself as an unsoldierly "worried pet" tightly gripping his Aunt Mary's hand in anxiety or fear at the soldierly fate of being away from home and in unfamiliar territory.) His childish indifference implicates him in several kinds of forgetting, which, as we'll see, the poem identifies with standard commemorations. Later, Heaney's interest in the monument grew, as did his interest in remembering Ledwidge. Those interests combine to rehabilitate memorial commemoration, which they revise by increasing its capacity to remember persons and events as monuments usually don't, that is, in all their inconvenient complications. In the meantime, the poem stresses the infidelity of the sculpture's memorial tribute to faithfulness. The Portstewart bronze depicts a generic Tommy bent aggressively forward in a bayonet charge at the front, but Heaney undercuts the statue's heroic fierceness: he observes that the soldier's bronze cape "crumples stiffly" in an imagined wind and can't respond to the "buff and sweep" of plural and contending real ones.

The sculpture seems false in other ways as well; supposedly it comprises Ledwidge within its generalizing memorial conventions, but Ledwidge died unheroically (not to say unbravely): he was killed by a stray shell while working on a road. Meanwhile, the message of the sculptural figure is underwritten by a bronze plaque listing "loyal, fallen names." Since contemporary Ulster unionists who favor maintaining political ties with Britain at any cost are known as loyalists, Heaney's echo of the term ironically conveys and interrogates a particular and still current strand of pro-British Ulster propaganda inscribed in the monument. The loyalists attempt to capture for their own position all the Irish soldiers who enlisted in World War I by forgetting the nationalist aspirations of many who fought for Britain; in the case of Ledwidge, this means ignoring the contending political winds that buffeted and swept him. On the other hand, a similar and competing form of Great War amnesia is practiced by some in the independent south and among nationalist Catholics in the north: this involves forgetting the actual extent of Irish participation in Britain's war. These groups forget Ledwidge by converting his life and work into the competing nostalgic and republican myths I've mentioned. (Fran Brearton traces the interlocking patterns of Ireland's World War I remembering and forgetting in *The Great War in Irish Poetry*.)

Again, while such matters meant little to Heaney as a child, they mean a great deal to him as an adult poet, and his memorial to Ledwidge remembers and commemorates the man and his political situation in all their unsolved complications. (Those persist, of course, and in similar forms, in Heaney's experience, and in Ulster.) To repeat, Heaney's ambition here is to create an unusually inclusive, revised form of commemoration that will balk his memorial's use as propaganda in any of the forgetful terms described above. He accomplishes that goal by remembering Ledwidge from many different angles without covering up his failures or resolving his contradictions, and while still (if tartly) performing elegy's task of memorial consolation. Heaney uses biographical facts to depict Ledwidge's rural, Catholic, Celtic roots, and his enervated, ghostly out-of-placeness as a Tommy, but he does so without demeaning Ledwidge's difficult and courageous decision to enlist. He also moves freely in space and time to imagine episodes contrasting the disruptive (masculine) rites of war with the persistent (feminine) rituals of rural life. In 1915 Ledwidge sucks stones to moisten his mouth in the Dardanelles, and in 1917 he's killed, but Heaney's aunt herds cows on the long acre in 1917 just as she had two years before. This respectfully imitates Ledwidge's typical compensatory pattern: his recourse in times of conflict to a flowery, feminized, permanent, supposedly transcendent Irish landscape. But it also shows the inadequacy of that response. By deliberately omitting 1916 from his annals, Heaney emphasizes the far-from-pastoral, troubled Ireland of that year and shows what Ledwidge, at least in his poetry's sentimentally gendered landscape tropes, couldn't address or account for: the Easter Rising, the executions, and his own mixed feelings. (They're conveyed in conflicting passages from letters Heaney also cites.)

Heaney's poem concludes with the harsh summary ("useless equilibrium," "dead enigma") quoted in full above—or nearly does. That judgment is accompanied, although not reversed, by some finely equilibrated closing gestures. These ameliorate and accuse at once, just as the poem's last lines provide and moderate the consoling resolution elegy requires. "In Memoriam Francis Ledwidge" begins by discrediting the Portstewart bronze and its "imagined wind." It ends in a passage of musical (not sculptural) images; harmonious and dissonant, they soothe and jangle nerves as well as ears. The monument tunes and is tuned by the actual wind. This restores it to a vigilance both guaranteed and compromised by its association with the contrarily "sure confusing drum" of war—and of Ledwidge's own enlistment, republican rebellions, and loyalist or Orange commemorations. The drum silences Ledwidge's quiet pastoral note. There's pathos in that: his twilit fluting is delicate and lovely. But there's justice in it, too, since his prettified music fails to convey the dissonant realities of his time and place and experience.

The final images are equally vexed and sympathetic. Ledwidge is given proper elegiac burial. Underground, beyond life's rough combat, he consorts harmoniously with his fellow soldiers, friend and foe alike, including the enemies of Irish independence he fought alongside. At the same time, this posthumous resolution is sharply out of tune: Ledwidge, the poem recalls, was differently pitched or keyed than his loyalist companions; disharmony persists and "consort" seems ironic. The result is a useful equilibrium different from Ledwidge's useless one of silence, stalemate, or transcendence. By moving in and out of tune, reaching and racking resolution, finding and disturbing balance, Heaney does what Ledwidge couldn't. He keeps all the competing strains of defection and commitment in play in verse as well as life, so that memorial remembering can do its consoling work without being conscripted or recruited by "the sure confusing" drums of contemporary wars founded on nationalist, loyalist, or nostalgic versions of the past. Mixing (or "marching") its English form with the Gaelic assonance and internal rhyme Ledwidge learned from MacDonagh ("altar," "flowers"; "Easter," "water"), and following the conventional conflation of poetry with music, Heaney's "In Memoriam" builds the sort of riddled, riddling monument he seems to have had in mind when he demanded some years later, "What's the use of a held note or held line / That cannot be assailed for reassurance." For Heaney, a monument's or memorial's reassurance comes from its being open to assault.[7]

Heaney is among the most congenial and affirming of poets, but he's never glib; his examinations of conscience are severe, but they're not relentless. My opening riff on Heaney's attraction to the Pantheon risks making his revisions of monumental power seem just clever, while my emphasis on the Ledwidge and Grauballe poems makes his attacks on memorials seem too grim. The truth is nearer this: throughout his career, Heaney assails his most convincing commemorative attainments both in dire distrust and for reassurance. Especially in the poems after *Field Work,* he achieves remarkable combinations of ease and distress while razing and revising the stiffly monumental and its involvements in authority, injury, and vengeance. He does so while making more provisional memorials of his own and while maintaining—with increasingly clarity, confidence, and skill—that margin of trust in art and civilization he attributes to Yeats and Zbigniew Herbert.[8] Here's an extreme example, a reminder that margins can be either wide or narrow. Amid the tense and abrasive strains of "Station Island," the unquiet ghost of Colum McCartney, a victim of Ulster violence, rises in dreadful accusation. Heaney's cousin was peacefully laid to rest in scapulars woven from rushes just gone green in "The Strand at Lough Beg." But now his unpacified spirit is angry and restless: he arraigns Heaney for confusing "evasion and artistic tact," and indicts him for trying to sweeten and whitewash his ugly actual death with selfish and fake consolatory gestures. That abuses faith of every kind. Yet even in this sometimes grisly, penitential poem, quotidian objects (a makeshift shrine of mussel shells, a carved face copied in plaster, a "haircracked" mug, or a cast-off trumpet) appear momentarily and marvelously transformed. In the face of art's indictment, these seemingly trivial, artfully converted, elevated, elevating things-as-signs provide consoling memorial replenishment before quietly returning to their plainer, actual levels.

Ordinary objects and occasions, miraculously transfigured and briskly deflated, characterize Heaney's commemorative procedures from the 1980s onward. Their intricately varied patterns are forecast in a companion poem to the elegy for Ledwidge. (It accompanies it in *Field Work* and may also allude to the Ledwidge lyric called "June," as Michael Parker suggests.[9]) The poem is "The Harvest Bow," named for a common piece of rural craftsmanship: a ritual wreath plaited from fresh-cut wheat by Heaney's father, brightened by his handling of it, and kept by his son as a talisman. The bow has memorial and visionary power. It grants "golden," commemorative access to the fading past, moving what was palpably signaled but left unspoken closer to being uttered, gleaning the elating "lift" of remembered people, times, and places. Still, threats remain: tongue-tied silence, an auction notice, a discarded plough, and a sadly abandoned bed. The harvest bow conserves somewhat, but its persistence isn't monumental: a love-knot, yes, but a "frail device," a gewgaw of "throwaway" straw. As loved ones age and rural customs vanish, it dwindles to a "drawn snare," a fragile and ineffective tool slipped by the harvest spirit it can neither catch nor hold. Even so, the memorial wreath is "burnished" by the spirit's passage and "still warm." Just such interpenetrating lowerings and lifts characterize the anti-monumental but commemorative objects and procedures of Heaney's later poems. They're brushed by a disappearing world as they lose it; like slipped snares they capture experience's traces rather than experience itself. Nevertheless, the poems, like the wreath, are burnished and warmed by what's passed through them and can burnish and warm in their turn. Meanwhile, polishing and heat require friction. Well-marked limits in Heaney's later poems constrain too-comforting monumental certainties that could lead to impasse or struggle and are out of tune with the fluid growth and decay of life in any event. The harvest bow is a relic in twinned and opposing senses: outworn and sacramental.

Even a partial list of later Heaney poems of the sort "The Harvest Bow" predicts would be too long, but it would include "Shelf Life," "On the Road," "Alphabets," "The Spoonbait," "The Mud Vision," "The Riddle," "Markings," "Wheels within Wheels," poems viii, xxx, and xxxviii of "Squarings," "The Rain Stick," and " 'Poet's Chair.' " In those poems and others, Heaney achieves memorial solace in harshly scoured but gleaming commemorations that are neither fraudulently fixed nor monumentally stable. Then he assails them again for reassurance against some deeply distressing background: family deaths, sectarian killing, or art's complicity in violence. (Heaney's dead parents focus "Clearances" and "Man and Boy," for example; additional Ulster murders alarm "Two Lorries" and "Keeping Going"; "Mycenae Lookout" witnesses wretched historical devastations and culture's embedded involvement in them.) The resulting memorial structures are elegant and ordinary; like Swiss cheese or the Pantheon, they're pierced and punctured but still substantial. A glance at a characteristic poem from each of Heaney's three most recent books can demonstrate.

Seeing Things was published in 1991. The title suggests both deluded and visionary sight and insight—but with less sense than before that the monumental and ordinary, earthed and heady can be or need be told or kept apart. Monuments are concerned with preserving inheritances from the past and handing them on unaltered. "The Settle Bed" describes a particularly plain and burdensome sort of heirloom. "Trunk-hasped, cart-heavy, painted an ignorant brown," it seems all daunting weight, constricting framework, and life-contracting measure: "unshiftably planked," "pew-strait," both crib and coffin. But the bed also conveys a richly nourishing past: "bin-deep," it recalls the meal-sunk scoop that, in "Mossbawn," brightens the bleakness of *North*. Its headboard carries forward the old, "Unpathetic," and comforting "Sigh-life of Ulster," a sound that mends though it doesn't quite heal the sectarian divisions it also signals. That restores the settle bed to a real, if troubled "worthiness." Still, the irreducible mass that the poem's substantial, stacked-up, hyphenated terms convey (the bed's "un-get-roundable weight") demands resistance. The imagination supplies it, conceiving an airy "dower of settle beds tumbled from heaven." But relief turns wretched; the fanciful image adds the whole of Irish and Ulster history to the actual bed's already stunning weight. Like a biblical plague, the rain of beds is a "vengeance come on the people."

An earlier Heaney poem might have ended there, with the private and public betrayals lurking within inheritance, consolation, and art all grievously laid open. Here, however, the imagination is less balked and exhausted by constraint than inspired to make additional alterations. Among other things, the imagined barrage of beds stands for such assaults on society and the self as the presumed "necessity" of inherited and ritualized political violence. This time, though, the recognition that those assaults are rooted in the imagination liberates rather than devastates; it teaches something beyond despair or well-hedged caution. "Whatever is given," it says (that is, whatever is inherited and assumed to be inevitable or "natural," the way things are and beyond the reach of change), is, in fact, constructed and "Can always be reimagined, however four-square." "The Grauballe Man" and "In Memoriam Francis Ledwidge" struggle to create and defend a slender margin of creative freedom where inherited cultural furniture can be taken apart and reconstructed. That margin is greatly broadened in "The Settle Bed," where it's confidently and comically asserted. The poem concludes with an open-ended antique joke or story; it's both repeated and artfully revised.

The atavistic and monumental burdens so often portrayed in Heaney's work are lightened indirectly in "The Settle Bed." "Tollund," from *The Spirit Level* (1996), revisits the resonant scapegoat victims of the bogs directly. Dated September 1994 to mark the Ulster cease-fire, "Tollund" revises the fatalistic fears of "The Tollund Man" and the bog poems of *North*. In those earlier works, resemblances between ancient Scandinavian scapegoat deaths and contemporary Ulster killings threaten endless reenactments of violence; they accuse the consolations of art and culture of complicity in the rites. Here, civilization's counterthrust or "creative push," its imaginative willingness to accommodate competing *tearmanns* without giving in to quarrel or to impasse, rejects such fatalism and restores free will. "Tollund" celebrates the human capacity to receive and respect the past but also to alter inheritance in order to make its outcomes less destructive. In the poem, an ancient and monumental "standing stone" is neither worshipped nor discarded; it's "resituated and landscaped, / With tourist signs in *futhark* runic script / In Danish and in English." Perhaps the shifting borders of Irish, Irish-English, English, and all that each implies could coexist as well.

Heaney's confidence in the capacity of politics, art, and culture to resituate and improve inherited conditions has grown along with his ability to replace destructive monumental or memorial structures with more malleable and fluid commemorative processes and objects (amenable in their turn to additional revisions). Still, even so joyful a memorial as "Tollund" recalls that imagination can weaken and that reality resists its transformations. Alertness to those blunt facts, along with Heaney's inherited Ulster reticence, holds joy in check. The conclusion of "Tollund" is modest: a curt, if firm, "not bad." In Heaney's most recent volume, *Electric Light* (2001), all the old and current challenges to peaceful commemoration are still intact as well as resisted. Part 4 of "Sonnets from Hellas" is called "The Augean Stables." Heaney describes a favorite work of art, a bas-relief that remembers Athena instructing Hercules. She shows him just where to divert the river Alpheus in order to flush the reeking stable yard with "Sweet dissolutions from the water tables" and accomplish his heroic, purifying task. But Heaney's consoling meditation on the lustral capacity of civilized efforts (poetry, sculpture, engineering) is interrupted by the memory of another contemporary murder whose foulness no aesthetic or civic labor can cleanse. The elegant sonnet staggers; an ellipsis breaks its stride; it seems defeated. But then the form recovers, and although it concludes unrhymed and unresolved, its confirming form is completed. Removed from the monumental machinery that necessitates and justifies revenge, it offers a fluid, temporary, insufficient, satisfying, and incomplete memorial release: "Hose-water smashing hard back off the asphalt / In the car park where his athlete's blood ran cold."

Afterword

Conclusions usually tie up loose ends. This one arranges some strands, but it doesn't knot them, for while the preceding chapters were conceived of and written as a book, they deliberately sustain an air of miscellany. Bishop, Lowell, Merrill, Walcott, and Heaney have a good deal in common within the terms of my discussion. Each addresses monuments and monumentality to consider the political, aesthetic, and more broadly cultural issues that monuments condense. They all share poetry's long history of seeing monuments as sites of cultural contestation as well as cultural cohesion. They share some portion of the postmodern distrust of monuments (and of art in general) for their involvement in civilization's often hierarchical and repressive disciplinary structures. And they share with many recent artists and thinkers the dual response to that distrust. That is, they critique actual and virtual monuments for their pretensions and shortcomings (excessive claims of authority, permanence, and completeness, for instance), but they also believe that monuments fulfill as well as violate human needs—and they therefore attempt to reconceive them for current use in more humble, provisional, and partial forms: forms less concerned with immortality than with a modest awareness of their own decay (a fate that's tempered by the sense that culture is compost, and decay a concomitant of growth). They share as well the hope that such modifications might constrain the contributions culture makes to oppression and violence. More narrowly, Bishop, Lowell, Merrill, Walcott, and Heaney honor the literary traditions they inherit by revising as well as embracing them, and they see the limitations of language and technique as sources of creativity and knowledge as well as obstructions. But beyond such loosely unifying generalizations, differences ramify, since the poets pursue their shared activities and interests in widely divergent ways.

Bishop first published "The Monument" in 1939, the year

Seamus Heaney was born. The structure she describes is notional and wooden rather than marble or bronze; her immediate political concerns include Depression-era economics and the coming war. Lowell addresses Saint-Gaudens's bronze memorial to Shaw and the men of the 54th, a conventional public monument in all but its brilliantly unconventional expression of conflicting meanings. The political issues Lowell addresses include the civic life of Boston, America's military and racial history, and the nation's threatened postwar decline toward affluent venality and a numbed use of force. Merrill's marbles and bronzes are private aesthetic objects as well as monumental ones, since those realms (irregularly) overlap; his political contexts are global: pollution, nuclear power, and the dangers of apocalyptic thinking. As of this writing, Walcott has never made a specific monument the focus of a poem, and Heaney has done so only once (if ever), yet each examines monumentality or commemoration throughout his work. They share postcolonial, anti-imperialist political concerns, and although Walcott's context is Caribbean and Heaney's Irish, each also has an acute internationalist aspect.

Additional lists of not very neat similarities and differences might be constructed. (For example, all five poets mix autobiographical with public material, but each does so differently; their takes on the meaning and value of nationhood vary.) Placing these poets and poems conclusively within a single, rigid border would violate the flexibility they have in common by trying to systematize and enforce it. I've tried instead to locate each poet in relation to sets of ideas and issues associated with monuments and monumentality while also defining those things (monuments and monumentality, I mean, whether understood as objects, attitudes, or tropes) in response to each poet's or poem's local conditions and considerations, and with the sort of shifting, competing, but coexisting boundaries Heaney calls "different *tearmanns.*" Meanwhile, I've also wanted to credit poetry as one of the devices human beings have for getting at reality (to echo Heaney)—and to attend to the poems in their own individual, idiosyncratic terms as well as in the terms that frame and organize my argument. I repeat my earlier remark that these writers help us to consider how the human impulse to build to last (and to reify our culturally derived and ideologically driven faiths) might coexist with current creeds of relativism, multiculturalism, and diversity. I add that they do so in incomplete and varying ways, and I give the poets the final, open-ended words: "But roughly but adequately it can shelter" (Bishop); "fame, a bouquet of forgetfulness" (Lowell); "All stone once dressed asks to be worn" (Merrill); "I decompose, but I composing still" (Walcott); "whatever is given // Can always be reimagined" (Heaney).

Notes

Introduction

1. David Ferry, Introduction to *The Odes of Horace* (New York: Farrar, Straus and Giroux, 1997), xi-xii.
2. Helen Vendler, *The Art of Shakespeare's Sonnets* (Cambridge: Harvard University Press, 1997), 268.
3. Michael North, *The Final Sculpture: Public Monuments and Modern Poets* (Ithaca: Cornell University Press, 1985).
4. Richard Poirier, *Robert Frost: The Work of Knowing* (New York: Oxford University Press, 1977), 230–38.
5. Kirk Savage, *Standing Soldiers, Kneeling Slaves: Race, War, and Monument in Nineteenth-Century America* (Princeton: Princeton University Press, 1997); Sanford Levinson, *Written in Stone: Public Monuments in Changing Societies* (Durham: Duke University Press, 1998); James E. Young, *Writing and Rewriting the Holocaust: Narrative and the Consequences of Interpretation* (Bloomington: Indiana University Press, 1988); James E. Young, *The Texture of Memory: Holocaust Memorials and Meaning* (New Haven: Yale University Press, 1993).
6. Alastair Fowler, *The Kinds of Literature: An Introduction to the Theory of Genres and Modes* (Cambridge: Harvard University Press, 1982); Ferry, Introduction to *The Odes of Horace*, x.
7. Thomas Gardner, *Region of Unlikeness: Explaining Contemporary American Poetry* (Lincoln: University of Nebraska Press, 1999), 1–31.

I
Elizabeth Bishop

1. Lloyd Schwartz, "Elizabeth Bishop, 1911–1979," *Elizabeth Bishop and Her Art,* ed. Lloyd Schwartz and Sybil P. Estess (Ann Arbor: University of Michigan Press, 1983), 254.
2. Elizabeth Bishop, *The Collected Prose* (New York: Farrar, Straus and Giroux, 1984), 140.
3. Bishop, *The Collected Prose,* 230, 241, 102.

4. Bishop, *One Art: Letters,* ed. Robert Giroux (New York: Farrar, Straus and Giroux, 1994), 54.

5. Quoted in Anne Stevenson, "Letters from Elizabeth Bishop," *Times Literary Supplement,* March 7, 1980, 261; Ashley Brown, "An Interview with Elizabeth Bishop," *Conversations with Elizabeth Bishop,* ed. George Monteiro (Jackson: University Press of Mississippi, 1996), 24; Bishop, *The Collected Prose,* 31–32; Bishop, *One Art: Letters,* 170, 256.

6. Bishop, *One Art: Letters,* 68–69, 73.

7. Robert von Hallberg, *American Poetry and Culture, 1945–1980* (Cambridge: Harvard University Press, 1985), 62–92; Margaret Dickie, *Stein, Bishop, and Rich: Lyrics of Love, War, and Place* (Chapel Hill: University of North Carolina Press, 1997), 107–8.

8. Quoted in Brett C. Millier, *Elizabeth Bishop: Life and the Memory of It* (Berkeley: University of California Press, 1993), 131.

9. Mary McCarthy, "Symposium," *Elizabeth Bishop and Her Art,* 267.

10. Bishop, *One Art: Letters,* 12, 311, 11; Marianne Moore, "A Modest Expert," *Elizabeth Bishop and Her Art,* 179; quoted in David Kalstone, *Becoming a Poet: Elizabeth Bishop with Marianne Moore and Robert Lowell,* ed. Robert Hemenway (New York: Farrar, Straus and Giroux, 1989), 106.

11. Bishop, *One Art: Letters,* 23, 301.

12. Bonnie Costello, *Elizabeth Bishop: Questions of Mastery* (Cambridge: Harvard University Press, 1991), 218.

13. Susan McCabe, *Elizabeth Bishop: Her Poetics of Loss* (University Park: Pennsylvania State University Press, 1994), 55; Lorrie Goldensohn, *Elizabeth Bishop: The Biography of a Poetry* (New York: Columbia University Press, 1992), ix; Costello, *Elizabeth Bishop,* 218–23; Millier, *Elizabeth Bishop,* 89; Bishop, *One Art: Letters,* 478; Elizabeth Bishop, *Exchanging Hats: Paintings,* ed. William Benton (New York: Farrar, Straus and Giroux, 1996), 66; Bishop, *One Art: Letters,* 135; George Starbuck, "A Conversation with Elizabeth Bishop," in *Conversations with Elizabeth Bishop,* 88.

14. Susan Schweik, "An Oblique Place: Elizabeth Bishop and the Language of War," in *A Gulf So Deeply Cut: American Women Poets and the Second World War* (Madison: University of Wisconsin Press, 1991), 213; Gary Fountain and Peter Brazeau, *Remembering Elizabeth Bishop: An Oral Biography* (Amherst: University of Massachusetts Press, 1994), 63; Bishop, *One Art: Letters,* 41, 45; Millier, *Elizabeth Bishop,* 130; Schweik, "An Oblique Place," 213–41; Dickie, *Stein, Bishop, and Rich,* 104–15.

15. Barbara Page, "Off-Beat Claves, Oblique Realities: The Key West Notebooks of Elizabeth Bishop," in *Elizabeth Bishop: A Geography of Gender,* ed. Marilyn May Lombardi (Charlottesville: University Press of Virginia, 1993), 202 (Lombardi makes a similar point in her *The Body*

and the Song: Elizabeth Bishop's Poetics [Carbondale: Southern Illinois University Press, 1995], 178); Bishop, *One Art: Letters,* 48.

16. Celeste Goodridge discusses connections between Wilson's poem and Bishop's "A Miracle for Breakfast" in her "Elizabeth Bishop and Wallace Stevens: Sustaining the Eye/I," *The Wallace Stevens Journal* 19 (Fall 1995): 139–40.

17. Bishop's comment on de Chirico is in a letter to Joseph and U. T. Summers, *One Art: Letters,* 478. My discussion of de Chirico's work is indebted to Robert Hughes, *The Shock of the New* (New York: Knopf, 1981), 215–21.

18. Millier, *Elizabeth Bishop,* 134.

19. C. K. Doreski suggests that the paired *a*'s and *p*'s create an "associative chain" that makes the "prince seem a product of his prospect and place" in her *Elizabeth Bishop: The Restraints of Language* (New York: Oxford University Press, 1993), 30.

20. Anne Colwell, *Inscrutable Houses: Metaphors of the Body in the Poems of Elizabeth Bishop* (Tuscaloosa: University of Alabama Press, 1997), 56.

21. Readings of "The Monument" as antimodernist and antimonumental appear in Page, "Off-Beat Claves, Oblique Realities," 202–3; Lombardi, *The Body and the Song,* 178–81; and Goldensohn, *Elizabeth Bishop,* 111–13. Costello, *Elizabeth Bishop,* 224; John Hollander, *The Gazer's Spirit: Poems Speaking to Silent Works of Art* (Chicago: University of Chicago Press, 1995), 7. I discuss "The Monument" in my *Reading and Writing Nature: The Poetry of Robert Frost, Wallace Stevens, Marianne Moore, and Elizabeth Bishop* (Boston: Northeastern University Press, 1991), 207–9.

2

Robert Lowell

1. Elizabeth Bishop, "North Haven," *The Complete Poems: 1927–1979* (New York: Farrar, Straus and Giroux, 1983), 189; Bidart's remark is reported in Ian Hamilton, *Robert Lowell: A Biography* (New York: Random House, 1982), 392; Robert Lowell, *Selected Poems,* rev. ed. (New York: Farrar, Straus and Giroux, 1977), 213; Seamus Heaney, in *Robert Lowell: Interviews and Memoirs,* ed. Jeffrey Meyers (Ann Arbor: University of Michigan Press, 1988), 246; Lowell, "Dear Sorrow," *Selected Poems,* 213; *Notebook* (New York: Farrar, Straus and Giroux, 1970), 264; *Collected Prose,* ed. Robert Giroux (New York: Farrar, Straus and Giroux, 1987), 248; *Collected Prose,* 289; Helen Vendler, "Last Days and Last Poems," in *Robert Lowell,* ed. Harold Bloom (New York: Chelsea House, 1987), 104.

2. Calvin Bedient, "Visions and Revisions—Three New Volumes by America's First Poet," *New York Times Book Review,* July 29, 1973, 15; Vendler, "Robert Lowell," in *The Given and the Made* (Cambridge: Harvard University Press, 1995), 26; Raban's remarks are reported in Hamilton, *Robert Lowell,* 431.

3. Robert Fitzgerald, in Meyers, *Robert Lowell,* 226.

4. Lowell, *Collected Prose,* 32.

5. Stanley Kunitz, in Meyers, *Robert Lowell,* 85.

6. Vereen M. Bell, *Robert Lowell: Nihilist as Hero* (Cambridge: Harvard University Press, 1983), 52.

7. Bell, *Robert Lowell,* 205; Vendler, *The Given and the Made,* 12.

8. The lines are from "My Death, 1," *Notebook,* 128; Lowell, *Collected Prose,* 175; Lowell, cited in Philip Cooper, *The Autobiographical Myth of Robert Lowell* (Chapel Hill: University of North Carolina Press, 1970), 42; Lowell, *Collected Prose,* 26.

9. John Crowe Ransom, "Robert Lowell," in *Concise Encyclopedia of English and American Poets and Poetry,* ed. Stephen Spender and Donald Hall (London: Hutchinson, 1963), 191.

10. Bishop, *One Art: Letters,* ed. Robert Giroux (New York: Farrar, Straus and Giroux, 1994), 351–52.

11. Richard Tillinghast, *Robert Lowell's Life and Work* (Ann Arbor: University of Michigan Press, 1995), 28, 35.

12. Quoted in Tillinghast, *Robert Lowell's Life and Work,* 56.

13. Alan Williamson, *Pity the Monsters: The Political Vision of Robert Lowell* (New Haven: Yale University Press, 1974), 1.

14. Robert von Hallberg, *American Poetry and Culture, 1945–1980* (Cambridge: Harvard University Press, 1985), 150, 149; Lowell, cited in Paul Mariani, *Lost Puritan: A Life of Robert Lowell* (New York: Norton, 1994), 248; Vendler describes the graves in Meyers, *Robert Lowell,* 309.

15. Lowell's unpublished note on the poem is quoted in William Doreski, *The Years of Our Friendship: Robert Lowell and Allen Tate* (Jackson: University Press of Mississippi, 1990), 131–32; Lowell, *Collected Prose,* 225.

16. Hamilton, 277–81; Steven Gould Axelrod, *Robert Lowell: Life and Art* (Princeton: Princeton University Press, 1978), 156–59; Philip Hobsbaum, *A Reader's Guide to Robert Lowell* (London: Thames and Hudson, 1988), 126–28; Mariani, *Lost Puritan,* 283–85.

17. Axelrod, *Robert Lowell,* 172–73; Bell, *Robert Lowell,* 95–97.

18. Quoted by A. Alvarez in Meyers, *Robert Lowell,* 78; Axelrod, *Robert Lowell,* 157.

19. Kirk Savage, *Standing Soldiers, Kneeling Slaves: Race, War, and Monument in Nineteenth-Century America* (Princeton: Princeton University Press, 1997), 193–207.

20. Savage, *Standing Soldiers,* 256, n.103.

21. Hamilton, *Robert Lowell*, 111.

22. Hamilton, *Robert Lowell*, 295.

23. Savage, *Standing Soldiers*, 205–7.

24. Axelrod, *Robert Lowell*, 164; Vendler, *The Given and the Made*, 13.

3

James Merrill

1. James Merrill, *A Different Person: A Memoir* (New York: Knopf, 1993), 65; "Divine Poem," *Recitative: Prose by James Merrill*, ed. J. D. Mc-Clatchy (Berkeley: North Point, 1986), 87; "Object Lessons," *Recitative*, 112.

2. Merrill, *The (Diblos) Notebook* (New York: Atheneum, 1965), 62; "Unreal Citizen," *Recitative*, 99.

3. There are strong discussions of Merrill's revisions of Yeats in Leslie Brisman, "Merrill's Yeats," in *James Merrill*, ed. Harold Bloom (New York: Chelsea House, 1985), 189–98; in Timothy Materer, *James Merrill's Apocalypse* (Ithaca: Cornell University Press, 2000); and in Jeff Westover, "Writing on the (Sur)face of the Past: Convivial Visions and Revisions in the Poetry of James Merrill," in *Critical Essays on James Merrill*, ed. Guy Rotella (New York: Hall, 1996), 215–30.

4. Stephen Yenser, *The Consuming Myth: The Work of James Merrill* (Cambridge: Harvard University Press, 1987), 30, 238; Henry Sloss, "James Merrill's The Book of Ephraim," parts 1 and 2, *Shenandoah* 27, 28 (1976): 63–91; 83–110 (the phrase itself is on 64); Judith Moffett makes similar points about matter and manner in Merrill's trilogy in her *James Merrill: An Introduction to the Poetry* [New York: Columbia University Press, 1984], 161, as does Lynn Keller, in her *Re-making It New: Contemporary American Poetry and the Modernist Tradition* [New York: Cambridge University Press, 1987], 245); "James Merrill," in *The Poet's Notebook*, ed. Stephen Kuusisto, Deborah Tall, and David Weiss (New York: Norton, 1995), 191; Yenser, *The Consuming Myth*, 6.

5. Helen Vendler, "Fears and Farewells," reprinted in *Critical Essays on James Merrill*, 67; Merrill, "Another Autumn," in his *Collected Poems*, ed. J. D. McClatchy and Stephen Yenser (New York: Knopf, 2001), 257; Merrill, "Object Lessons," *Recitative*, 113.

6. James Merrill, "For Proust," *Collected Poems*, 140; *The (Diblos) Notebook*, 20; "Yánnina," *Collected Poems*, 380–84 (the quoted phrase is on 383); Jean Lunn, [Interview with James Merrill], *Sandscript* 6 (1982): 6.

7. Brisman, "Merrill's Yeats," 198; Merrill, "An Interview with Fred Bornhauser," *Recitative*, 56; *A Different Person*, 192; J. D. McClatchy, "Braving the Elements," reprinted in *Critical Essays on James Merrill*, 238.

8.   Merrill, "Notes on Corot," *Recitative,* 156, 153; *The (Diblos) Notebook,* 36; *A Different Person,* 236.

9.   Merrill, "The Broken Home," *Collected Poems,* 197–200 (the quoted passage is on 199); "An Interview with John Boatwright and Enrique Ucelay DaCal," *Recitative,* 38; Richard Saez, "James Merrill's Oedipal Fire," *Parnassus: Poetry in Review* (Fall/Winter 1974): 183–84; Merrill, *A Different Person,* 67; "Divine Poem," *Recitative,* 87; "The Transparent Eye," *Recitative,* 129.

10. Merrill, "The Transparent Eye," *Recitative,* 125; "An Interview with Donald Sheehan," *Recitative,* 28; "On Literary Tradition," *Recitative,* 9; Lunn, [Interview], 12; Merrill, "Overdue Pilgrimage to Nova Scotia," *Collected Poems,* 666; "The Transparent Eye," *Recitative,* 127 (the Bishop poem to which Merrill refers is her "Visits to Saint Elizabeth's").

11. This material is partly borrowed from my introduction to *Critical Essays on James Merrill,* 2–4.

12. Mutlu Blasing, "Rethinking Models of Literary Change: The Case of James Merrill," reprinted in *Critical Essays on James Merrill,* 99–115; David Bromwich, "Answer, Heavenly Muse, Yes or No," reprinted in *Critical Essays on James Merrill,* 55.

13. Robert Polito's discussion of Merrill's revisions of modern masters is especially good: see "Afterword," in his *A Reader's Guide to James Merrill's The Changing Light at Sandover* (Ann Arbor: University of Michigan Press, 1994), 231–63. Merrill, "The Thousand and Second Night," *Collected Poems,* 176–185 (the cited passage is on 179); "Syrinx," *Collected Poems,* 355–56.

14. Merrill, "An Interview with Donald Sheehan," *Recitative,* 35; *A Different Person,* 138; "Graffito" and "Self-Portrait in Tyvek © Windbreaker," *Collected Poems,* 567, 669–73.

15. Merrill "Object Lessons," *Recitative,* 111; Lee Zimmerman, "Against Apocalypse: James Merrill's The Changing Light at Sandover," reprinted in *Critical Essays on James Merrill,* 186; Merrill "The Beaten Path," *Recitative,* 151; "Little Fanfare for Felix Magowan," *Collected Poems,* 201.

16. Merrill, "The Will," *Collected Poems,* 392–98 (the cited passage is on 394); Stephen Yenser cites Rilke (in Stephen Mitchell's translation) in *The Consuming Myth,* 331; Merrill, *The (Diblos) Notebook,* 34; The Poet's *Notebook,* 193; "After the Fire," *Collected Poems,* 296–98 (the passage quoted is on 296).

17. The early version of "The Broken Bowl" is in Merrill, *Collected Poems,* 4, and the revised version is in *Selected Poems 1946–1985* (New York: Knopf, 1992), 6; James Merrill, *The Changing Light at Sandover* (New York: Atheneum, 1982), 229; *The Changing Light at Sandover,* 118.

18. Merrill, "Unreal Citizen," *Recitative,* 99.

19. Discussions of the recovery and exhibit of the Riace bronzes appear in Carol C. Mattusch, *The Victorious Youth* (Los Angeles: Getty Museum

Studies on Art, 1997), 16–19, and *Greek Bronze Statuary* (Ithaca: Cornell University Press, 1988), 8–9; Joseph Alsop's comment appears in his "Warriors from a Watery Grave: Glorious Bronzes from Ancient Greece," *National Geographic,* 163 (June 1983): 820–27; a good example of the formalist approach to the bronzes is Susan Woodford, *An Introduction to Greek Art* (Ithaca: Cornell University Press, 1986).

20. See the books by Carol C. Mattusch cited above as well as Mattusch, *Classical Bronzes: The Art and Craft of Greek and Roman Statuary* (Ithaca: Cornell University Press, 1996). The muscular diktat comment is from Nigel Spivey, *Understanding Greek Bronzes: Ancient Meanings, Modern Readings* (London: Thames and Hudson, 1996), 39. Spivey is particularly good on the case for the statues' place within a larger group at Delphi and for discussion of the role of Phidias in the statues' reception and in art history in general. Mattusch's comment on the color of the Riace statues is in *Classical Bronzes,* 27; for Merrill's preference for convalescent over redemptive strategies, see Guy Rotella, "James Merrill's Poetry of Convalescence," *Contemporary Literature,* 38 (1997): 307–24.

21. Lurie's case is made in *Familiar Spirits: A Memoir of James Merrill and David Jackson* (New York: Viking, 2001); the fullest discussion of Merrill's relationship with Count Morra is in Merrill, *A Different Person,* 108–9, 207–16; as to the phrase "sculpture museum," an early Merrill poem is called "Dream (Escape from the Sculpture Museum) and Waking"—this additional intertextual detail suggests a revision: escape isn't the issue here. Readings of "Bronze" which contributed to mine include those in Vendler, "Fears and Farewells," and Yenser, *The Consuming Myth,* as well as Stephen Sandy, "Of 'Bronze,' " *Verse* 5 (July 1988): 56–59, and Ruth Thompson, "Merrill's 'Bronze,' " *The Explicator* 47 (Fall 1988): 48–50.

4

Derek Walcott

1. For Walcott's analysis of history as synchronic rather than sequential, see "The Muse of History," in his *What the Twilight Says* (New York: Farrar, Straus and Giroux, 1998), 36–64.

2. For Walcott's ideas on mimicry as characteristic and constructive rather than a matter of diminishment or lack, see his essay "The Caribbean: Culture or Mimicry?" in *Critical Perspectives on Derek Walcott,* ed. Robert D. Hamner (Boulder: Lynne Rienner, 1997), 51–57. The strongest critical discussion of Walcott's understanding and practice of mimicry is Rei Terada, *Derek Walcott's Poetry: American Mimicry* (Boston: Northeastern University Press, 1992).

3. Timothy Hofmeister, "Classical Analogy as Discursive Act: A Reading of Derek Walcott's 'As John to Patmos,' " *The South Atlantic Quarterly (SAQ)* 96 (Spring 1997): 276; Walcott, "The Muse of History," 44.

4. Walcott, "The Muse of History," 38; "Reflections on *Omeros*," *The South Atlantic Quarterly* 96 (Spring 1997): 239.

5. Walcott, "Ruins of a Great House," *Collected Poems: 1948–1984* (New York: Farrar, Straus and Giroux, 1986), 19–21; "The Muse of History," 36.

6. Walcott, "From This Far," *Collected Poems,* 414; "The Schooner *Flight,*" *Collected Poems,* 347; "A Propertius Quartet," *The Arkansas Testament* (New York: Farrar, Straus and Giroux, 1987), 98; "The Villa Restaurant," *The Arkansas Testament,* 25 and 26; "The Gulf," *Collected Poems,* 106; *Omeros* (New York: Farrar, Straus and Giroux, 1990), 284; "An Interview with Nancy Schoenberger," *Conversations with Derek Walcott,* ed. William Baer (Jackson: University Press of Mississippi, 1996), 89.

7. Walcott, "Tarpon," *Collected Poems,* 61–62; "The Fortunate Traveller," *Collected Poems,* 456–63; "A Change of Skin," *The Gulf* (London: Jonathan Cape, 1969), 26; *Another Life,* Book One, Chapter 1, section II, *Collected Poems,* 148–49.

8. Walcott, "XLIII: Tropic Zone," *Midsummer, Collected Poems,* 496–501.

9. Walcott, "The Caribbean: Culture or Mimicry?" 51.

10. Walcott, "Reflections on *Omeros*," 237.

11. Paul Breslin, *Nobody's Nation: Reading Derek Walcott* (Chicago: University of Chicago Press, 2001), 5–6; Terada, *Derek Walcott's Poetry,* 82–118.

12. J. P. White, "An Interview with Derek Walcott," *Conversations with Derek Walcott,* 158–59; Derek Walcott, "I," *Midsummer* (New York: Farrar, Straus and Giroux, 1984), n.p.; "A Village Life," *Collected Poems,* 81; "A Propertius Quartet," *The Arkansas Testament,* 98.

13. Walcott, *Another Life,* Book Two, Chapter 12, section I, *Collected Poems,* 217; "The Master of the Ordinary: Philip Larkin," *What the Twilight Says,* 169; "The Road Taken: Robert Frost," *What the Twilight Says,* 210; "On Robert Lowell," *What the Twilight Says,* 106; "On Robert Lowell," 89; "The Hotel Normandie Pool," *Collected Poems,* 439–45; the University of Milan remarks are reported by Paula Burnett, *Derek Walcott: Politics and Poetics* (Gainesville: University Press of Florida, 2000), 319; "The Road Taken: Robert, Frost," 202; "On Robert Lowell," 97; "Elegy," *Collected Poems,* 109; "The Master of the Ordinary: Philip Larkin," 169.

14. Walcott's best critics include: Edward Baugh, *Derek Walcott: Memory as Vision: Another Life* (London: Longman, 1978); Ned Thomas, *Derek Walcott: Poet of the Islands/Derek Walcott: Barrd yr Ynysoedd* (Cardiff: Welsh Arts Council, 1980); Rei Terada, *Derek Walcott's Poetry;* Robert D. Hamner, *Epic of the Dispossessed: Derek Walcott's*

Omeros (Columbia: University of Missouri Press, 1997); John Thieme, *Derek Walcott* (Manchester: Manchester University Press, 1999); Paul Breslin, *Nobody's Nation;* and Jahan Ramazani, *The Hybrid Muse: Post-colonial Poetry in English* (Chicago: University of Chicago Press, 2001); as well as the contributors to the special issue of *The South Atlantic Quarterly,* cited in note 3. Walcott, "An Interview with Nancy Schoenberger," 91; Edward Hirsch, "An Interview with Derek Walcott," *Conversations with Derek Walcott,* 59; Robert D. Hamner, "Conversation with Derek Walcott," *Conversations with Derek Walcott,* 32; Walcott, "The Muse of History," 62; Leif Sjöberg, "An Interview with Derek Walcott," *Conversations with Derek Walcott,* 83; Walcott, "Ted Hughes," *What the Twilight Says,* 176; Sjöberg, "An Interview with Derek Walcott," 83; David Montenegro, "An Interview with Derek Walcott," *Conversations with Derek Walcott,* 148; J. P. White, "An Interview with Derek Walcott," 154; Derek Walcott, "The Master of the Ordinary: Philip Larkin," 163; "The Road Taken: On Robert Frost," 203.

15. Sjöberg, "An Interview with Derek Walcott," 79; Anthony Milne, "This Country is a Very Small Place," *Conversations with Derek Walcott,* 74–75; Sjöberg, "An Interview with Derek Walcott," 79.

16. Walcott, "The Antilles: Fragments of Epic Memory," *What the Twilight Says,* 76; "The Muse of History," 43; "Origins," II, *Collected Poems,* 12; "Names," II, *Collected Poems,* 306–7; "This Country is a Very Small Place," 76; "This Country is a Very Small Place," 75; "What the Twilight Says," *What the Twilight Says,* 16; *Another Life,* Book Two, Chapter 12, section II, in *Collected Poems,* 219, 220; "The Muse of History," 36; "The Muse of History," 40–41; "The Antilles: Fragments of Epic Memory," 69; "History and Picong . . . in the Middle Passage," in *Critical Perspectives on Derek Walcott,* 19.

17. Walcott, *Another Life,* Book Three, Chapter 13, section IV, in *Collected Poems,* 230; *Another Life,* Book Three, Chapter 14, section III, in *Collected Poems,* 236; *Another Life,* Book One, Chapter 7, section III, 186; Montenegro, "An Interview with Derek Walcott," 136; Walcott, *Another Life,* Book One, Chapter 7, section III, *Collected Poems,* 186; "Islands," in *Collected Poems,* 52; "Nearing Forty," in *Collected Poems,* 136; "Cul de Sac Valley," in *The Arkansas Testament,* 9; "The Gulf," in *Collected Poems,* 106; "The Schooner *Flight,*" in *Collected Poems,* 360; *Omeros,* 183.

18. Walcott, "XXV," *Midsummer, Collected Poems,* 484; Edward Hirsch, "The Art of Poetry XXXVII," *Conversations with Derek Walcott,* 99; *Another Life,* Book Two, Chapter 8, sections II and III, in *Collected Poems,* 194–96; White, "An Interview with Derek Walcott," 165; Walcott, "The Art of Poetry XXXVII," 105; Sjöberg, "An Interview with Derek Walcott," 79; Walcott, "The Art of Poetry XXXVII," 105; *Another Life,* Book Four, Chapter 23, section IV, in *Collected Poems,* 294; Hirsch, "An Interview with Derek Walcott," 52; Robert Brown and Cheryl

Johnson, "Thinking Poetry: An Interview with Derek Walcott," *Conversations with Derek Walcott*, 182; Derek Walcott, "XVI," *Midsummer*, n.p.; *Omeros*, 227; "The Antilles: Fragments of Epic Memory," 82.

19. Walcott, "The Antilles: Fragments of Epic Memory," 69; "The Caribbean: Culture or Mimicry?" 55; "The Art of Poetry XXXVII," 114; "The Antilles: Fragments of Epic Memory," 65–66.

20. Walcott, "The Bounty," ii, *The Bounty* (New York: Farrar, Straus and Giroux, 1997), 5; "Landfall, Grenada," *Collected Poems*, 125; Gregson Davis, " 'With No Homeric Shadow': The Disavowal of Epic in Walcott's *Omeros*," *The South Atlantic Quarterly* 96 (Spring 1997): 321–33; Walcott, "Eulogy to W.H. Auden," *The Arkansas Testament*, 61; for details on the critics of *Omeros* mentioned, see notes 13 and 14 above; Walcott, *Omeros*, 182–84; *Omeros*, 189–93; *Omeros*, 193–96; *Omeros*, 204–205; Walcott, *Tiepolo's Hound* (New York: Farrar, Straus and Giroux, 2000), 158; the phrase "Deciduous beauty" appears in "Ruins of a Great House," *Collected Poems*, 19; "What the Twilight Says," 14.

5

Seamus Heaney

1. Paul Muldoon, "Caprices des Deux;" "Seamus Heaney: The Art of Poetry LXXV," *Paris Review* 144 (1997): 120–21. Details of the Pantheon's structure and history come from standard guidebooks; comments on the Pantheon's siting and on its merger of architectural, theological, and political dimensions come from the descriptions and analysis in Spiro Kostof, *A History of Architecture: Setting and Ritual* (Oxford: Oxford University Press, 1985), 217–18.

2. Seamus Heaney, "Something to Write Home About," *Finders Keepers: Selected Prose, 1971–2001* (New York: Farrar, Straus and Giroux, 2002), 51; Heaney quotes Anthony Storrs on Jung in "Place and Displacement," Finders Keepers, 122; the phrase "earthed and heady" is from "The Loose Box" in Heaney's *Electric Light* (New York: Farrar, Straus and Giroux, 2001), 15; Heaney's comments on *pagus* and *disciplina* are in "The God in the Tree," in his *Preoccupations: Selected Prose, 1968–1978* (New York: Farrar, Straus and Giroux, 1980), 183.

3. Heaney, "Something to Write Home About," 51–62; "Place and Displacement: Recent Poetry from Northern Ireland," *Finders Keepers*, 129; "Crediting Poetry," *Opened Ground: Selected Poems, 1966–1996* (New York: Farrar, Straus and Giroux, 1998), 418; Eagleton is quoted in Henry Hart, *Seamus Heaney: Poet of Contrary Progressions* (Syracuse, N.Y.: Syracuse University Press, 1992), 180; Bernard O'Donoghue, *Seamus Heaney and the Language of Poetry* (New York: Harvester Wheatsheaf, 1994), 121; Heaney, "Yeats as an Example?," *Finders Keepers*, 117.

4. Many of Heaney's critics discuss his use of *deibidhe* and *dinnseanchas* traditions: O'Donoghue's comments are especially helpful; the best discussion of centers in Heaney's work is Daniel Tobin, *Passage to the Center: Imagination and the Sacred in the Poetry of Seamus Heaney* (Lexington: University Press of Kentucky, 1999).

5. The most powerful attack on *North* is Edna Longley, " 'Inner Émigré' or 'Artful Voyeur'? Seamus Heaney's *North*," in *Poetry and the Wars* (Newcastle-upon-Tyne: Bloodaxe, 1986), 140–69; for a survey and digest of responses to the volume, see "Poetry and Politics," in *The Poetry of Seamus Heaney: Essays, Articles, Reviews,* ed. Elmer Andrews (New York: Columbia University Press, 1998), 80–119.

6. Neil Corcoran, *A Student's Guide to Seamus Heaney* (London: Faber and Faber, 1986), 98–99; Helen Vendler, "Seamus Heaney: The Grammatical Moment," in *The Breaking of Style* (Cambridge: Harvard University Press, 1995), 52–60; Heaney, "W. B. Yeats and Thoor Ballylee," *Finders Keepers,* 260; Thomas Docherty "Ana-; or Postmodernism, Landscape, Seamus Heaney," in *Seamus Heaney,* ed. Michael Allen (New York: St. Martin's, 1997), 211; Tobin discusses Heaney's Girardian sense of the relationship of violence and the sacred in *Passage to the Center,* 118–24—I'm indebted to his reading of "The Grauballe Man"; quoted in Dennis O'Driscoll, " 'Steady Under Strain and Strong Through Tension,' " *Parnassus: Poetry in Review* 26, no. 2 (2002): 154; for readings of "The Grauballe Man" as an attack on art, see Corcoran, *A Student's Guide to Seamus Heaney,* 114–15, and Elmer Andrews, *The Poetry of Seamus Heaney: All the Realms of Whisper* (New York: St. Martin's, 1998), 84–86.

7. Heaney, "Introduction," in *Francis Ledwidge: Selected Poems,* ed. Dermot Bolger (Dublin: New Island Books, 1992), 11–20 (see also Heaney's "The Labourer and the Lord: Francis Ledwidge and Lord Dunsany," in *Preoccupations,* 202–6); Fran Brearton, *The Great War in Irish Poetry: W. B. Yeats to Michael Longley* (Oxford: Oxford University Press, 2000); Heaney, poem xxii, in the "*Settings*" section of "Squarings," *Opened Ground,* 346.

8. Heaney, "Atlas of Civilization," *Finders Keepers,* 168.

9. Michael Parker, *Seamus Heaney: The Making of the Poet* (Iowa City: University of Iowa Press, 1993), 262, n.74.

Index